LAWMAN

A Companion to the Classic TV Western Series

By Bill Levy

BearManor Media

Orlando, Florida

Lawman: A Companion to the Classic TV Western Series
© 2020 Bill Levy. All Rights Reserved.

No part of this book may be reproduced in any form or in any means, electronic, mechanical, digital, photocopying or recording except for the inclusion in a review, without permission in writing from the publisher.

With the exception of the cover photo and the seven photographs gifted to the author from Michael F. Blake, Robert Colbert, Michael Dante, Joyce Meadows, Roberta Shore, Jan Shepard, and Olive Sturgess for the "Recollections" chapter, all of the photographs in this book were courtesy of The Doug Abbott Collection. (www.westerntvphotos.com)

The cover photograph is a scene from "Yawkey" (1961) courtesy of The Doug Abbott Collection. The spine photograph is a Lawman publicity still gifted to the author from Nancy Dale.

Published in the USA by
BearManor Media
1317 Edgewater Dr. #110
Orlando, FL 32804
www.BearManorMedia.com

Softcover Edition
ISBN-10: 1-62933-526-6
ISBN-13: 978-1-62933-526-1

Printed in the United States of America

This book is dedicated to James Robert Parish,

my advisor, editor, mentor, and friend

for thirty years

and to

Nancy Dale,

a new friend and advisor.

Table of Contents

1.	Acknowledgements	ix
2.	Foreword by Will "Sugarfoot" Hutchins	xi
3.	Preface by Boyd Magers	xv
4.	Introduction	xvii
5.	Photo Gallery I: The Three Leads	1
6.	Creating *Lawman*	9
7.	The Appeal of *Lawman*	17
8.	Photo Gallery II: Supporting Cast and Guest Stars	29
9.	The Episodes	35
10.	Recollections	169
11.	*Lawman* Miscellanea	181
12.	Epilogue	185
13.	Recommended Readings	187
14.	Index	189
15.	About the Author	225

Acknowledgments

From the beginning of this project, BearManor Media's publisher Ben Ohmart and media historian James Robert Parish consistently provided me with significant support. I thank Will Hutchins and his wife Babs for the book's Foreword and their friendship. I thank Nancy Dale, the founder and administrator of Facebook's *Lawman* TV Series Fan Group and Facebook's John Russell Fan Group, for sharing her *Lawman* passion and expertise with me. Television westerns guru Boyd Magers was extremely kind to share his encyclopedic knowledge, to help me connect with most of the actors and actresses in the "Recollections" chapter, and to write the Preface to this book. I thank Doug Abbott for his vivid photographs and generosity, and Allan Duffin for the book's design and layout. I also thank the three J's: Janice Allen, Julienne Marks, and Jasper Housman, for everything they did to aid this endeavor.

I wish to thank Robert Colbert, Michael Dante, Roberta Shore, Olive Sturgess, Jan Shepard, Joyce Meadows, and Michael F. Blake for sharing their memories of *Lawman*.

Others I wish to thank are Diana Levy, Michelle Levy, Mark Poisella, Mike "The Rabbit" Berry, Ted Michelfelder, Gerrianne Delaney, Suzie McKibben, Roger Crowley, Robert Fells, William Darby, Greg Shepard, Tom Weaver, Martin Grams, Marlene and Michael Falken, Marsha and Gary Feldman, Lou Sabini, Dave Johnson, Matthew Hendryx, Stewart Marks, Robin and Sharon McNutt, Frank and Marilyn Fredo, Pete Housman, Buddy of Photofest, Genevieve Maxwell, Jos Ullian, Robert Ullian, David Wilson, the librarians at Fort Wayne's Main and Georgetown Library branches, the librarians at Sarasota's Selby and Fruitville Libraries, Zach Eccles, Barry Ranish, Karen and Jerry Koch, Dick and Pauline Augsburger, Jason Housman, and, finally, Jeffrey C. Levine, researcher par excellence.

(The Doug Abbott Collection)

Foreword
By Will "Sugarfoot" Hutchins

I can't believe it's been over sixty years since the fall of 1958 when *Lawman* first aired on ABC-TV.

It was my second year of playing the young 'easy lopin'' and 'cattle ropin'' Tom Brewster on *Sugarfoot*, and I was so happy for my good friends, John Russell and Peter Brown, to have their own series. John was a tall fellow Californian who was a hardworking and generous actor. Peter was a guy who took his role very seriously and quickly became an expert with both a pistol and a horse. *Lawman* was a change from the four established Warner's western series, *Cheyenne*, my *Sugarfoot*, *Maverick* and *Colt .45*, because its two main characters were not drifters seeking out adventure and romance but, instead, a marshal and his deputy trying to keep the peace in Laramie. I witnessed the construction of Laramie's main street on the Warner Bros. backlot and watched the father-son relationship between John's Marshal Dan Troop and Peter's Deputy Johnny McKay develop into a solid friendship.

I never did a *Lawman* episode, but Peter did two *Sugarfoot* shows, "The Hideout" and "The Trial of the Canary Kid," and John was in "Ring of Sand." The three of us saddled up to ride together in the *Maverick* crossover episode, "Hadley's Hunters." Although the studio kept us busy working non-stop on episodes and personal appearances, I had lots of opportunities to spend quality time with John and Peter.

A note about Warner Bros. and the way we were treated. You may recall that *Cheyenne's* Clint Walker, *Maverick's* Jim Garner, *77 Sunset Strip's* Edd Byrnes, and *Colt .45's* Wayde Preston each had serious contract differences with the studio. Let me put it this way. The worst gang in the Old West wasn't the James Gang, the Dalton brothers, or the Youngers; the toughest gang was the Warner Brothers. They rode us hard and put us away wet. On weekdays, they worked us relentlessly from dawn to dark; on weekends, they'd send us out on public appearances and rodeos for which they were paid handsomely and we were paid ugly.

Over the years, I've met a lot of folks who have good memories of *Lawman* and now, with its availability on cable and DVD, the series has attracted many new fans. This book was written for them and anyone who likes the Old West. It not only provides readers with all the information they would want to know about the show, but it also explores the reasons for its popularity.

My favorite part of the book is when Bill Levy describes the joy of watching *Lawman* and recognizing familiar faces like veteran film stars Robert Armstrong, Tom Drake, and Wayne Morris in featured roles and such former western heroes as Bob Steele, Allan Lane, Jack Buetel, and

Foreword

Kermit Maynard in bits. The entire book illustrates Bill's passion for those thrilling days of yesteryear.

So buckaroos, enjoy riding down memory lane with Marshal Dan Troop, Deputy Johnny McKay, and the lovely Lily.

Preface
by Boyd Magers

Author of *A Gathering of Guns: 50 Years of the TV Western* and "Western Clippings"

John Russell – Marshal Dan Troop; Peter Brown – Deputy Johnny McKay... the television team that maintained law and order in ABC and Warner Bros. Laramie, Wyoming on Sunday nights for four years and 156 episodes.

When it all began, Russell sat down with Peter Brown and said, "Look, we got ourselves a series. I think between us we can make it the best TV series in the country."

And to my way of thinking, they *did* make it *the best* half hour TV Western!

Now, thanks to Bill Levy, you will be able to relive all those terrific episodes as well as gain an insight into the lives of John Russell, Peter Brown, and lest we not overlook, Peggie Castle, who added sex appeal to the series.

So once again, let's ride back to 1958 where TV western evil violently flowed as we send for the badge and the gun of The Lawman!

Introduction

In the first edition of Richard West's book, *Television Westerns: Major and Minor Series, 1946-1978*, West concludes his introduction with this short paragraph:

"To those of us who grew up in that far simpler time before Viet-Nam, before Nixon and Watergate, before disco and punk rock, before those awful music videos and home computers, this book is dedicated. And almost certainly to Matt, Davy, Major Adams, Bret, Bart, and all the others who made those days such a pleasant time in which to spend our youth."

When I was a teenager growing up on Long Island, New York during the late 1950s and early 1960s, I loved television westerns. My favorite series was ABC-TV's *Lawman* (1958-62) starring John Russell as Laramie's Marshal Dan Troop and Peter Brown as Deputy Johnny McKay.

I identified with Peter Brown's loyal deputy, open to learning the ropes so he could become a successful peace officer. I admired John Russell's laconic marshal who had little patience for outlaws or hypocrites, but would stand up for underdogs and outsiders. Marshal Troop also displayed a warmer side with his mentoring of his young deputy and, beginning in the second season, in his relationship with Peggie Castle's beautiful Lily Merrill.

I relished this show because it was tightly written. Unlike most of its hour-long contemporaries, *Lawman* episodes lasted thirty minutes. Marshal Troop was faced with a dilemma or a menacing adversary, and after some initial problems, the predicament was resolved while his deputy Johnny learned a lesson or two.

I relished this show because it told its stories without gimmicks. There were no special guns, no corny sidekicks, just a marshal and his deputy doing their jobs and combatting whatever evils confronted them.

In recent years, after decades when it was not accessible to the public, (*Lawman* was never released on VHS), episodes of the series have been aired on Encore's Western Channel and other cable networks. DVDs of all four seasons are now available. Once barely remembered except by its aficionados, there's been a recent resurgence of interest that has resulted in a Facebook's *Lawman* TV Series Fan Group, with a current membership of over 950 passionate participants. This resurgence has also resulted in the latest edition of Richard West's book displaying John Russell's Marshal Troop alone on the cover.

After watching all 156 episodes on DVD, I approached BearManor Media's Ben Ohmart who had previously published my book, *Lest We Forget: The John Ford Stock Company* in 2013. I asked if he would be interested in a book on *Lawman*. He was.

Hopefully, *Lawman: A Companion to the Classic TV Western Series* will stimulate veteran viewers and new fans to experience this exceptional western series and its three-dimensional leads.

Bill Levy
Sarasota, Florida 2019

Photo Gallery I: The Three Leads

John Russell

Lawman Publicity Still

(The Doug Abbott Collection)

Peter Brown

Lawman Publicity Still

(The Doug Abbott Collection)

Peggie Castle

Lawman Publicity Still

(The Doug Abbott Collection)

John Russell, Peter Brown, Peggie Castle

Lawman Publicity Still

(The Doug Abbott Collection)

Photo Gallery I

Peter Brown, John Russell
Lawman Publicity Still
(The Doug Abbott Collection)

Peggie Castle
Lawman Publicity Still
(The Doug Abbott Collection)

Peter Brown, John Russell, Peggie Castle
Scene from "The Second Son," 1960
(The Doug Abbott Collection)

Peter Brown, John Russell, Peggie Castle
Scene from "The Second Son," 1960
(The Doug Abbott Collection)

John Russell
Lawman Publicity Still
(The Doug Abbott Collection)

Peter Brown
Lawman Publicity Still
(The Doug Abbott Collection)

John Russell, Peggie Castle
Lawman Publicity Still
(The Doug Abbott Collection)

Peggie Castle
Lawman Publicity Still
(The Doug Abbott Collection)

PHOTO GALLERY I

John Russell, Peter Brown
Lawman Publicity Still
(The Doug Abbott Collection)

Peter Brown, John Russell
Scene from "The Long Gun," 1962
(The Doug Abbott Collection)

John Russell, Peggie Castle, Peter Brown
Lawman Publicity Still
(The Doug Abbott Collection)

Peggie Castle
Scene from "The Ugly Man," 1960
(The Doug Abbott Collection)

John Russell, Peggie Castle
Lawman Publicity Still
(The Doug Abbott Collection)

Peggie Castle, John Russell
Lawman Publicity Still
(The Doug Abbott Collection)

Peter Brown, John Russell
Lawman Publicity Still
(The Doug Abbott Collection)

John Russell, Peter Brown
Lawman Publicity Still
(The Doug Abbott Collection)

PHOTO GALLERY I

John Russell
Scene from "Homecoming," 1961
(The Doug Abbott Collection)

John Russell
Scene from "The Catalog Woman," 1961
(The Doug Abbott Collection)

John Russell, Peggie Castle
Lawman Publicity Still
(The Doug Abbott Collection)

Peggie Castle
Lawman Publicity Still
(The Doug Abbott Collection)

Creating *Lawman*

Lawman debuted on Sunday evening, October 5, 1958 at 8:30 on ABC-TV with the episode, "The Deputy." Seven very different people, Jack L. Warner, William T. Orr, Jules Schermer, Harry Whittington, John Russell, Peter Brown, and Peggie Castle, created and/or shaped this television western series that has stood the test of time.

By the mid-1950s, Hollywood's "Golden Era" was drawing to a close and the motion picture studios were facing serious competition from television. Warner Bros. had experienced popular and financial success for over a quarter of a century. With memorable and lucrative motion pictures featuring such stars as Rin Tin Tin, Al Jolson, George Arliss, James Cagney, Bette Davis, Errol Flynn, Paul Muni, Edward G. Robinson, Humphrey Bogart, and Olivia de Havilland, Warner Bros. had achieved a firm fiscal base culminating in a net profit of twenty million dollars in 1947 (230 million dollars in 2019 dollars).

In 1948, Warner Bros. (and other studios) lost an antitrust case,

United States v. Paramount Pictures, Inc., forcing the studios to separate production from the theatrical exhibition and distribution of their films. In addition, Warner Bros.' 3-D and widescreen movie ventures had failed to counter the public's infatuation with television, and the studio's net profit for 1954 was down to two million dollars.

Warner Bros. studio head Jack L. Warner always had great disdain for the smaller screen. But after observing the 1954 success of Walt Disney's "Disneyland" television program, Warner decided to explore an involvement with television's third network, ABC-TV. Warner was known for his lack of respect for actors and writers, his penny-pinching cost-cutting, and his studio's rapid assembly-line schedule ("I don't want it good; I want it Tuesday!"). But he had a good eye for making money. In 1955, he hired his son-in-law, William T. Orr, to organize a television wing of the studio and produce low-cost black and white one-hour dramas.

****

Ron Simon, the curator of television and radio at the Paley Center for Media located in New York City and Los Angeles, declared, "Television began as a step-child. But because of Orr, it became equal with film in creating revenue and jobs." Orr had the vision to appreciate television's potential for airing entertaining and lucrative productions, and to initiate direct relationships with sponsors. He transformed Warner Bros. movie production into an even faster-paced television mode and engaged motion picture writers, directors, and producers to create and recreate countless storylines for television. He was responsible for even more cost savings by filling these new Warner Bros. series with scenes from earlier movies. According to Hollywood observer Bob Thomas, the popular joke around Hollywood during the 1950s was, "If you see more than two characters in a Warners TV show, it's stock footage."

Orr supervised the production of *Warner Bros. Presents*, which debuted during the fall of 1955. It featured three new alternating one-hour dramas, *Casablanca*, *King's Row*, and the western *Cheyenne*. *Cheyenne* (1955-63) survived the first year, lasted six seasons, and initiated the surge of Warner Bros. television western series on ABC-TV: *Maverick* (1957-62), *Sugarfoot* (1957-61), *Colt .45* (1957-60), and in the fall of 1958, *Bronco* (1958-62), and *Lawman* (1958-62).

****

Meanwhile, during the spring of 1957, pulp novelist Harry Whittington was in Hollywood writing a screenplay for Warner Bros. based on his western novel, *Trouble Rides Tall*, which would be published in England by Abelard-Schuman and in the United States as a Crest paperback in June of that year. This was to be a tough film about an uncompromising, seasoned peace officer, a "trouble marshal," confronting rampant crime and criminals in a frontier community. The movie was to be directed and produced by Roy Del Ruth who had helmed *The Babe Ruth Story* (1948) and *On Moonlight Bay* (1951). Gary Cooper or John Wayne were said to be possibly starring in the production.

Although the film was never made, Orr, his executive assistant Hugh Benson, and their underlings liked the concept of a television series based on Whittington's script. Seeing the popularity of *Gunsmoke* (1955-75) and *The Life and Legend of Wyatt Earp* (1955-61), Orr decided to create a serious Warner Bros. adult western that didn't have a protagonist wandering the west as in the studios' other westerns, but rather one with a marshal who remained in one locality.

Lawman's Marshal Dan Troop owes much to Whittington and the protagonist of *Trouble Rides Tall* (1958), Bry Shafter. Troop and Shafter are taciturn men, forced by their chosen profession to isolate themselves from others. Both are wary of becoming involved with a woman because each fears he may die at any time. Whittington described Shafter's reflections of the precariousness of being a lawman: "He thought about... the quiet and peace that he had made – and he alone, walking the streets in the dark, standing up to men who had never backed down, seeing them back down or draw." But unlike Troop, Shafter has a cantankerous relationship with his deputy, similar to the one that Sheriff Walt Longmire had with Deputy Branch Connally on the cable television series *Longmire* (2012-17). And unlike Shafter, Troop has Johnny and Lily to add light and warmth to his life.

****

To oversee his new series, Orr brought in Jules Schermer, a veteran Hollywood insider who had co-written the movie *The Fighting Sullivans* (1944), and produced the films *The Man from Colorado* (1949) and *Pickup on South Street* (1953). Orr declared, "Jules Schermer produced *Lawman* – and very well. He loved sparse dialogue. He was a good choice to produce it because he liked very sparse scenes. His whole career he had done pictures that were kind of that way."

Schermer vowed to make *Lawman* special and from the beginning, he worked hard on establishing a quality product. He called *Lawman* a "thinking western," one that allowed the relationship between the characters to reach a deeper intensity. He aimed to assemble a cast and crew who worked closely together and had good chemistry. Schermer received substantial support from his two stars, John Russell and Peter Brown. Brown recalled, "It took a lot of determination on our part to maintain the integrity of the show and characters while dealing with a parade of ever-changing writers and directors, a bare-bones budget, and what can only be described as a frantic shooting schedule." In a *TV Guide* interview, Brown added, "When we started, he [Russell] sat down with me and said, 'Look, we've got ourselves a series. I don't know how you feel, but I think we can make it the best TV series in the country.' I said, 'I'm with you.' That's why you never see us pull a gun we don't intend to use, take unnecessary risks like phony heroes, or stage any long, drawn-out fist fights."

Schermer, Russell, and Brown provided consistency during the four-year run of the series. Schermer was executive producer or producer for 153 of the 156 episodes. He was always extremely protective of *Lawman* and did everything he could to provide support for his cast and crew amid the organized chaos of Warner Bros. frenetic assembly-line production and studio politics. Schermer was constantly at odds with directors, who he described in a *Variety* article as "more concerned with meeting a schedule than getting value out of a script... Too often, directors played scenes too broadly, giving the entire episode the appearance of cliché or caricature." Schermer's loyalty to the series and his efforts to maximize its quality proved contagious; unlike many of the other Warner Bros. series, there were no actor walkouts on Schermer's watch.

****

Lawman's three lead actors, John Russell, Peter Brown, and Peggie Castle, were each influential in shaping the series. In very different ways, they each added to the tone, depth, and uniqueness of *Lawman*.

John Russell had been acting in films since the late 1930s with only a stint in the Marine Corps during World War II breaking up his acting career. He had small parts in *Forever Amber* (1947), John Ford's *The Sun Shines Bright* (1953), and *The Last Command* (1955). He often played villains; his outlaw Lengthy in the gritty western, *Yellow Sky* (1948), was a typical role for Russell. In 1955, he had the opportunity to star in the syndicated television series, *Soldiers of Fortune*, playing a heroic adventurer for hire, Tim Kelly. The show was aired for two years and then rerun throughout the 1950s and 1960s. It consisted of fifty-two episodes.

In February 1958 in the *Cheyenne* episode, "The Empty Gun," Russell portrayed a sincere man of honor, a former gunslinger with a crippled gun hand attempting to go straight. Orr and Schermer were very impressed with Russell's performance. Orr recalled, "We liked John. We tested him and kept his style that way. He had no vestige of anything but dedication to duty, directness, and lacked any small talk – very monosyllabic."

Schermer and Russell worked on Russell's character for *Lawman* and agreed on Dan Troop's single-mindedness: Marshal Dan Troop was portrayed as a man who rarely followed the path of least resistance. In an interview with *TV Guide*, aptly titled, "He Had All the Expression of a Rock," Russell explained, "Troop is a man doing a job at the expense of everything else. He doesn't make himself winning or witty, or do anything else to make people like him. Unbending isn't his duty." Russell even had a white streak put into his hair to age his character.

Mass media observer Rita Parks' depiction of the Western hero encapsulates Marshal Troop: "He is generally a loner. He is, however, a man in command of things, persons, and events, handling them skillfully but with a certain aloofness that preserves his integrity. He is a man with a mysterious and frequently melancholy past; his future is tenuous and foreboding. He is almost always a man with one foot in the wilderness and the other in civilization, moving through life belonging to neither world."

****

1958 was a pivotal year for twenty-two year-old Peter Brown. He signed a contract with Warner Bros., had small parts in three films, *Darby's Rangers*, *Marjorie Morningstar*, and *Onionhead*, and got the role of his lifetime as Deputy Johnny McKay. *Onionhead* had been produced by Jules Schermer, and when searching for a young actor to play McKay, Schermer remembered Brown and cast him as the youngster who yearned to be a lawman like Marshal Dan Troop.

Brown maintained that Russell taught him the ropes: "'Focus on the camera,' he'd always say. 'Use your eyes to tell the story, not always your mouth. That's where your focus should be. Your eyes are the tool.'" Brown also remembered that Russell was "always thinking how to make the show better, causing me to do the same."

Brown worked hard on perfecting his quick draw until he was

considered one of the fastest in Hollywood. He was an excellent rider, but because *Lawman* was filmed on the Warner Bros. backlot in Burbank, he didn't have many opportunities to demonstrate his equestrian skills on his horse, Houdini. He did well enough with his characterization of a youth quickly becoming a man that after *Lawman's* first season, he won "The Most Outstanding Newcomer Award" from the Theater Owners of America.

******

During *Lawman's* first season (1958-59), Schermer tried out two actresses to play romantic interests for Dan Troop, but neither Bek Nelson nor Barbara Lang provided the right chemistry with the marshal. Nelson's widow and café owner appeared too docile while Lang's newspaper editor was too adversarial. At the beginning of the second season (1959-60), Peggie Castle was brought in to play Lily Merrill, the owner and proprietress of "The Birdcage Saloon." It was immediately apparent that she blended well with Russell and Brown.

Castle worked as a Universal and United Artists contract player before signing with Warner Bros. in 1956. Among her films were *I, the Jury* (1953), *Jesse James' Women* (1954), *Miracle in the Rain* (1956), and *The Seven Hills of Rome* (1957). She was known as "the poor man's Claire Trevor," since she often played a blonde in distress in B-movies. After she appeared in several Warner Bros. films and television series, Schermer decided to cast her as the marshal's lady at the beginning of *Lawman's* second season. Castle's Lily not only added beauty to the show; she added wit, humor, and compassion, and brought out these traits in Troop. Hollywood columnist Erskine Johnson called her effect on the marshal, "defrosting of the character."

Castle described Lily as "a jolly friendly person with a heart as big as a bus. She has a kind word and a smile for everyone.... But when she wants to be, she is as tough as Dan Troop." Her only reservation about playing Lily was that she had to sing, a skill she knew she wasn't adept at: "For the first time in my life, I was a singer – that was the producer's opinion, not mine."

****

The contributions of these seven diverse individuals resulted in top-thirty Nielsen ratings of twenty seven, fifteen, and twenty-six during *Lawman's* first three years even though it was slotted against the second half of the popular *The Ed Sullivan Show*. For almost four years, a large, loyal audience tuned into *Lawman* on Sunday evenings at 8:30 to watch the reticent marshal, his loyal deputy, and his lady fair confront the latest threat to the peace of Laramie.

The Appeal of *Lawman*

Lawman has always had avid fans, from viewers of the series' initial broadcasts between 1958 and 1962 to contemporary audiences enjoying each show on cable and DVDs. There are many reasons for its appeal, but the contributions of the three leads, John Russell, Peter Brown, and Peggie Castle, were crucial in the creation of such a special viewing experience.

When asked about the reasons for *Lawman's* success, co-star Peter Brown replied, "John Russell, John Russell, John Russell." Without a doubt, *Lawman* is driven by Russell's Marshal Dan Troop, a tall, handsome, no-nonsense protagonist with a chiseled face and body. Troop is depicted as an ethical and courageous peace officer who refuses to give in to evil adversaries or political pressures. He is also a realist; he understands that he could die at any time, but he refuses to allow this to dissuade him.

Christopher Anderson, author of *Hollywood: The Studio System in the Fifties* (1994), pictures Troop as, "A towering, solemn figure, armed with a piercing stare and an unwavering sense of dignity. . . . a frontier patriarch," while Robert Malsbary, co-author of *Warner Bros. Television* (1985), calls him, "the personification of law and order in its purest, most unadulterated form."

Russell's marshal is also complex which adds to his appeal. He is a charismatic leader who possesses excellent detective skills, has a nose for trouble, and displays an abundance of courage and insight. At first glance, he appears to be uncompromising, but he's more than a tough fighter and a fast gun willing to confront outlaw gunmen, hysterical mobs, bigots, and confidence men. Troop is a compassionate man; note his kind, fatherly mentoring of his deputy, his reserved but loving relationship with Lily, and his sympathetic championing of various underdogs and outsiders.

Listening to his words of advice to Johnny and observing his actions, one realizes that Dan Troop is an exceptional individual. In the episode, "The Gang" (1959), it's revealed that the girl Troop once loved was an innocent bystander killed in a meaningless gunfight years before. Troop dedicates his life to upholding the law and preventing future tragedies.

Russell's Marshal Troop may appear impassive when he shoots to kill, but note the usually steel-eyed marshal's desolation while cradling James Drury's character in his arms at the end of the episode "The Gang" (1959) or feel his sadness for his love-sick rejected deputy at the conclusion of "Girl from Grantsville" (1960). Troop is usually pictured as very serious and somber, but in "The Return of Owny O'Reilly" (1960) and "Mountain Man" (1962), his sense of humor is on full display.

All of these attributes create an intriguing and extremely watchable leading man and an intriguing and extremely watchable show. John Russell was a very powerful presence; he was the only actor to stand up as an equal to the two greatest western movie icons, John Wayne and Clint Eastwood (in *Rio Bravo* [1959] and *Pale Rider* [1985]). Perhaps the best tribute to Russell's portrayal of Marshal Dan Troop was written by Gary Yoggy in *Riding the Video Range: The Rise and Fall of the Western on Television* (1995): "If Jim Arness is television's John Wayne then it is not stretching too much to liken John Russell's Dan Troop to Gary Cooper's Will Kane, the western roles for which each is best remembered."

The promos for the series describe the marshal as "a lawman of strength and purpose" and his deputy as "the boy he trained to fight by his side." From the first episode, Peter Brown's young Deputy McKay is more than a boy, much more than a callow youth. Compare him with the brash, impulsive, hero-worshipping Bat Masterson (Mason Alan Dinehart) in the early episodes of *The Life and Legend of Wyatt Earp* (1955-61). From the beginning, McKay exhibits self-confidence, bravery, and a dogged determination to succeed. As the series evolves, he demonstrates a consistent growth in maturity. He makes his mistakes, but he learns from them. He grows into a thoughtful and responsible young man who isn't quite a facsimile of his marshal; the deputy displays more humor and optimism. It's these two traits, along with his good looks, that make the Johnny McKay so likeable and memorable.

By the middle of the first season, Johnny has earned the respect of the marshal and the community, and is given more responsibilities. Troop has no problem leaving him in charge of policing the town. At the end of "The Young Toughs" (1959), Troop compliments Johnny for standing up alone to three troublemakers: "Sometimes it's not possible to back down. You did right to go ahead. It was the right choice – for a man."

Peggie Castle's Lily Merrill displays admirable personal qualities throughout her three seasons on the show. She shows her courage after an outlaw gang intimidates the entire town from serving on a jury; she volunteers to serve in "The Juror (1961)." She repeatedly demonstrates her empathy for others in her dealings with strays, the emotionally wounded, and others in need of a shoulder. She reveals a wonderfully wry sense of humor in her interactions with the marshal, and she exhibits her pluck when she volunteers to be Laramie's fire chief in "Firehouse Lil" (1961) and substitute teacher in "The Substitute" (1961).

Lily Merrill's presence adds to the show and increases its appeal. As Peter Brown declared, she was "a great fit for the cast." In a variety of scenarios ranging from tense situations when she is in danger to lighter moments when she flirts with Troop or jokes with Johnny, Lily consistently provides a feminine radiance that melds with the marshal and his deputy's masculinity without distracting from them or the storylines. In addition, it is her presence that warms up Troop and helps pull him away from his solitary, glacial remoteness.

Castle stated, "I've tried to give Lily the glamour and presence of the famous English actress Lily Langtry, and the fire and sexiness of the one and only Maria Montez, the famous dancer of the turn of the century." She succeeded. With her peaches and cream complexion, spectacular figure, and stunning wardrobe, Castle's earthy but classy portrayal of an independent woman enhances the show.

Another important draw to *Lawman* is the fact that each episode lasts only twenty-six minutes. There is no time for fluff. The story revolves around the three leads and one, possibly two additional characters. Marginal subplots are kept to a minimum. There is no opportunity for anyone or anything who isn't involved in the basic plot to pull attention away from the pace and tension of the narrative. In this way, conflicts, misunderstandings, and complex issues can be addressed and resolved quickly.

Although there are often veteran and younger actors and actresses guest-starring, the focus rarely departs from at least one of the three leads. Recognizable faces may give memorable performances, but these are integrated into the show, unlike *Wagon Train* and *Gunsmoke* when big-name stars often monopolized the storylines.

One of the joys of *Lawman* is watching the many recognizable faces visiting the streets of Laramie. Among them are noteworthy actors from the 1930s, 1940s, and 1950s including John Carradine, Wayne Morris, Robert Armstrong, Philip Carey, Dick Foran, Bill Williams, Lon Chaney Jr., Marie Windsor, and Tom Drake, as well as former cowboy stars Bob Steele, Jack Buetel, Kermit Maynard, Allan Lane, and John Agar. Future television and film stars like Troy Donahue, Edd Byrnes, Chad Everett,

Martin Landau, Shirley Knight, James Coburn, James Drury, Joel Grey, Dorothy Provine, Robert Fuller, and Dawn Wells appear too. Also, there are the myriad of beautiful young actresses who appear briefly, infatuating a certain young deputy.

Good villains are a necessity for good drama and *Lawman's* episodes are filled with determined and menacing antagonists for Marshal Troop to face. Among the strong actors whose characters threaten the law and order of Laramie are Jack Elam, Lee Van Cleef, Robert Wilke, Arch Johnson, Larry Blake, Ray Danton, Frank de Kova, R.G. Armstrong, James Griffith, Marc Lawrence, and Jack Lambert.

Producer Jules Schermer's insistence on high quality production values is apparent in *Lawman*. There is no sense that the series was rushed, and the continuity in the stories is always strong. Actress Jan Shepard, who co-starred in the episode "Change of Venue" (1962), recalled the positive and supportive comradery of the cast, the expertise of the wardrobe and make-up crews, and the professionalism of the music and photography departments.

The musical background to *Lawman* boosts the series in a variety of ways. Composer Jerry Livingston and lyricist Mack David's theme song is addictive and the music is often used in different tempos to capture diverse moods, tensions, and situations. For example, oboes and clarinets are played to highlight the humorous scenes. Much of the music in *Lawman* and most Warner Bros. series is taken from western classics, and the melodies of "Oh Susanna," "The Streets of Laredo," and "Buffalo Gals" provide nostalgia to many scenes in and out of "The Birdcage Saloon."

Another element of *Lawman* that makes it distinct is the superior photography. Renowned cinematographer Bert Glennon, who shot John Ford's *Young Mr. Lincoln* (1939), *Stagecoach* (1939), *Drums Along the Mohawk* (1939), and *Rio Grande* (1950), photographed sixty-four *Lawman* episodes. These films reveal Glennon's mastery of lighting, close-ups, and use of rain, wind, sun, shadows, and perspective to highlight his stark, gritty, textured black-and-white visuals. Emmy winning photographer

Ralph Woolsey, who shot *The Iceman Cometh* (1973) and *The Great Santini* (1979), did twenty-six *Lawman* episodes, always trying to keep it simple. He later recalled, "We had crews who had been working on pictures for years, so sometimes they would tend to be a little too fancy or elaborate for a television show. In other words, you had to say, 'Forget the frosting on the cake, and let's take care of the meat and potatoes first.'"

The basic strength and attraction of *Lawman* is that it's a serious "meat and potatoes" show revolving around the trials and tribulations of two men attempting to keep the peace in the frontier west. Extraneous humor is kept to a minimum. Troop, Johnny, and Lily have their fun with one another, but few other characters are given the opportunity to lighten the series' dramatic tensions. Warner Bros. television production head, William Orr, has stated he attempted to pressure Jules Schermer to include more comedy in the series with the barber (Roscoe Ates) or the hotel clerk (Grady Sutton), but Schermer was able to avoid implementing Orr's suggestions.

Another reason for *Lawman's* appeal is its relevancy. During its four-year run, *Lawman* proved itself one of the best adult westerns by addressing complex and controversial topics that are still pertinent today. These include Post Traumatic Stress Disorder in "Battle Scar" (1959); the ramifications of brain injury in "Explosion" (1962); the dangers of using the media to find romance in "The Catalog Woman" (1961); domestic violence in "Whiphand" (1961) and "Heritage of Hate" (1962); alienated youths in "The Young Toughs" (1959) and "The Town Boys" (1960); the use of psychology to promote fear in "The Thimblerigger" (1960) and "The Threat" (1961); the dangers of modern weaponry in "Trojan Horse" (1961); hostage-taking in "Thirty Minutes" (1960); and prejudice and discrimination against minorities in "The Intruders" (1958), "Warpath" (1959), and "The Outsider" (1959).

Lawman continually offers its viewers a blueprint for using intelligence, forcefulness, and compassion to combat violence, hatred, and prejudice. As the marshal mentors his deputy, the show gives its audience a multitude of "teachable moments" that can lead to the contemplation of solutions to a wide variety of problems and dilemmas.

Finally, *Lawman* has always offered its audience comfort and relief. In our modern world filled with anger and angst, and aptly described by actor Michael Dante's father as "far more interested in making a killing than making a living," it's a pleasure to watch a morality play where even though there may be shades of grey, good does overcome evil.

****

The same strengths of *Lawman*, which numerous television commentators applauded during the late 1950s and early 1960s and which western genre writers over the years have admired in their books and essays, still hold true today. Below are perspectives of the cast, entertainment writers, and members of Facebook's *Lawman* TV Series Fan Group voicing their opinions as to why the show was and is so special:

John Russell: "*Lawman* was a pure Western that employed standard weapons rather than gold-headed canes or tricked-up rifles. Its stories began with 'A,' proceeded straight to 'B,' and stopped neatly at 'C' without any fussy complications."

Peter Brown: "I think John and I had a classic mentor/protégé arrangement in *Lawman*. Some people have described it more as a father-son relationship."

Nancy Dale, founder and administrator of Facebook's *Lawman* TV Series Fan Group: "To me, it was John Russell's compelling and mesmerizing eyes that made him and the series so appealing. He didn't need to say a word. Those dark eyes spoke volumes with their powerful and compelling intensity. They were so fixated! They never blinked or flinched; Russell's Marshal Dan Troop never blinked or flinched."

Writer Tise Vahimagi: "In the breed of Warners' 'adult' Westerns, this is a direct-hit actioner with little time given to the psychology behind the action. The characterization is strong and the production above average, and John Russell is a hard-bitten, shoot-to-kill lawman."

Christina Dale, co-administrator of Facebook's *Lawman* TV Series Fan Group: "I love the comradery between Dan, Johnny, and Lily. Their friendship is truly one of a kind. When you watch an episode, there's always a lesson to be learned that can still be applied in today's world. *Lawman* draws a vast array of audiences, from the younger generation (like myself) to the mature generation that watched it on prime time. And coming from a feminist's stand point, I admire Lily's bravery and courage. She is not afraid to stand up for what she believes is right. I feel that the writers dug deep within themselves to write of a variety of emotions. No matter what episode you watch, you will always walk away having learned something."

Westerns enthusiasts Dick and Pauline Augsburger: "We recently discovered the series and found it to be a refreshing no-frills western with strong characters. Fun to watch!"

Marvin Diamond, member of Facebook's *Lawman* TV Series Fan Group: "Strong cast, strong storylines, and strong production values have made *Lawman* so enduring."

Writer Michael F. Blake, son of *Lawman* actor, Larry Blake who played numerous villains on the show: "For a half-hour show, *Lawman* managed to create believable characters and interesting story plots. The scripts were tight, to the point, and entertaining. And, the show had the actors – John Russell and Peter Brown – and that was what separated the show from others."

Sandra Miller, member of Facebook's *Lawman* TV Series Fan Group: "I think the reason that it endures today is because the stories were believable, well portrayed, and there's an absent of crude language, horrendous violence, and moronic humor. The lead characters were admirable and had great respect for one another. New fans can appreciate a well-written story that leaves you with the satisfaction that the heroes won the West!"

TV.com: "This western was a highly professional show in the midst of a time when formula westerns were the norm."

Rick du Bise, member of Facebook's *Lawman* TV Series Fan Group: "The acting and writing were way above par. The taciturn image of Marshal Troop contrasted nicely with the more lighthearted Deputy – even with the *Bride of Frankenstein* blaze on his [Troop's] head!!"

Actor Michael Dante: "*Lawman* was special because the plots were tight and they adhered to dialogue; they didn't wander. John Russell has a great western face; chiseled cheekbones, dark eyes. The series accurately depicted two men of integrity and principle willing to risk everything to protect a lawful and peaceful American way of life."

Francis Taylor, member of Facebook's *Lawman* TV Series Fan Group: "Everything in the show is sincere."

Writer Jim Willard: "Perhaps it was the thin mustache accompanied by the steely-eyed gaze that drew me to the lead. . . . The series of half-hour shows didn't unfold any tricks or gimmicks during its run, just uncomplicated stories of bad men brought to justice by a guy with a slim moustache and a string tie, my kind of lawman."

Guy Guenin, member of Facebook's *Lawman* TV Series Fan Group: "*Lawman* is/was about as straight-laced as you get, not a whole lot of gray area – I prefer things that way."

Writers Neil Summers and Roger M. Crowley: "A classic TV western, *Lawman* was a straight forward, no frills series. . . . Of the hundreds of westerns that have been on the air, *Lawman* is a standout and Peter Brown and John Russell can be proud of their time spent on the dusty streets of Laramie."

Writer Gary Yoggy: "All in all, *Lawman* was a superior Western filled with adult situations, a minimum of dialogue, and plenty of old-fashioned action. *Lawman* depicted the keeping of law and order on the frontier as it could have been – indeed, as it must have been."

Sue Shearer, member of Facebook's *Lawman* TV Series Fan Group: "I like the way John Russell can seem so unemotional and then physically touch someone in such a gentle caring way. Best example was when he cradled Clay's (James Drury) head after Clay died saving him. I liked *Gunsmoke* but never saw that kind of compassion/feeling demonstrated by James Arness."

Gary Feldman, TV westerns enthusiast: "I find Marshal Troop particularly engaging and appealing. He is not only heroic; he is an instinctive detective who often employs ingenious ploys to capture a criminal. I also enjoy the series' fast pace, the comradery between the two lawmen, and the relationship between Dan and Lily."

George Moore, member of Facebook's *Lawman* TV Series Fan Group: "*Lawman* has been a favorite of mine since my dad and I would watch it together. Back then Westerns were all over the TV with many great shows, but *Lawman* stood out from the rest. John Russell was a man who made his badge reflect the law."

Writer Robert Malsbary: "This Western was different from the others. One might say that *Lawman* was *Gunsmoke*, *The Lone Ranger*, and *Father Knows Best* all rolled into one."

Michael Shields, member of Facebook's *Lawman* TV Series Fan Group: "A lot of it, for me, was that the show was believable. It was totally realistic with John Russell voicing what law enforcement was really all about, and the production staff paid attention to detail, unlike some of the other programs of that era (like nine-shot six shooters and so on). There was also the element of the experienced marshal taking the time to teach his new deputy about things, rather than using the old premise of everyone knowing everything. *Lawman*, being a half hour, had to tighten things up and tell a story at its basic level.... I thought it was a good thing to keep some mystery about each character and make the home audience think about, and guess about their backgrounds."

****

Michael Shields makes an excellent point in his above final statement. One of *Lawman's* biggest strengths is that sense of mystery which permeates the show and makes this series a thought-provoking adult western. We know some of the personal histories of the three leads, but there are voids in their pasts which the contemplative viewer must speculate about: Is Troop doing some sort of penance dedicating his life to upholding the law because he feels responsible for the love of his life's death in a gunfight? What was it in Johnny's past that enabled him to become the heroic man he became? How and why is Lily so strong yet so vulnerable at the same time? These questions and others prove that *Lawman* is a multifaceted western series that should be watched and re-watched, savored and shared.

**Photo Gallery II:
Supporting Cast and Guest Stars**

Bek Nelson, John Russell
Lawman Publicity Still
(The Doug Abbott Collection)

John Russell, Barbara Lang, Peter Brown
Lawman Publicity Still
(The Doug Abbott Collection)

Peter Brown, Roscoe Ates
Scene from "The Breakup," 1959
(The Doug Abbott Collection)

John Russell, Joel Grey
Scene from "The Return of Owny O'Reilly," 1960
(The Doug Abbott Collection)

PHOTO GALLERY II

John Russell, Lee Van Cleef
Scene from "The Actor," 1962
(The Doug Abbott Collection)

Peter Brown, John Carradine, John Russell
Scene from "Man on a Mountain," 1960
(The Doug Abbott Collection)

Dawn Wells, Peter Brown
Publicity Still from "No Contest," 1962
(The Doug Abbott Collection)

John Russell, Ray Danton
Publicity Still from "Lily" 1959
(The Doug Abbott Collection)

John Russell, Edd Byrnes
Scene from "The Mad Bunch," 1960
(The Doug Abbott Collection)

Troy Donahue, John Russell
Scene from "The Payment," 1960
(The Doug Abbott Collection)

John Russell, Louise Fletcher
Publicity Still from "The Encounter," 1959
(The Doug Abbott Collection)

Peter Brown, Lon Chaney Jr.
Scene from "The Tarnished Badge," 1962
(The Doug Abbott Collection)

PHOTO GALLERY II

Peter Brown, Sammy Davis Jr.
Scene from "Blue Boss and Willie Shay," 1961
(The Doug Abbott Collection)

John Russell, Don Drysdale
Publicity Still from "The Hardcase," 1960
(The Doug Abbott Collection)

John Russell, Tom Drake
Scene from "The Hunch," 1959
(The Doug Abbott Collection)

John Russell, William Joyce,
Kathie Browne, Peggie Castle
Scene from "Heritage of Hate," 1962
(The Doug Abbott Collection)

The Episodes

The following 156 *Lawman* capsules include the original broadcast date, the principal cast and crew, a brief synopsis, a commentary, and a trivia section for each episode.

The cast and crew's names are listed exactly as they were on screen in the credits at the end of each episode.

William T. Orr was the Executive Producer for all 156 episodes of *Lawman*. Gordon Bau was the makeup supervisor throughout the run of the show. Jerry Livingston composed the music and Mack David wrote the lyrics to the song "Lawman," which was sung at the beginning and at the end of each show. These four men are not listed in the episode summaries.

Each synopsis is deliberately brief so it won't reveal any plot points or surprise hooks.

Each commentary includes a description of how the common themes in *Lawman* are depicted in that episode. This section also discusses how the acting, music, photography, lighting, action, dialogue, body language, sets, and costumes enrich and enhance the storyline.

The trivia section offers biographical background information about the cast and crew and production particulars. Whenever possible, credits in western movies and television shows are included.

Lawman was produced by Warner Bros. and broadcast on ABC-TV on Sundays from 8:30 to 9:00 PM from October 5, 1958 to April 1, 1962. From April 8, 1962 to June 24, 1962, original shows were broadcast on ABC-TV on Sundays from 10:30 to 11:00 PM. Repeats were shown during the summer and early fall of the four year run of the series.

The episodes were twenty-six minutes in length. The additional four minutes were taken up by commercials for the main sponsor of the series, R.J. Reynolds Tobacco Company, and the secondary sponsor, General Mills. John Russell and Peter Brown did commercials endorsing Camel cigarettes and Cheerios.

Season One

Episode 1: "The Deputy" October 5, 1958.

Starring John Russell (Dan Troop) and Peter Brown (Johnny McKay). Supporting Cast: Bek Nelson (Dru Lemp), Edward Byrnes (Lacy Hawks), Jack Elam (Flynn Hawks), Lee VanCleef [Van Cleef] (Walt Hawks), Stanley Farrar (Judge Patterson), Lane Chandler (Tom Pike), Rankin Mansfield (Carl Shoemaker).

Directed by Montgomery Pittman, Teleplay by Dean Riesner, from a novel by Harry Whittington, Produced by Jules Schermer, Director of Photography: Ralph Woolsey, Art Director: Howard Campbell, Supervising Film Editor: James Moore, Film Editor: Elbert K. Hollingsworth, Production Manager: Oren W. Haglund, Sound: Stanley Jones, Set Decorator: Fay Babcock, Assistant Director: C. Carter Gibson.

Synopsis: Dan Troop is hired as the new town marshal of Laramie,

Wyoming Territory, in 1879. He investigates the murder of the previous marshal and searches for a deputy.

Commentary: The first episode establishes the characters of the two main protagonists: the strong, uncompromising marshal and the young, eager, loyal deputy. Bek Nelson's Dru Lemp, the widow of the slain marshal, provides a potential romantic partner for Troop. This episode and the four years of *Lawman* are loosely based on the structure of Harry Whittington's 1958 novel, *Trouble Rides Tall*. The book depicts the challenges facing a legendary peace officer who's hired to "clean up" a town overrun by criminals and crime. It's fitting that two of the most well-known movie and television western villains, Jack Elam and Lee Van Cleef, appear in this episode, as well as a young Warner Bros. television star, Edward "Kookie" Byrnes. Warner Bros. used all of their television shows to showcase their young contracted players. The scene in the cemetery is photographed so that the majority of the shots are clean over-the-shoulder set-ups (no shoulder of the other character is seen), isolating Troop and McKay, in contrast to later shared interactions.

Trivia: Elam was featured in five *Lawman* episodes, Van Cleef in four, and Byrnes in two. The Judge Patterson character is listed in the credits but isn't in the episode. Lane Chandler appeared in five *Lawman* episodes as townsman, Tom Pike. Chandler was a silent film star during the late 1920s. He co-starred with Clara Bow in *Red Hair* (1928), but by the 1930s he had reverted to supporting and bit parts. In Howard Hawks' classic western, *Red River* (1948), Chandler played the neighbor, Meeker, whom John Ireland's character leaves to go on the cattle drive.

Episode 2: "The Prisoner" October 12, 1958.
Starring John Russell and Peter Brown. Supporting Cast: Bek Nelson (Dru Lemp), John Doucette (Dick Sellers), William Henry (Doug Sutherland), Harry Cheshire (Judge Trager), Jon Lormer (Harry Tate), K.L. Smith (Hank), Phil Tully (Jody), Lane Chandler (Tom Pike), Robert Williams (Caddo Colin).

Directed by Richard L. Bare, Teleplay by Edmund Morris, Story by Frank Gruber, Produced by Jules Schermer, Director of Photography: Ralph Woolsey, Art Director: Howard Campbell, Supervising Film Editor: James Moore, Film Editor: Robert Watts, Production Manager: Oren W. Haglund, Sound: B.F. Ryan, Set Decorator: Jerry Welch, Assistant Director: Eddie Prinz.

Synopsis: Marshal Troop arrests a loud-mouthed, fast-drawing cowboy who provokes his victims into drawing on him before he shoots them.

Commentary: In each *Lawman* episode, a character must face a serious moral dilemma or challenge. Sometimes it's the marshal or his deputy, but usually it's someone else who gets help and aid from Laramie's lawmen. Troop gives Johnny his first lesson of being vigilant around prisoners. The flirtatious relationship between Troop and Dru continues. Troop's hair looks a bit grayer in this episode. Johnny's belt buckle on his side expanded a fashion trend.

Trivia: Fred Graham is uncredited as the bartender. Graham and William Henry were members of director John Ford's stock company of actors and actresses. Thirteen other players (who were in at least three Ford productions) appeared in *Lawman*: John Carradine, Willis Bouchey, Frank Albertson, John Qualen, Charles Tannen, Mickey Simpson, Steve Pendleton, Harry Tyler, Olive Carey, Harry Carey Jr., Chuck Roberson, Harry Strang, and Denver Pyle. Jules Schermer was the producer or supervising producer for all but three *Lawman* episodes. This was the first of 106 *Lawman* episodes in which Eddie Prinz was the assistant director. He worked on many of the other contemporary Warner Bros. television productions. He was also active as a choreographer and dance instructor in numerous Hollywood feature musicals during the 1940s and 1950s, including *Hellzapoppin'* (1941), *Tea for Two* (1950), and *Lullaby of Broadway* (1951).

THE EPISODES

Episode 3: "The Joker" October 19, 1958.
Starring John Russell and Peter Brown. Supporting Cast: Jeff York (Barney Tremain), Bek Nelson (Dru Lemp), Jon Lormer (Harry Tate), Emile Meyer (Sheriff Giles), Dub Taylor (Larry), I. Stanford Jolley (Gil Breck).

Directed by Stuart Heisler, Written by Finlay McDermid, Produced by Jules Schermer, Director of Photography: Ralph Woolsey, Art Director: Howard Campbell, Supervising Film Editor: James Moore, Film Editor: Elbert K. Hollingsworth, Production Manager: Oren W. Haglund, Sound: Francis J. Scheid, Set Decorator: Jerry Welch, Assistant Director: Eddie Prinz.

Synopsis: A boisterous and notorious outlaw convinces Johnny that he is Johnny's father.

Commentary: Marshal Troop trusts Johnny with the town when Troop has to visit a distant ranch.

Trivia: Jeff York's most famous role was Mike Fink, "King of the Keelboatmen," in *Davy Crockett and the River Pirates* (1956). He also co-starred in the Warner Bros. television series, *The Alaskans* (1959-60). For over fifty years, Dub Taylor played rustic and western characters; he had noticeable parts in *Bonnie and Clyde* (1967) and *The Wild Bunch* (1969). Taylor also appeared (with his son, fellow actor Buck Taylor) in Sam Elliott's *Conagher* (1991).

Episode 4: "The Oath" October 26, 1958.
Starring John Russell and Peter Brown. Supporting Cast: Barbara Stuart (Lola Bordeaux), Whit Bissell (Thornton Eggles), Don Kelly (Lou Menke), Stephen Courtleigh (Doc Walter Brewer), Betty Lynn (Edna Philips), John Cliff (Hurley).

Directed by Leslie H. Martinson, Teleplay by William Leicester, Story by Irving Rubine, Produced by Jules Schermer, Director of Photography: Ralph Woolsey, Art Director: Howard Campbell, Supervising Film Editor: James Moore, Film Editor: Leo Shreve, Production Manager:

Oren W. Haglund, Sound: M.A. Merrick, Set Decorator: Jerry Welch, Assistant Director: Eddie Prinz.

Synopsis: Marshal Troop and Johnny transport two prisoners to the penitentiary. A chance meeting with a stagecoach changes the circumstances.

Commentary: This is the first of numerous storylines when Troop, Johnny, or both lose their prisoners or are taken hostage. Troop's hair now has a white streak indicating his age.

Trivia: Whit Bissell, who acted in four *Lawman* episodes, was the funeral director early in *The Magnificent Seven* (1960). Barbara Stuart was best known for her role as Bunny, Sergeant Carter's girlfriend on *Gomer Pyle* (1964-69), while Betty Lynn played Barney Fife's patient sweetheart Thelma Lou on *The Andy Griffith Show* (1961-66).

Episode 5: "The Outcast" November 2, 1958.
Starring John Russell and Peter Brown. Supporting Cast: Dick Foran (Ed Kelly), Martin Landau (Bob Ford), Tony Romano (Guitar Player), Stuart Randall (Stan Jackson), Emory Parnell (Hank), James Lydon (Nat Davis), Harry Harvey Jr. (Willy Davis).

Directed by Stuart Heisler, Teleplay by William Leicester, Story by William Leicester and Jack Emanuel, Produced by Jules Schermer, Director of Photography: Ralph Woolsey, Art Director: Howard Campbell, Supervising Film Editor: James Moore, Film Editor: Robert T. Sparr, Production Manager: Oren W. Haglund, Sound: Theodore B. Hoffman, Set Decorator: Jerry Welch, Assistant Director: Eddie Prinz.

Synopsis: Marshal Troop attempts to protect Bob Ford, the man who killed Jesse James, from a lynching.

Commentary: This episode is an example of Troop defending someone universally scorned, combatting prevalent public opinion.

Trivia: Martin Landau was best known for his role as Rollin Hand in the first three years of the television series, *Mission: Impossible* (1966-73). He also played a hilarious Indian in *The Hallelujah Trail* (1965) and a memorable villain in *Nevada Smith* (1966). Actor-singer Dick Foran was the first of many 1930s and 1940s movie notables who were featured in *Lawman*. Foran had a small supporting role in this episode but had a more significant part in the fourth season's "The Wanted Man." James Lydon had the lead in the 1940s Henry Aldrich film comedies and also had the title role in *Tom Brown's School Days* (1940) and played the college-bound son in *Life with Father* (1947).

Episode 6: "The Jury" November 9, 1958.
Starring John Russell and Peter Brown. Supporting Cast: Jean Willes (Kate Wilson), Anthony George (Larry Bennett), John Reach (Carter Knox), Harry Cheshire (Judge Trager), Jon Lormer (Harry Tate), Don Beddoe (Jim Tyler), Tom Jackson (Warden).

Directed by Richard L. Bare, Teleplay by William Leicester, Written by Edmund Morris, Produced by Jules Schermer, Director of Photography: Wesley Anderson, Art Director: Howard Campbell, Supervising Film Editor: James Moore, Film Editor: David Wages, Production Manager: Oren W. Haglund, Sound: B.F. Ryan, Set Decorator: Jerry Welch, Assistant Director: Robert Farfan.

Synopsis: An attractive female continuously bamboozles male juries into finding her innocent of her crimes.

Commentary: Jean Willes' character is the first of numerous beautiful, wily, female criminals Troop and Johnny are forced to confront. Troop demonstrates his ingenuity in the way he uses the law to defeat her.

Trivia: Willes had a long career playing tough, brassy, notorious women. She appeared in two *Lawman* storylines, most of the Warner Bros. series, and such westerns as *Son of Paleface* (1952), *Four Queens and a King* (1956), and *Bite the Bullet* (1975). Kermit Maynard had an uncredited bit in this and six other *Lawman* episodes, usually as a townsman or barfly. He was the brother of cowboy movie star Ken Maynard. Kermit was a former world champion rodeo rider who had a long career in the movies as a stuntman, a B-western star, a cowboy character actor, and a bit player. He starred in one of the earliest television western series, *Saturday Roundup* (1951), which dramatized James Oliver Curwood's frontier stories.

Episode 7: "Wanted" November 16, 1958.
Starring John Russell and Peter Brown. Supporting Cast: Pat McVey (Red Barrington), Bek Nelson (Mrs. Dru Lemp), Robert Wilke (Fallon), Russ Thorson (Wilson), Ralph Reed (Roy Barrington), Kelly Thordsen (Carver), I. Stanford Jolley (Gil Breck).

Directed by Leslie H. Martinson, Written by Finlay McDermid, Produced by Jules Schermer, Director of Photography: Edwin DuPar, Art Director: Howard Campbell, Supervising Film Editor: James Moore, Film Editor: Frank O'Neill, Production Manager: Oren W. Haglund, Sound: M.A. Merrick, Set Decorator: John P. Austin, Assistant Director: Eddie Prinz.

Synopsis: A brutal and corrupt bounty hunter arrives in Laramie.

Commentary: The theme of Marshal Troop protecting someone who has rehabilitated himself is repeated numerous times in *Lawman*. Although Troop will never compromise his principles and give in to intimidation or corruption, he will skirt the letter of the law to help someone he thinks deserves a second chance, as he does in this episode.

Trivia: Robert Wilke was a great western villain. He was one of the three desperados (along with Lee Van Cleef and Shep Woolley) waiting at the station for their henchman in *High Noon* (1952). His most memorable cowboy role was in *The Magnificent Seven* (1960) when he stupidly challenged James Coburn's character to a gun vs. knife fight.

Episode 8: "The Badge" November 23, 1958.
Starring John Russell and Peter Brown. Supporting Cast: Gary Vinson (Bill Andrews), Wesley Lau (Rick Andrews), Venetia Stevenson (Molly Matson), Charles Bateman (Tim Bucknell), Phil Tead (Mr. Seymour),

Kenneth R. MacDonald (Banker Matson), Peter Breck (1st Ranchhand), John Cason (2nd Ranchhand), James McCallion (Shorty).

Directed by Lee Sholem, Written by Bernard C. Schoenfeld and Finlay McDermid, Produced by Jules Schermer, Director of Photography: Harold Stine, Art Director: Howard Campbell, Supervising Film Editor: James Moore, Film Editor: Leo Shreve, Production Manager: Oren W. Haglund, Sound: B.F. Ryan, Set Decorator: Jerry Welch, Assistant Director: Eddie Prinz.

Synopsis: A youth whose father was hung is accused of theft and attempted manslaughter. The entire town believes he's guilty, but Johnny has his doubts.

Commentary: Johnny shows maturity by refusing to compromise his beliefs.

Trivia: This was the first of three *Lawman* appearances for Peter Breck, each one a larger part. Breck co-starred in two western series, *Black Saddle* (1959-60) and *The Big Valley* (1965-69), and played in most of the Warner Bros. television westerns including portraying Doc Holliday in five *Maverick* episodes in 1961 and 1962.

Episode 9: "The Bloodline" November 30, 1958.
Starring John Russell and Peter Brown. Supporting Cast: Bek Nelson (Dru Lemp), Will Wright (Luke Saint), Paul Langton (Matt Saint), Chuck Courtney (Mark Saint), Jon Lormer (Harry Tate), Emory Parnell (Hank), James Hope (Sloane).

Directed by Leslie H. Martinson, Teleplay by Finlay McDermid, Story by Burt Arthur and Budd Arthur, Produced by Jules Schermer, Director of Photography: Ralph Woolsey, Art Director: Leo K. Kuter, Supervising Film Editor: James Moore, Film Editor: Basil Wrangell, Production Manager: Oren W. Haglund, Sound: Samuel F. Goode, Set Decorator: Jerry Welch, Assistant Director: Eddie Prinz.

Synopsis: Marshal Troop attempts to stop a young gunman from challenging his famous father to a gunfight.

Commentary: This is another episode when Troop and Johnny find themselves in the middle of a family feud.

Trivia: Although Will Wright played crusty old argumentative characters in scores of westerns, perhaps his most memorable part was as the corrupt politician in *All the King's Men* (1949). In this storyline, his Luke Saint is the ultimate curmudgeon; in another *Lawman* episode, "The Inheritance" (1961), he portrayed the definitive skinflint. Paul Langton was most famous for his Leslie Harrington character on the television drama, *Peyton Place* (1964-69).

Episode 10: "The Intruders" December 7, 1958.
Starring John Russell and Peter Brown. Supporting Cast: Frances Fong (May Ling), Philip Ahn (Wong), John Hoyt (Thomas Clemens), Bek Nelson (Dru Lemp), Lane Bradford (Cotty), Mickey Simpson (Porter), Fred Graham (Hart), Howard Negley (Bartender), David McMahon (Bill Butler).

Directed by Stuart Heisler, Teleplay by David Lang and Edmund Morris, Story by David Lang, Produced by Jules Schermer, Director of Photography: Warren Lynch, Art Director: Howard Campbell, Supervising Film Editor: James Moore, Film Editor: Leo Shreve, Production Manager: Oren W. Haglund, Sound: Samuel F. Goode, Set Decorator: Ben Bone, Assistant Director: Eddie Prinz.

Synopsis: Marshal Troop and Johnny investigate the murder of a Chinese laborer and the extortion of the entire Chinese community.

Commentary: This is the first of several episodes where Troop comes to the aid of minorities; during the run of the show, he defends Native Americans, an innocent black man, a brain-damaged youth, and numerous immigrants and outsiders.

Trivia: Mickey Simpson and Fred Graham took part in the classic donnybrook against Victor McLaglen's Sergeant Quincannon in *She Wore a Yellow Ribbon* (1949). Simpson was in six *Lawman* episodes including the title role in "Samson the Great" (1960).

Episode 11: "Short Straw" December 14, 1958.
Starring John Russell and Peter Brown. Supporting Cast: Jack Lambert (Lon Haggert), Ted De Corsia (Jess Crowthers), Bek Nelson (Dru Lemp), John Hubbard (Jake Biddle), Charles Fredericks (Orin Smith), David Alpert (Lester White), Tom McKee (Joe Haslip).

Directed by Stuart Heisler, Written by Clair Huffaker, Produced by Jules Schermer, Director of Photography: Carl Berger, Art Director: Leo K. Kuter, Supervising Film Editor: James Moore, Film Editor: Lee C. Hall, Production Manager: Oren W. Haglund, Sound: Theodore B. Hoffman, Set Decorator: William. Kuehl, Assistant Director: Eddie Prinz.

Synopsis: Unhappy with Troop's strict law enforcement policies, which they think are hurting their businesses, a group of Laramie residents draw straws to see who will kill him.

Commentary: An underlying theme throughout the four years of *Lawman* is the dissatisfaction some of Laramie's citizens have with Troop. Some are uncomfortable with the often violent way he is forced to uphold the peace and prevent crime; others fear that a peaceful town will not attract young cowboys and miners into spending their money in Laramie. Harry Whittington's novel, *Trouble Rides Tall* (1958), is the basis for the *Lawman* series. It focuses on the paradox that occurs when a peace officer does his job, but then seemingly is no longer needed.

Trivia: Jack Lambert played villains in countless westerns, and was the first mate, Joshua McGreevy, in the television series, *Riverboat* (1959-61). Menacing thick-necked Ted de Corsia portrayed powerful heavies in scores of westerns. One of his most memorable movie appearances was as the Texas cattle baron, Shanghai Pierce, who was backed down by Burt Lancaster's Wyatt Earp in *Gunfight at the O.K. Corral* (1957). Clair Huffaker was a prolific western writer of novels and screenplays. Among his western screenplays were *Flaming Star* (1960), *The Comancheros* (1961), *Rio Conchos* (1964), *The War Wagon* (1967), and *100 Rifles* (1969). He scripted eighteen *Lawman* episodes.

Episode 12: "Lady in Question" December 21. 1958.
Starring John Russell and Peter Brown. Featuring Bek Nelson (Dru Lemp), Michael Connors (Hal Daniels), Dorothy Provine (Julie Preston), Harry Cheshire (Judge Trager), Lane Chandler (Mr. Pike), Ken Christy (Sims), Steven Jay (Jimmy Hines), Ann Staunton (Mrs. Hines).

Directed by Alan Crosland, Jr., Written by David Lang, Produced by Jules Schermer, Director of Photography: Ralph Woolsey, Art Director: Howard Campbell, Supervising Film Editor: James Moore, Film Editor: David Wages, Production Manager: Oren W. Haglund, Sound: B.F. Ryan, Set Decorator: Jerry Welch, Assistant Director: Eddie Prinz.

Synopsis: Johnny is accused of murder when the gun of the man he shot can't be found.

Commentary: Throughout the run of *Lawman*, Johnny continuously falls in love with various comely ladies.

Trivia: The object of his infatuation this time is Dorothy Provine who later starred in two Warner Bros. television series, *The Alaskans* (1959-60) and *The Roaring Twenties* (1960-62). Her most memorable movie role was as Milton Berle's zany wife in *It's a Mad Mad Mad Mad World* (1963). Mike Connors is best remembered for his television series, *Mannix*, (1967-75).

Episode 13: "The Master" December 28, 1958.
Starring John Russell and Peter Brown. Featuring Wayne Morris (Tod Hogan), Bek Nelson (Dru Lemp), Rusty Lane (Brady), Tom Holland (Farley Brent), Lonie Backman (Lucy Brent), William Meigs (Johnson), Ray Walker (Sheehan), Duane Grey (Willard).

Directed by Anton M. Leader, Teleplay by Finlay McDermid and Edmund Morris. Story by Finlay McDermid. Produced by Jules Schermer, Director of Photography: Edwin DuPar, Art Director: Howard Campbell, Supervising Film Editor: James Moore, Film Editor: Lee C. Hall, Production Manager: Oren W. Haglund, Sound: Dolph Thomas, Set Decorator: Ben Bone, Assistant Director: Eddie Prinz.

Synopsis: Troop comes into conflict with his former mentor who has been hired by the local cattle barons to scare off homesteaders.

Commentary: This is the last of nine appearances that Bek Nelson made as Dru Lemp, the widow of the previous marshal and a potential romantic partner for Troop. It appears the producers didn't like the chemistry between Nelson and Russell and elected to write her out of the series. She was replaced by Barbara Lang who played the newspaper editor, Julie Tate, for four episodes later in Season One and then disappeared from the series. Peggie Castle's Lily Merrill co-starred in the second, third, and fourth years of *Lawman* portraying the strong-willed but vulnerable owner of "The Birdcage Saloon." All three woman added beauty to the show as well as a lighter touch in their flirting and bantering with the marshal, but Lily's chemistry with the marshal was obvious from the beginning. This episode is one of several that features storylines that depict renowned lawmen who have crossed the line and become lawbreakers.

Trivia: Wayne Morris was another former leading man who guest starred on *Lawman*. Morris was a World War II ace who starred or co-starred in many A and B westerns. His greatest role was playing a coward in Stanley Kubrick's *Paths of Glory* (1957).

Episode 14: "The Outsider" January 4, 1959.
Starring John Russell and Peter Brown. Featuring Miranda Jones (Rene Lebeau), Barry Kelley (Josh Teller) James Drury (Stan Bates), Mike Road (Herbie Teller), Rosa Rey (Mrs. Lebeau), Jon Lormer (Harry Tate), Earle Hodgins (Fane), Michael Macready (Talby).

Directed by Stuart Heisler, Written by William Leicester, Produced by Jules Schermer, Director of Photography: Harold Stine, Art Director: Leo K. Kuter, Supervising Film Editor: James Moore, Film Editor: David Wages, Production Manager: Oren W. Haglund, Sound: Samuel F. Goode, Set Decorator: Gene S. Redd, Assistant Director: Eddie Prinz.

Synopsis: A rich cattleman attempts to pressure a widowed Indian and her beautiful daughter into selling their ranch to him by scaring off their help, spreading lies, and spouting prejudice to the townspeople.

Commentary: The strong antagonists who Troop and Johnny are forced to face provide the lawmen with repeated opportunities to exhibit their courage and moral fiber. Heavy-set, gruff Barry Kelley is a perfect foil and adversary with his intimating presence and convincing ability to peddle hate.

Trivia: Beautiful, intense Miranda Jones who resembled Jean Simmons had significant roles in three *Lawman* episodes. James Drury later starred in the western series, *The Virginian* (1962-71). Mike Road, an Efrem Zimbalist Jr. look-alike, made appearances in most of Warner Bros. television westerns and dramas including four *Lawman* episodes. He co-starred as Marshal Tom Sellers in *Buckskin* (1958-59) and policeman Joe Switolski in *The Roaring Twenties* (1960-61) series. Famed guitarist Tony Romano was the guitar player in this story.

Episode 15: "The Captives" January 11, 1959.
Starring John Russell and Peter Brown. Featuring Edgar Buchanan (Jess Miller), James Bell (Doc Stewart), Michael Dante (Jack McCall), Phil Tead (Mr. Seymour), Dee Carroll (Mrs. Mitchell), Tom Fadden (Mr. Slade), James Dobson (Jody Peters).

Directed by Stuart Heisler, Written by Edmund Morris, Produced by Jules Schermer, Director of Photography: William Margulies, Art Director: Leo K. Kuter, Supervising Film Editor: James Moore, Film Editor: Thomas Neff, Production Manager: Oren W. Haglund, Sound: Francis E. Stahl, Set Decorator: William L. Kuehl, Assistant Director: Eddie Prinz.

Synopsis: Troop and Johnny are forced to confront Jack McCall, the murderer of Wild Bill Hickok, and now a kidnapper.

Commentary: This episode contains some time discrepancies. Wild Bill Hickok was murdered by Jack McCall on August 2, 1876 in Deadwood and the events in this story supposedly take place right after the shooting. However, the first episode of *Lawman* is set in 1879. There are additional historical inconsistencies in other episodes when Civil War events are described as occurring six or seven years previously when they should have occurred at least fourteen years before. Michael Dante's Jack McCall is one of several villains depicted as psychopaths in *Lawman*; another is Jack Elam's character in "Thirty Minutes."

Trivia: Edgar Buchanan had been a practicing dentist for eight years before turning to acting. He made scores of westerns and starred in the title role of the series, *Judge Roy Bean* (1955-56) and as Uncle Joe Carson in a total of 222 episodes of *The Beverly Hillbillies* (1962-71), *Petticoat Junction* (1963-70), and *Green Acres* (1965-71). Buchanan made scores of movie and television westerns often portraying a sly scoundrel such as his Sheriff "Bravo" Trimble in Randolph Scott's *Abilene Town* (1946). Michael Dante played Crazy Horse in the 1967 *Custer* television series and had the starring role in the film *Winterhawk* (1975). Dante, who was signed by the Boston Red Sox after graduating from high school in Stamford, Connecticut, is one of two honorary Arizona Rangers; the other is George W. Bush. Dante's other western films include *Westbound* (1959), *Apache Rifles* (1964), and *Arizona Raiders* (1965).

Episode 16: "The Encounter" January 18, 1959.
Starring John Russell and Peter Brown. Featuring Louise Fletcher (Betty Horgan), Donald Buka (Cole Hawkins), Russell Johnson (Wade Horgan).

Directed by Stuart Heisler, Written by Clair Huffaker, Produced by Jules Schermer, Director of Photography: Ralph Woolsey, Art Director: Howard Campbell, Supervising Film Editor: James Moore, Film Editor: Robert T. Sparr, Production Manager: Oren W. Haglund, Sound: J. A. Goodrich, Set Decorator: William L. Kuehl, Assistant Director: Eddie Prinz.

Synopsis: After Troop is severely mauled by a bear, he is rescued and cared for by a young woman who turns out to be the sister of one of the outlaws Troop has been pursuing.

Commentary: Each *Lawman* begins with a pan or teaser, a brief introductory scene. Until "The Encounter," it had always been a representative scene from the show, but this scene begins the narrative and is not repeated. Here, Johnny brings Troop a telegram informing him that two outlaws have murdered again. After this episode, these introductory scenes vary; some begin the story and are not seen again while others are repeated during the show.

Trivia: Louise Fletcher won an Academy Award for her work in *One Flew Over the Cuckoo's Nest* (1975) but began her career with 1958 television appearances in such western series as *Bat Masterson* (1958-61) and *Yancy Derringer* (1958-59). Russell Johnson was best known for his role as Professor Roy Hinkley on *Gilligan's Island* (1964-67), but he played numerous outlaws on the big and small screen during the 1950s before portraying Marshal Gib Scott in forty-one episodes of *Black Saddle* (1959-60). Stuart Heisler directed twenty-seven *Lawman* episodes. As a film director, he had helmed *The Biscuit Eater* (1940), *The Glass Key* (1942), *Storm Warning* (1951) and *The Lone Ranger* (1956).

Episode 17: "The Brand Release" January 25, 1959.
Starring John Russell and Peter Brown. Featuring R.G. Armstrong (Gabe Dallas), Russ Thorson (Sheriff Lang), Lee Farr (Ben Greene), Stewart Bradley (Chad Williams), Phil Tead (Mr. Seymour), Zon Murray (Charles Bay), Tom Palmer (Dr. Stewart Russell), Harry Tyler (Seth Billings).

Directed by Stuart Heisler, Teleplay by Oliver Crawford and Edmund Morris, Story by Oliver Crawford, Produced by Jules Schermer, Director of Photography: Ralph Woolsey, Art Director: Leo K. Kuter, Supervising Film Editor: James Moore, Film Editor: Robert T. Sparr, Production Manager: Oren W. Haglund, Sound: Francis J. Scheid, Set Decorator: William L. Kuehl, Assistant Director: Eddie Prinz.

Synopsis: Pursued by a sheriff, a wounded stranger claims that a cattle baron sold livestock to him and then had him shot.

Commentary: This is one of several episodes when Troop helps rehabilitate a lawman who has compromised his principles. R.G. Armstrong is yet another powerful antagonist Troop must face.

Trivia: Armstrong made many appearances on western television series during the 1950s and 1960s and had memorable supporting roles in several Sam Peckinpah western classics including *Ride the High Country* (1962), *Major Dundee* (1965), and *Pat Garrett and Billy the Kid* (1973). Set decorator William L. Kuehl was involved in seventeen *Lawman* episodes as well as most of the other Warner Bros. series. Kuehl created the sets for such western films as Paul Newman's *The Left Handed Gun* (1958), Jeffrey Hunter's *The Man from Galveston* (1963), Troy Donahue's *A Distant Trumpet* (1964), and James Stewart's *Firecreek* (1968).

Episode 18: "The Runaway" February 1, 1959.
Starring John Russell and Peter Brown. Featuring Karl Lukas (Sgt. Blaney), Joyce Taylor (Dora Mahan), James Kirkwood, Jr., (Ben Steed), Hugh Sanders (Col. Steed), Paul Lukather (Cpl. Breen).

Directed by Stuart Heisler. Written by William F. Leicester, Produced by Jules Schermer, Director of Photography: Ralph Woolsey, Art Director: Howard Campbell, Supervising Film Editor: James Moore, Film Editor: Elbert K. Hollingsworth, Production Manager: Oren W. Haglund, Sound: John K. Kean, Set Decorator: William L. Kuehl, Assistant Director: Eddie Prinz.

Synopsis: Troop attempts to locate Fort Laramie's commanding officer's son who has deserted from the army.

Commentary: In Troop's relationships with other authoritarian leaders, he is usually friendly, but in circumstances when he encounters rigidity as with the commanding officer, the marshal can be adversarial. Burly Karl Lukas' Sgt. Blaney provides Troop with another manipulative and dangerous opponent.

Trivia: Lukas usually played villains in his many television and movie roles but his most well-known character was Private Stash Kadowski in ninety-seven episodes of *The Phil Silvers Show* (1955-59). Joyce Taylor was one of many beautiful ladies featured on *Lawman*. Her biggest claim to fame was co-starring in eight episodes of the 1959-60 television drama, *Men into Space*.

Episode 19: "Warpath" February 8, 1959.
Starring John Russell and Peter Brown. Featuring Murvyn Vye (Tom Cardigan), William Fawcett (Billy Bright), Lew Gallo (Weed), Howard Caine (Newt Whittaker), Michael Forest (Chief Little Wolf), Ted Jacques (Lew Bush), Eugene Iglesias (Blanket), Iron Eyes Cody (Scarfaced Brave).

Directed by Stuart Heisler, Written by Dean Riesner, Produced by Jules Schermer, Director of Photography: William Margulies, Art Director: Howard Campbell, Supervising Film Editor: James Moore, Film Editor: Leo Shreve, Production Manager: Oren W. Haglund, Sound: Theodore B. Hoffman, Set Decorator: William L. Kuehl, Assistant Director: Eddie Prinz.

Synopsis: Troop attempts to prevent a war between Indian-hating buffalo hunters and the Shoshone tribe.

Commentary: This is another example of Troop being forced to combat mass hysteria and prejudice egged on by immoral men. It also illustrates Troop's compassion and sympathy for outsiders and underdogs.

Trivia: The buffalo hunters' leader was played by Vye, who often portrayed villains. Two memorable roles were his evil outlaw opposing Alan Ladd in *Whispering Smith* (1948) and a comic Merlin in Bing Crosby's *A Connecticut Yankee in King Arthur's Court* (1949). Iron Eyes Cody had a bit part in this episode. He played Indians in scores of western films and television series. He is best known as the Native American shedding a tear after observing devastating pollution in the "Keep America Beautiful" television ad of the 1970s and 1980s.

Episode 20: "The Gunman" February 15, 1959.
Starring John Russell and Peter Brown. Featuring Richard Arlen (Kurt

Monroe), Gordon Jones (Chalk Hennesey), Hal Baylor (Harlan Smith), Frank Sully (Jenks Edwards), Baynes Barron (Al Horn), Paul Brinegar (Stage Line Clerk), Howard Negley (Hank), Dorothy Partington (Lucy Benson).

Directed by Stuart Heisler, Written by Clair Huffaker, Produced by Jules Schermer, Director of Photography: William Margulies, Art Director: Leo K. Kuter, Supervising Film Editor: James Moore, Film Editor: Walter S. Stern, Production Manager: Oren W. Haglund, Sound: Francis E. Stahl, Set Decorator: William L. Kuehl, Assistant Director: Eddie Prinz.

Synopsis: Troop attempts to defuse a potentially violent scenario when a reformed gunfighter is pressured by an old crony to shoot it out with the marshal.

Commentary: *Lawman* has numerous episodes when a legendary shootist attempts to stop participating in life-or-death showdowns. The end of the acting credits states, "And Richard Arlen as Kurt Monroe."

Trivia: Arlen teamed with Andy Devine in fourteen action-comedy *Aces of Action* B-westerns during the late 1930s and early 1940s, but is best remembered for his featured role as a pilot in *Wings* (1927). Gordon Jones often played a loud lout who instigated trouble. He portrayed a similar character in the *Lawman* episode, "The Last Man" (1959). His best known character was Lou Costello's nemesis on *The Abbott and Costello Show* television series (1952-54). Paul Brinegar, who had a bit part as the stage line clerk in this episode, played the cantankerous cook, Wishbone, on the television series, *Rawhide* (1959-65).

Episode 21: "The Big Hat" February 22, 1959.
Starring John Russell and Peter Brown. Featuring Barbara Lang (Julie Tate), Jay Novello (Frank Slater), Rita Lynn (Lily Keats), Jon Lormer (Harry Tate), Richard Reeves (Marty Brattle), Robert B. Williams (Big Hat Anderson), James Parnell (Miner).

Directed by Stuart Heisler, Written by William F. Leicester, Produced by Jules Schermer, Director of Photography: Ralph Woolsey, Art Director: Howard Campbell, Supervising Film Editor: James Moore, Film Editor: Fred M. Bohanan, Production Manager: Oren W. Haglund, Sound: Dolph Thomas, Set Decorator: William L. Kuehl, Assistant Director: Eddie Prinz.

Synopsis: Troop investigates the shooting of Laramie's newspaper editor.

Commentary: This is the first appearance for Barbara Lang who plays the newspaper editor, Julie Tate, who takes over for her murdered father. Initially, there's friction between Julie and Marshal Troop, but soon there appears to be potential mutual chemistry. Situations involving mistaken identity are utilized several times in the series. For example, in "No Contest," Johnny's cousin from Boston, a dead ringer for Billy the Kid, visits Laramie.

Trivia: Sad-faced character actor Jay Novello had a pivotal role in this episode and in *Lawman's* final one, "The Witness" (1962).

Episode 22: "The Chef" March 1, 1959.
Starring John Russell and Peter Brown. Featuring Sig Ruman (Hans Steinmayer), Lee Patrick (Mary Young), John Doucette (Ira Young), Bryon Foulger (Harry Dorn), Harry Cheshire (Judge Trager), Charles Meredith (Territorial Governor), Jean Harvey (Governor's Wife).

Directed by Stuart Heisler. Teleplay by Edmund Morris, Story by Mortimer Braus, Produced by Jules Schermer, Director of Photography: William Margulies, Art Director: Howard Campbell, Supervising Film Editor: James Moore, Film Editor: Fred M. Bohanan, Production Manager: Oren W. Haglund, Sound: B.F. Ryan, Set Decorator: William L. Kuehl, Assistant Director: Eddie Prinz.

Synopsis: Troop intervenes in a dispute involving a popular German chef that may lead to violence.

Commentary: Although the majority of their work in *Lawman* involves dramatic conflicts, both Russell and Brown are excellent in their support of comedic actors and humorous situations. This is one of the lighter episodes of the first season, filled with Sig Ruman, Lee Patrick, and John Doucette's overacting. Doucette is surprisingly silly in his role as a pompous cattleman dominated by his wife.

Trivia: Doucette had played a very different sort of man, an insensitive murderer, in *Lawman's* second episode, "The Prisoner" (1958). His characters were usually villains, but he did play a sheriff friend of John Wayne's in *Big Jake* (1971). Ruman was famous for his appearances in several Marx Brothers comedies. He played the chef again in another *Lawman* episode, "The Young Toughs" (1959). Lee Patrick was Humphrey Bogart's secretary, Effie Perine, in *The Maltese Falcon* (1941).

Episode 23: "The Posse" March 8, 1959.
Starring John Russell and Peter Brown. Featuring Pernell Roberts (Fent Harley), Jean Allison (Beth Hunter), Tol Avery (Bliss Carter), Dick Rich (Arch Devereaux), Emerson Treacy (Blinker), Dick Wessell (Jed Thomas), Michael Macready (Tracy Hunter).

Directed by Stuart Heisler, Written by William F. Leicester, Produced by Jules Schermer, Director of Photography: Edwin DuPar, Art Director: Howard Campbell, Supervising Film Editor: James Moore, Film Editor: Leo Shreve, Production Manager: Oren W. Haglund, Sound: Theodore B. Hoffman, Set Decorator: Ralph S. Hurst, Assistant Director: Eddie Prinz.

Synopsis: Troop and Johnny attempt to solve a murder case before an innocent man is hung.

Commentary: Tol Avery does an excellent job playing Carter, the vociferous, bullying know-it-all leader of the posse convinced the accused is guilty. When Troop demands that justice be served, Carter asks, "What kind of lawman are you?" Troop answers, "The right kind, I hope. I'm trying to get at the truth."

Trivia: Pernell Roberts, who played Adam Cartwright during the first six years of *Bonanza* (1959-73), had a small part as a sarcastic and cynical member of the posse.

Episode 24: "The Visitor" March 15, 1959.
Starring John Russell and Peter Brown. Featuring Charles Cooper (Jack Rollins), Vivi Janiss (Mrs. Welch), Ned Weaver (Welch), Roscoe Ates (Old Timer), Stephen Talbot (Jamie), Doug McClure (Jed Ryan).

Directed by Stuart Heisler. Written by Edmund Morris, Produced by Jules Schermer, Director of Photography: Ralph Woolsey, Art Director: Howard Campbell, Supervising Film Editor: James Moore, Film Editor: Leo Shreve, Production Manager: Oren W. Haglund, Sound: Samuel F. Goode, Set Decorator: William L. Kuehl, Assistant Director: Eddie Prinz.

Synopsis: Troop tries to prevent bloodshed when a well-known gunfighter comes to Laramie on "personal business."

Commentary: This is one of several *Lawman* stories where a parent who had previously abandoned their son seeks to reclaim him. It is also another episode depicting the trials and tribulations of an aging, infamous gunman – similar to Gregory Peck's in *The Gunfighter* (1950) – attempting to stop the killing, but thwarted by the challenges of a youngster, in this case played by a sneering Doug McClure.

Trivia: McClure later starred as Trampas in *The Virginian* television series (1962-71) and had supporting but memorable scenes in Burt Lancaster's *The Unforgiven* (1960) and James Stewart's *Shenandoah* (1965). *The Simpsons'* character Troy McClure's name is supposedly based on the names, Troy Donahue and Doug McClure.

Episode 25: "Battle Scar" March 22, 1959.
Starring John Russell and Peter Brown. Featuring R.G. Armstrong (Major Ben Rogers), Catherine McLeod (Cynthia Rogers), Robert Conrad (Davey Catterton), Walter Coy (Colonel French).

The Episodes

Directed by Stuart Heisler, Teleplay by Edmund Morris, Story by Larry Menkin and Don Tait, Produced by Jules Schermer, Director of Photography: Edwin DuPar, Art Director: Howard Campbell, Supervising Film Editor: James Moore, Film Editor: Elbert K. Hollingsworth, Production Manager: Oren W. Haglund, Sound: Samuel F. Goode, Set Decorator: George James Hopkins, Assistant Director: Eddie Prinz.

Synopsis: Troop is forced to deal with a former Army major turned prosperous rancher who is haunted by the trauma of his Civil War experiences and is exhibiting uncontrollable bouts of rage.

Commentary: Once again Troop demonstrates substantial patience and sympathy for someone acting out of the fold, in this case, R.G. Armstrong's character, a man suffering from combat stress due to his traumatic wartime experiences.

Trivia: Robert Conrad starred in Warner Bros. *Hawaiian Eye* (1959-63) but his role as secret agent James West in the television series, *The Wild Wild West* (1965-69), was his most memorable. Walter Coy played John Wayne's brother in *The Searchers* (1956).

Episode 26: "The Gang" March 29, 1959.
Starring John Russell and Peter Brown. Featuring James Drury (Clay), Barbara Lang (Julie Tate), Roscoe Ates (Ike), Karl Davis (Hayes), Emory Parnell (Hank), Tom Palmer (Doc Stewart), Dick Wessell (Jed Thomas), Guy Wilkerson (Smith).

Directed by Stuart Heisler, Written by Clair Huffaker, Produced by Jules Schermer, Director of Photography: Ralph Woolsey, Art Director: Howard Campbell, Supervising Film Editor: James Moore, Film Editor: Robert T. Sparr, Production Manager: Oren W. Haglund, Sound: Stanley Jones, Set Decorator: George James Hopkins, Assistant Director: Eddie Prinz.

Synopsis: The Hayes Gang intends to kill Troop for standing up to them. His only allies against these seven killers are Johnny and a mysterious stranger named Clay.

Commentary: Significant information about Troop's life history is revealed in this episode. Johnny shows his sand when without words he lets Troop know he will stand by him. The initial flirtatious scene between Clay and Julie features oboes and clarinets in the background; this music will characterize many future humorous scenes in the series. This episode contains a surprise hook at the end.

Trivia: This was James Drury's second appearance in the series; this time, in a much bigger role. Emory Parnell played Hank the bartender in twelve *Lawman* episodes. He had a small but memorable bit as the corrupt sheriff in *Tall in the Saddle* (1944).

Episode 27: "The Souvenir" April 5, 1959.
Starring John Russell and Peter Brown. Featuring Jeanette Nolan (Ma Carey) Barbara Lang (Julie Tate), Don Kelly (Virgil Carey), Jan Harrison (Nan Brooks), Brett King (Boone), Robert Fuller (Davey), Tom Palmer (Doc Stewart), Harry Cheshire (Judge Trager), Emory Parnell (Hank), Lane Chandler (Tom Pike), Ken Christy (Carl Shoemaker).

Directed by Stuart Heisler, Teleplay by Edmund Morris, Story by Frederick Louis Fox, Produced by Jules Schermer, Director of Photography: Wesley Anderson, Art Director: Howard Campbell, Supervising Film Editor: James Moore, Film Editor: Clarence Kolster, Production Manager: Oren W. Haglund, Sound: Robert B. Lee, Set Decorator: George James Hopkins, Assistant Director: Eddie Prinz.

Synopsis: After a killer escapes on Johnny's watch, the young deputy learns a lot about himself and Troop.

Commentary: This episode depicts a rarity – friction between Johnny and Troop. Their misunderstanding reveals much about the character of the two lawmen. The souvenir in the title is a bullet.

Trivia: Jeanette Nolan made movies for fifty years, ranging from Orson Welles' *Macbeth* in 1948 to *The Horse Whisperer* in 1998, and also acted in hundreds of television dramas. She co-starred with Earl Holliman in twenty-nine episodes of the western series, *Hotel de Paree* (1959-60).

THE EPISODES

Episode 28: "The Young Toughs" April 12, 1959.
Starring John Russell and Peter Brown. Featuring Sig Ruman (Hans), Barbara Lang (Julie Tate), Tom Gilson (Hoak Barnes), Van Williams (Zachary Morgan), Eric Morris (Joey Young), Morris Ankrum (Ike Smith), Emory Parnell (Hank).

Directed by Leslie H. Martinson, Written by Clair Huffaker, Produced by Jules Schermer, Director of Photography: Perry Finneman, Art Director: Howard Campbell, Supervising Film Editor: James Moore, Film Editor: Elbert K. Hollingsworth, Production Manager: Oren W. Haglund, Sound: Joseph T. Wissmann, Set Decorator: William Wallace, Assistant Director: Eddie Prinz.

Synopsis: The marshal leaves town on business and Johnny must confront three young thugs by himself.

Commentary: Warner Bros. produced numerous other television westerns and dramas during the late 1950s and early 1960s including *Cheyenne* (1955-63), *Maverick* (1957-62), *Sugarfoot* (1957-61*)*, *Colt .45* (1957-59), *77 Sunset Strip* (1958-64), *Bronco* (1958-62), *Hawaiian Eye* (1959-63), *Bourbon Street Beat* (1959-60), *The Alaskans* (1959-60), *SurfSide 6* (1960-62), and *The Roaring Twenties* (1960-62). To attract viewers' interest in young attractive contract players, many of these actors and actresses made guest appearances on these shows.

Trivia: Van Williams' part in *Lawman* was an example of the opportunities Warner Bros. provided for its contract players. After showing off his shirtless chest and sparkling smile, Williams was soon co-starring in *Bourbon Street Beat* (1959-60) and *SurfSide 6* (1960-62).

Episode 29: "Riding Shotgun" April 19, 1959.
Starring John Russell and Peter Brown. Featuring Allen Case (Larry DeLong), Paul Fix (Pop Marraday), Jack Lomas (Jess Brubaker), Ron Soble (Jake), Lane Chandler (Pike), Roy Barcroft (Feeney), Terry Rangno (Tommy), George Bellows (Ott).

Directed by Alan Crosland Jr., Teleplay by William F. Leicester, Story by Kenneth Perkins, Produced by Jules Schermer, Director of Photography: Ralph Woolsey, Art Director: Howard Campbell, Supervising Film Editor: James Moore, Film Editor: Leo Shreve, Production Manager: Oren W. Haglund, Sound: Samuel F. Goode, Set Decorator: Jerry Welch, Assistant Director: Robert Farfan.

Synopsis: An ex-con Troop has befriended is accused of shooting a stagecoach driver.

Commentary: This is another story revolving around Troop's supporting an outsider and standing up against prevalent public opinion.

Trivia: Allen Case played the title role in Henry Fonda's western series, *The Deputy* (1959-61). Of his scores of westerns, Paul Fix was best known for his role as the marshal in *The Rifleman* (1958-63) and as the cowboy, Keeler, in *Red River* (1948). He also played the judge in *To Kill a Mockingbird* (1962). Barcroft was in nineteen *Gunsmoke* episodes between 1959 and 1969 and had hundreds of supporting and bit appearances in western movies and television series over a forty-year career.

Episode 30: "The Journey" April 26, 1959.
Starring John Russell and Peter Brown. Featuring Robert J. Wilke (Tom Haddon), J. Pat O'Malley (Owen Muldoon), Willis Bouchey (Jabez Bentham), Harry Millard (Philip Bentham), Nesdon Booth (Mr. Kenyon).

Directed by Stuart Heisler, Written by Edmund Morris, Produced by Jules Schermer, Director of Photography: Wesley Anderson, Art Director: Howard Campbell, Supervising Film Editor: James Moore, Film Editor: Thomas Neff, Production Manager: Oren W. Haglund, Sound: M.A. Merrick, Set Decorator: William Wallace, Assistant Director: Eddie Prinz.

Synopsis: Troop travels to New Mexico to help out a friend and is soon confronted by a corrupt marshal, and a packet of lies.

Commentary: This is another storyline involving a dishonest peace officer and a scenario when Troop must face many adversaries by himself. This episode is similar to "The Post" (1960).

Trivia: Bob Steele, the star of numerous B-westerns in the 1930s and 1940s, made an uncredited appearance as the telegraph operator. Steele later had small supporting bits in numerous television and movie westerns including playing Trooper Duffy in *F Troop* (1965-67). Willis Bouchey made several John Ford westerns during the late 1950s and early 1960s; in *The Man Who Shot Liberty Valance* (1962), he was the train conductor who delivers the ironic line to James Stewart's senator, "Nothing's too good for the man who shot Liberty Valance."

Episode 31: "The Huntress" May 3, 1959.
Starring John Russell and Peter Brown. Featuring Andra Martin (Lorna), John Pickard (Jim Pearce), Olive Sturgess (Wanda), Keith Bryon (Frank Pierce), John Clarke (Cowboy), Harry Swoger (Blum), Harry Tyler (Jake Smith), Mickey Simpson (Bill Crowthers), Dub Taylor (Man).

Directed by Stuart Heisler, Written by Clair Huffaker, Produced by Jules Schermer, Director of Photography: Wesley Anderson, Art Director: Howard Campbell, Supervising Film Editor: James Moore, Film Editor: Robert B. Warwick Jr., Production Manager: Oren W. Haglund, Sound: B.F. Ryan Set Decorator: George James Hopkins, Assistant Director: Eddie Prinz.

Synopsis: A beautiful woman seeks revenge for the murder of her boyfriend.

Commentary: This episode is one of several *Lawman* episodes that depicts the repercussions of taking the law into one's own hands.

Trivia: Andra Martin was another contract player for Warner Bros. who made the rounds of almost all their television series. She was once married to Ty Hardin, the star of *Bronco* (1958-62). Pretty Olive Sturgess also made appearances in most of the small tube western series of the late

1950s and early 1960s and co-starred in *Requiem for a Gunfighter* (1965) with Rod Cameron and Stephen McNally.

Episode 32: "The Return" May 10, 1959.
Starring John Russell and Peter Brown. Featuring Frank Albertson (Clint Porter), Burt Douglas (Ben Adams), Nan Peterson (Nancy Porter), Joan Granville (Rose Gentry), Harry Landers (Wes Blaine), Lane Bradford (Roy Blaine), Don Wilbanks (Ryan), Tom Fadden (Cartwright), Emory Parnell (Hank), Jack Shea (Triplett).

Directed by Stuart Heisler, Teleplay by Finlay McDermid, Story by Jules Schermer and Jim Barnett, Produced by Jules Schermer, Director of Photography: Harold Stine, Art Director: Howard Campbell, Supervising Film Editor: James Moore, Film Editor: William Zeigler, Production Manager: Oren W. Haglund, Sound: Theodore B. Hoffman, Set Decorator: Frank M. Miller, Assistant Director: Don Page.

Synopsis: Marshal Troop contends with the town's disapproval when he refuses to run an ex-con out of Laramie.

Commentary: Troop's moustache is markedly grayer. For all his toughness and cynicism, Troop is a strong believer in rehabilitation. Whenever there's a happy ending, the musical theme to *Lawman* is played softly in an upbeat rhythm as in this episode.

Trivia: Lane Bradford played outlaws in scores of movie and television westerns during the 1940s and 1950s; a representative role was his Curly Bill Brocius in George Montgomery's *Toughest Gun in Tombstone* (1958).

Episode 33: "The Senator" May 17, 1959.
Starring John Russell and Peter Brown. Featuring Jack Elam (Spence), Donald Barry (Shorty), Ted de Corsia (Barrett), Grandon Rhodes (Fergus), Dan Sheridan (Clegg Willis), Paul Keast (Senator Wellborn), Emory Parnell (Hank), Cecil Elliott (Mrs. Ashborne), Walter Baldwin (Telegraph Clerk).

Directed by Stuart Heisler, Teleplay by Clair Huffaker and Booker McClay, Story by Booker McClay, Produced by Jules Schermer, Director of Photography: Ralph Woolsey, Art Director: Howard Campbell, Supervising Film Editor: James Moore, Film Editor: Walter S. Stern, Production Manager: Oren W. Haglund, Sound: M.A. Merrick, Set Decorator: Frank M. Miller, Assistant Director: Eddie Prinz.

Synopsis: Troop is warned that there's a plot to assassinate a senator who will be arriving by train at midnight.

Commentary: In several *Lawman* episodes, Troop is warned of an upcoming crime. He proves once again that he is an excellent detective – although he initially suspects the wrong man – as well as a superb enforcer of the law. The trio of murderers represent three kinds of outlaws: the scheming leader (de Corsia's Barrett), the cold-blooded killer (Elam's Spence), and the weak link of the team (Barry's Shorty).

Trivia: This was Dan Sheridan's first appearance on the show; he would later play the bartender Jake Summers in thirty-nine *Lawman* episodes beginning with the fourth episode of Season Three (1960). Donald "Red" Barry was involved with oaters for over forty years from *Wyoming Outlaw* in 1939 to *Little House on the Prairie* (1974-82), including the title role in *Adventures of Red Ryder* (1940). He also wrote the stories to several movie westerns including *Jesse James' Women* (1954) – co-starring Peggie Castle – which he also directed.

Episode 34: "The Ring" May 24, 1959.
Starring John Russell and Peter Brown. Featuring Richard Long (Zachary), Hillary Brooke (Claire Adams), Byron Palmer (Link), Roscoe Ates (Mr. Jenkins), Roy Baker (Albert Tishkin), Tom Palmer (Doc Stewart), Ruth Warren (Angie Spender).

Directed by Leslie H. Martinson, Teleplay by Edmund Morris, From a novel by Harry Whittington, Produced by Jules Schermer, Director of Photography: Harold Stine, Art Director: Howard Campbell, Supervising Film Editor: James Moore, Film Editor: Fred M. Bohanan, Production

Manager: Oren W. Haglund, Sound: Joseph T. Wissmann, Set Decorator: George James Hopkins, Assistant Director: Eddie Prinz.

Synopsis: The only clue Troop has about a dancehall girl's brutal murder is her missing diamond ring.

Commentary: This storyline is derived from Harry Whittington's dark 1958 western novel, *Trouble Rides Tall*, which is the basis for the entire *Lawman* television series. This episode reveals a great deal about Dan Troop: his compassion for a troubled youngster; his refusal to judge the murdered girl – "she was wild but she wasn't bad;" – his patience with fools and gossipers like the barber; and his ability to think outside the box in his scheme to trick the murderer. This episode's storyline and the novel each have different surprise conclusions.

Trivia: Richard Long had a recurring role as Gentleman Jim Darby in four *Maverick* episodes in 1958 and 1959 before starring as Rex Randolph in *Bourbon Street Beat* (1959-60) and *77 Sunset Strip* (1960-61). He later portrayed Jarrod Barkley in *The Big Valley* (1965-69), and Professor Everett in *Nanny and the Professor* (1970-71). Tom Palmer played a Laramie doctor eight times on *Lawman*. Other actors who played physicians on *Lawman* were Don Beddoe, John Qualen, Harry Antrim, Ralph Moody, James Bell, Tom Drake, Stephen Ellsworth, and Stephen Courtleigh.

Episode 35: "The Bandit" May 31, 1959.
Starring John Russell, Peter Brown. Featuring Skip Homeier (Ches Ryan), Lurene Tuttle (Matt's Wife), Anne Anderson (Jenny Gibbons), Don Beddoe (Dr. Morros), Jimmy Baird (Bobby Gibbons).

Directed by Lee Sholem, Written by Oliver Crawford, Produced by Jules Schermer, Director of Photography: Harold Stine, Art Director: Howard Campbell, Supervising Film Editor: James Moore, Film Editor: David Wages, Production Manager: Oren W. Haglund, Sound: M.A. Merrick, Set Decorator: Mowbray F. Berkeley, Assistant Director: Eddie Prinz.

Synopsis: A bank robber fleeing from Troop and Johnny comes across two critically ill youngsters in an isolated cabin.

Commentary: The story is reminiscent of Joel McCrea's *Four Faces West* (1948). Troop's open-mindedness is depicted again: "Seems like I started out chasing one kind of man and caught up with another." The end of the acting credits states, "And Skip Homeier as Ches Ryan."

Trivia: Homeier, along with Richard Boone and Henry Silva, were the trio of killers in Randolph Scott's *The Tall T* (1953). Homeier's other western films included *The Gunfighter* (1950), *Day of the Badman* (1958), and *Comanche Station* (1960).

Episode 36: "The Wayfarer" June 7, 1959.
Starring John Russell, Peter Brown and Adam West as Doc Holliday. Featuring Jeff York (Sam Cates), Debby Hengen (Toby), Ken Becker (Treb Cates), Emory Parnell (Hank), Tom Palmer (Doc Stewart), John Harmon (Gordy).

Directed by Lee Sholem, Teleplay by William F. Leicester and Edmund Morris, Story by William F. Leicester, Written by Clair Huffaker, Produced by Jules Schermer, Director of Photography: J. Peverell Marley, Art Director: Howard Campbell, Supervising Film Editor: James Moore, Film Editor: Robert Watts, Production Manager: Oren W. Haglund, Sound: Joseph T. Wissmann, Set Decorator: George James Hopkins, Assistant Director: Eddie Prinz.

Synopsis: Troop attempts to protect the legendary Doc Holliday when two brothers vow revenge against Doc after he kills their brother in self-defense.

Commentary: Every few shows, Troop protects a famous gunfighter. As in almost every storyline, there is at least one well-written, strong antagonist for Troop; in this case it is Jeff York's character. For the first time, another name is listed in the opening credits: "And Starring Adam West as Doc Holliday.

Trivia: West, most famous for playing Batman on the small screen, also played Holliday in a *Colt .45* episode, "The Devil's Godson" (1959) and a *Sugarfoot* episode, "The Trial of the Canary Kid" (1959). He was to play Holliday in a Warner Bros. series titled *Doc Holliday* and a pilot was made in the late 1950s, but it never came to fruition. According to West, "The studio liked the plot a lot, but it [the dental scenes] was a little too realistic for the tube at that time."

Episode 37: "Conclave" June 14, 1959.
Starring John Russell and Peter Brown. Featuring Lawrence Dobkin (Buck Walsh), Denver Pyle (Glen Folsom), Carl Milletaire (Ramirez), Lee Van Cleef (Ned Scott), John Hubbard (Abel Clark), Emory Parnell (Hank), Rayford Barnes (Ken Tompkins), Donald Elson (Mr. Oliver).

Directed by Mark Sandwich, Jr., Written by Edmund Morris, Produced by Jules Schermer, Director of Photography: Harold Stine, Art Director: Howard Campbell, Supervising Film Editor: James Moore, Film Editor: David Wages, Production Manager: Oren W. Haglund, Sound: Francis E. Stahl, Set Decorator: George James Hopkins, Assistant Director: Eddie Prinz.

Synopsis: Troop attempts to stop the robbery of a large gold shipment headed for Laramie via stagecoach.

Commentary: Troop doesn't break the law, but he will push the rules to get the job done. Here, he uses a character's weakness for alcohol to get at the truth.

Trivia: Chuck Roberson, a John Ford stock company member and stuntman, had a bit as the stagecoach shotgun guard; his most famous western role was Sheriff Jeff Lord, the lucky man who married Yvonne DeCarlo in *McLintock!* (1963).

Episode 38: "Red Ransom" June 21, 1959.
Starring John Russell and Peter Brown. Featuring Grace Raynor (White

Cloud), George Wallace (Nat Gruber), Francis J. McDonald (Red Horse), Walter Burke (Whiskey Jimmie).

Directed by Leslie H. Martinson, Written by William F. Leicester, Produced by Jules Schermer, Director of Photography: Harold Stine, Art Director: Howard Campbell, Supervising Film Editor: James Moore, Film Editor: Marsh Hendry, Production Manager: Oren W. Haglund, Sound: Howard Fogetti, Set Decorator: George James Hopkins, Assistant Director: Claude E. Archer.

Synopsis: When Troop and Johnny return the body of a chief's slain son to an Indian village, Johnny is taken hostage, and Troop is given a day to find the murderer.

Commentary: Troop continues to treat Native Americans as equals. Extramarital and romantic entanglements resulting in tragedy are repeated throughout the first season.

Trivia: Walter Burke made four appearances on *Lawman*, each time depicting a little man getting into big trouble. Burke had small roles in dozens of movie and television productions; a memorable one was in *Support Your Local Sheriff* (1969) as a member of the town counsel.

Episode 39: "The Friend" June 28, 1959.
Starring John Russell and Peter Brown. Featuring Robert Fuller (Buck Harmon), Robert F. Simon (Mr. Harmon), Nestor Paiva (Jack Gorman), Roscoe Ates (Jenkins), Emory Parnell (Hank), Brad Von Beltz (Harry), Paul Lukather (Mack).

Directed by Mark Sandwich, Jr., Written by Clair Huffaker, Produced by Jules Schermer, Director of Photography: Carl Berger, Art Director: Howard Campbell, Supervising Film Editor: James Moore, Film Editor: Thomas Neff, Production Manager: Oren W. Haglund, Sound: Joseph T. Wissmann, Set Decorator: Jerry Welch, Assistant Director: Claude Binyon, Jr

Synopsis: Johnny's childhood friend returns to Laramie to scout out the town and the bank for his outlaw gang.

Commentary: Troop is in this episode for only the initial two minutes when he is uncharacteristically tricked by the outlaws to lead a posse on a wild goose chase. When Johnny requests to go along with the posse, Troop compliments his deputy by stating, "You're worth more here." Johnny later demonstrates substantial maturity and growth, and successfully stops the robbery.

Trivia: Robert Fuller appeared in two *Lawman* episodes and acted in scores of television westerns culminating in a major role in the series *Laramie* (1959-63) where he played Jess Harper, a fast-drawing gunfighter, who assisted the Sherman brothers (John Smith and Robert Crawford) with their ranch and relay station outside of Laramie during the 1880s. From 1963 to 1965, Fuller starred in *Wagon Train* as the frontier scout, Cooper Smith. Fuller and Peter Brown were good personal friends.

Season Two

Episode 40: "Lily" October 4, 1959.
Starring John Russell, Peter Brown, Ray Danton (Len Farrell), and Peggie Castle (Lily Merrill). Featuring Nan Peterson (Annette), Dan Sheridan (Barney Tate), Clancy Cooper (Timmo McQueen), Charles Maxwell (Lonzo Grey), Mina Vaughn (Sarabelle).

Directed by Leslie H. Martinson, Teleplay by Dean Riesner, Story by Clair Huffaker, Produced by Jules Schermer, Production Manager: Oren W. Haglund, Sound: Ross Owen, Director of Photography: Perry Finnerman, Art Director: LeRoy Deane, Supervising Film Editor: James Moore, Film Editor: Harold Minter, Set Decorator: Frank M. Miller, Assistant Director: William Lasky.

Synopsis: Lily Merrill takes over ownership of "The Birdcage Saloon" and initially comes into conflict with Troop.

Commentary: This is the first appearance in *Lawman* for Peggie Castle, and along with her beauty and wit, she brings warmth and humor that permeates the entire show and helps to humanize the marshal. In addition, there's obvious chemistry between the two. Troop displays his common sense and empathy when Lily asks him if one of her dancehall girls will stand trial. "What trial?" he replies, "She just fell in love with the wrong man, that's all." Johnny's shirt is unbuttoned revealing more chest than in Season One. Ray Danton is given third billing in the starring credits, above Peggie Castle.

Trivia: In the introductory segment, "The Birdcage Saloon's" bartender, played by Clancy Cooper, describes the saloon to a friendly trapper played by Dan Sheridan. Cooper would leave the show at the end of Season Two and Sheridan would replace him behind the bar beginning with the fourth episode of Season Three. Actress Nan Peterson declared in Boyd Magers' book, *A Gathering of Guns: A Half Century of TV Westerns* (1949-2001), that she was considered to play a consistent role in the series as Brown's girlfriend, but it never came to be.

Episode 41: "The Hunch" October 11, 1959.
Starring John Russell, Peter Brown, Peggie Castle, and Tom Drake (Frank Judson). Featuring Strother Martin (Jack Foley), Howard Petrie (Hal Mead), Kim Charney (Peter Judson).

Directed by Robert T. Sparr, Written by William F. Leicester, Produced by Jules Schermer, Director of Photography: Perry Finnerman, Art Director: LeRoy Deane, Supervising Film Editor: James Moore, Film Editor: Carl Pingitore, Production Manager: Oren W. Haglund, Sound: Stanley Jones, Set Decorator: Stephen A. Potter, Assistant Director: William Lasky.

Synopsis: All the evidence indicates that a man who passed out drunk is guilty of a bank robbery, but Troop has the feeling he's been set up.

Commentary: Troop's compassion for the underdog continues as he refuses to give up on a man he thinks might be innocent. Howard Petrie's pompous villain makes another formidable opponent for Troop.

Trivia: Tom Drake, who appeared in three *Lawman* episodes, had his most memorable film role as the boy-next-door in Judy Garland's *Meet*

Me in St. Louis (1944). He portrayed a very different person, an outlaw, in Henry Fonda's *Warlock* (1959). Strother Martin played bandits and rascals for thirty years in westerns and dramas including several classics directed by John Ford and Sam Peckinpah. His most famous character was the prison captain in *Cool Hand Luke* (1967). Gerald Perry Finnerman, the son of Perry Finnerman, this episode's director of photography, was also a cinematographer. In 1969, the son was scouting locations by plane for the television show *Star Trek* (1966-69) when it crashed, killing Robert Sparr, the director of this episode. Sparr helmed thirty-three *Lawman* shows and edited another five.

Episode 42: "Shackled" October 18, 1959.
Starring John Russell, Peter Brown, and Peggie Castle. Featuring Robert McQueeney (Bench Ryan), Kasey Rogers (Maggie Ryan), John Milford (Frank Krohl), Alfred Shelby (Ben Lang).

Directed by Leslie H. Martinson, Written by William F. Leicester, Produced by Jules Schermer, Director of Photography: Perry Finnerman, Art Director: Howard Campbell, Supervising Film Editor: James Moore, Film Editor: Elbert K. Hollingsworth, Sound: Howard Fogetti, Set Decorator: William Wallace, Production Manager: Oren W. Haglund, Assistant Director: Claude E. Archer.

Synopsis: Johnny is transporting an outlaw to the penitentiary when the prison wagon is attacked by the outlaw's partner and Johnny is taken prisoner.

Commentary: This is one of many *Lawman* shows in which Troop or Johnny loses a prisoner and then spend the rest of the show trying to regain custody. Although she's listed in the credits, Peggie Castle doesn't appear in this episode, while John Russell is in it for only a few minutes.

Trivia: Many of the Warner Bros. young contract players resembled established movie stars. For example, Robert McQueeney looked a great deal like Barry Sullivan. McQueeney had roles in four *Lawman* episodes, most of the Warner Bros. television productions, and co-starred in the short-lived 1962-63 Warner Bros. World War II series, *The Gallant Men*. Kasey Rogers' most memorable characters were Farley Granger's estranged wife in *Strangers on a Train* (1951), Barbara Perkins' mother on the *Peyton Place* series (1964-69), and the second Louise Tate in *Bewitched* (1966-72). Rogers also used the stage name Laura Elliot(t). Under that name she co-starred with Edmond O'Brien and Sterling Hayden in the western, *Denver and Rio Grande* (1952).

Episode 43: "The Exchange" October 25, 1959.
Starring John Russell, Peter Brown, and Peggie Castle. Featuring Mike Road (Frank Quinlivan), J. Edward McKinley (Mr. Worth), Paul Comi (Williams), James Parnell (Hanson), Bryan Russell (Tommy Quinlivan), Clancy Cooper (Timmo), Roscoe Ates (Ike Jaenkins).

Directed by Robert T. Sparr, Written by Edmund Morris, Produced by Jules Schermer, Director of Photography: Harold Stine, Art Director: Carl Macauley, Supervising Film Editor: James Moore, Film Editor: Fred M. Bohanan, Sound: Ross Owen, Set Decorator: Glenn P. Thompson, Production Manager: Oren W. Haglund, Assistant Director: Rusty Meek.

Synopsis: Lily's estranged ex-con husband shows up in Laramie and blackmails her to help aid him in a bank robbery.

Commentary: This episode depicts Lily's backstory and provides a major test for Troop and Lily's relationship. Troop's ability to read people and predict trouble is apparent: Lily: "What makes you think there's trouble?" Troop: "I've developed a nose for it." The storyline also provides Lily with the opportunity to sing and display a lot of leg.

Trivia: Roscoe Ates added some humor to each of his eight *Lawman* appearances. During his long career, he appeared in fifteen westerns as Soapy Adams, comic sidekick to singing cowboy, Eddie Dean. Ates was also in *Cimarron* (1931), John Wayne's *Three Texas Steers* (1939), and *Gone With the Wind* (1939) as a wounded Confederate soldier.

Episode 44: "The Last Man" November 1, 1959.
Starring John Russell, Peter Brown, and Peggie Castle. Featuring Henry Brandon (Joshua Haney), Gordon Jones (Sergeant Hanks), Steve Darrell (Torn Cloud), Herman Rudin (Gen. Iron Jack Miller), Clancy Cooper (Timmo), Robert Clark (Captain Graves).

Directed by Robert T. Sparr, Written by Clair Huffaker, Produced by Jules Schermer, Director of Photography: Ray Fernstrom, Art Director: Carl Macauley, Supervising Film Editor: James Moore, Film Editor: George C. Shrader, Sound: Charles Althouse, Set Decorator: Steve A. Potter, Production Manager: Oren W. Haglund. Assistant Director: William Lasky.

Synopsis: Troop attempts to stop two men from blocking a peace treaty.

Commentary: The townspeople's disrespect for Native Americans and Troop's efforts to defuse this hate is a theme repeated throughout *Lawman*. In this episode, Henry Brandon's Joshua Henry, a white man raised by the Sioux and caught between the two cultures, is one of several such characters depicted in this series. Brandon is magnificent in his role here.

Trivia: Brandon played two of the most different yet memorable villains in Hollywood history: Barnaby Barnicle in Laurel and Hardy's *Babes in Toyland/March of the Wooden Soldiers* (1934) and Scar in *The Searchers* (1956).

Episode 45: "The Breakup" November 8, 1959.
Starring John Russell, Peter Brown, and Peggie Castle. Featuring Donald Buka (Harry Jensen), Nan Peterson (Annie), Hal Baylor (Poke), Roscoe Ates (Jenkins), Clancy Cooper (Timmo), John Clarke (Chaw), Rayford Barnes (Bill Watts), Andrew Colmar (Jessie Watts).

Directed by Paul Guilfoyle, Written by Clair Huffaker, Produced by Jules Schermer, Director of Photography: Perry Finnerman, Art Director: LeRoy Deane, Supervising Film Editor: James Moore, Film

Editor: Robert T. Sparr, Sound: Samuel F. Goode, Set Decorator: Steven A. Potter, Production Manager: Oren W. Haglund, Assistant Director: William Lasky.

Synopsis: Johnny resigns after he's forced to kill two brothers he's known all his life.

Commentary: Johnny resigns a total of three times during the series – in this episode, "The Joker" (1958) and "The Souvenir" (1959) – but always returns to duty. The concluding scene with Troop nodding with approval and opening the door for Johnny to enter the marshal's office with the *Lawman* theme playing in the background provides an extremely satisfactory conclusion to this episode.

Trivia: Paul Guilfoyle was a character actor who appeared in over 130 films and television productions. He was probably best known as the sly gangster trying to kill James Cagney in *White Heat* (1949). He also directed over sixty television programs including two *Lawman* episodes, "The Shelter" (1959) and "Man on a Mountain" (1960).

Episode 46: "Shadow Witness" November 15, 1959.
Starring John Russell, Peter Brown, and Peggie Castle. Featuring Herbert Rudley (Clint Baker), Percy Helton (Oren), Walter Burke ("Specs" Toynby), Barbara Bestar (Beth Harvey).

Directed by Everett Sloane, Written by William F. Leicester, Produced by Jules Schermer, Director of Photography: J. Peverell Marley, Supervising Art Director: Perry Ferguson, Art Director: LeRoy Deane, Supervising Film Editor: James Moore, Film Editor: Robert B. Warwick Jr., Music Supervision: Paul Sawtell and Bert Shefter, Music Editor: Erma E. Levin, Sound: Charles Althouse, Set Decorator: Steve A. Potter, Production Manager: Oren W. Haglund, Assistant Director: William Lasky.

Synopsis: The only witness to the murder of a dancehall girl is a near-sighted bartender whose glasses were broken by the killer.

Commentary: This is another episode in which Troop creates a scenario to push the lawbreaker to show his hand. Lily displays warmth and empathy with a wounded man and an obvious affection for the marshal: "I'm kinda partial to the strong, silent type." The crew credits begin listing music supervisors, Paul Sawtell and Bert Shefter, and different music editors with this episode.

Trivia: Percy Helton made scores of appearances in television and film westerns, usually playing a timid townsman or crime victim. He had a memorable bit as Sweetface in *Butch Cassidy and the Sundance Kid* (1969). The director of this episode, Everett Sloane, was most famous for his acting; for example, his work in Orson Welles' *Citizen Kane* (1940). Sloane also directed; he helmed a 1946 Broadway play, *The Dancer*, and five television shows.

Episode 47: "The Prodigal" November 22, 1959.
Starring John Russell, Peter Brown, and Peggie Castle. Featuring Tony Young (Mark), Clancy Cooper (Timmo), Ken Lynch (Al Feller), Arthur Batanides (Vince Semby), Bill Challee (Bill Porter), Dal McKennon (Randy).

Directed by Paul Stewart, Written by William F. Leicester, Produced by Jules Schermer, Director of Photography: Carl Berger, Supervising Art Director: Perry Ferguson, Art Director: Carl Macauley, Supervising Film Editor: James Moore, Film Editor: Ted Bellinger, Music Supervision: Paul Sawtell and Bert Shefter, Music Editor: Theo W. Sebern, Sound: Stanley Jones, Set Decorator: Steve Potter, Production Manager: Oren W. Haglund, Assistant Director: Dave Marks.

Synopsis: Lily's bartender's son comes to Laramie with a chip on his shoulder.

Commentary: Troop verbalizes his view of successful parenting: "What that boy needs is a father's loving hand. Right across the seat of his pants." At the end of the show, Troop once again allows someone who's rehabilitated themselves to get on with their life.

Trivia: This episode's director, Paul Stewart, usually played gangster roles in movies and on television; one of his more memorable characters was the mobster Zepp in Cary Grant's *Mr. Lucky* (1943). Tony Young was the son of character actor Carleton G. Young. Tony briefly starred in the 1961 television western series, *The Gunslinger*.

Episode 48: "The Press" November 29, 1959.
Starring John Russell, Peter Brown, and Peggie Castle. Featuring Robert Wilke (Lal Hoard), Vinton Hayworth (Oren Slauson), Wendell Holmes (Cal Nibley), Robert Riordan (Arthur Grey).

Directed by Robert T. Sparr, Written by Ric Hardman, Produced by Jules Schermer, Director of Photography: Ray Fernstrom, Supervising Art Director: Perry Ferguson, Art Director: Carl Macauley, Supervising Film Editor: James Moore, Film Editor: George E. Luckenbacher, Music Supervision: Paul Sawtell and Bert Shefter, Music Editor: Sam E. Levin, Sound: Arthur Kirbach, Set Decorator: Glenn P. Thompson, Production Manager: Oren W. Haglund, Assistant Director: James T. Vaughn.

Synopsis: An ex-con whom Troop had sent to prison vows revenge against the marshal.

Commentary: This isn't the first time Troop's marshalling is disparaged by the local newspaper; when Julie Tate took over "The Free Press" during the first season, she was also critical of Troop. This episode successfully balances a light, whimsical touch involving Lily's lace curtains with Wilke's reptilian villain's scheme to gain revenge against Troop and his "ramrod sense of duty." The marshal once again shows his moral flexibility when he allows another character in the story a second chance because, as Troop states, "A man has the right to change." The town's appreciation for Troop and his method of keeping the peace is illustrated at the end of this episode.

Trivia: This was the first of twenty-six *Lawman* episodes written by Ric Hardman, sometimes under the pseudonym Bronson Howitzer. He also authored the scripts for such western films as Tab Hunter's *Gunman's*

Walk (1958) and James Stewart and Maureen O'Hara's *The Rare Breed* (1966); He also wrote such novels as *Fifteen Flags* (1968) and *Sunshine Rider* (1998), the first "vegetarian" western.

Episode 49: "9:05 to North Platte" December 6, 1959.
Starring John Russell, Peter Brown, and Peggie Castle. Featuring Harry Shannon (Pa Jutes), Richard Rust (Rood Jutes), Don C. Harvey (Harry Banks), Walter Baldwin (Cal Satler), Joann Manley (Mrs. Buckner), Charlie Briggs (Logan Jutes), Jimmy Baird (Joey Buckner), Jack Hogan (Lester Jutes), Robert J. Nelson (Jack Buckner).

Directed by Robert T. Sparr, Written by Clair Huffaker, Produced by Jules Schermer, Director of Photography: Warren Lynch, Supervising Art Director: Perry Ferguson, Art Director: Carl Macauley, Supervising Film Editor: James Moore, Film Editor: George E. Luckenbacher, Music Supervision: Paul Sawtell and Bert Shefter, Music Editor: Erma E. Levin, Sound: Eugene Irvine, Set Decorator: Gene Redd, Production Manager: Oren W. Haglund, Assistant Director: James T. Vaughn.

Synopsis: A prisoner's outlaw father kidnaps Lily and a boy, and demands that Troop free his son.

Commentary: Troop and Johnny again uses chicanery to defeat the bad guys. Troop's feelings for Lily are obvious after he rescues her. Harry Shannon provides the show with another strong-willed opponent opposing the marshal.

Trivia: Shannon played memorable old codgers on both sides of the law; one notable role was Orson Welles' alcoholic father in *Citizen Kane* (1940).

Episode 50: "The Hoax" December 20, 1959.
Starring John Russell, Peter Brown, and Peggie Castle. Featuring Paula Raymond (Paula), Willard Waterman (The Deacon), John Hubbard (Candy Kid), Maudie Prickett (Laura Tate), Tom Palmer (Dr. Stewart), Nolan Leary (Rev. Aaronson), Andrea Smith (Rosie).

Directed by Robert T. Sparr, Written by Dean Riesner, Produced by Jules Schermer, Director of Photography: Warren Lynch, Art Director: Carl Macauley, Supervising Film Editor: James Moore, Film Editor: Robert Crawford, Music Supervision: Paul Sawtell and Bert Shefter, Music Editor: Erma E. Levin, Sound: Don McKay, Set Decorator: Gene Redd, Production Manager: Oren W. Haglund, Assistant Director: James T. Vaughn.

Synopsis: Two con-men pose as ministers to steal funds raised to build a new church in Laramie.

Commentary: This is one of several *Lawman* episodes in which Troop encounters and confronts con artists and their schemes.

Trivia: Stunning Paula Raymond turned down the role of Kitty in *Gunsmoke* which eventually went to Amanda Blake. She co-starred in the westerns *Devil's Doorway* (1950) and *The Gun That Won the West* (1955). Maudie Prickett had a long career portraying busy-bodies and nosy, gossipy neighbors, and was the inspiration for comic Johnathan Winters' character, Maude Frickert. Due to holiday scheduling, the previous Sunday, December 13, 1959, was the only time during in its run that *Lawman* was not televised in its regular slot.

Episode 51: "The Shelter" December 20, 1959.
Starring John Russell and Peter Brown. Featuring Chris Alcaide (Ben Moray), John Alderson (Jack Brace), Anna Navarro (Tucupita).

Directed by Paul Guilfoyle, Written by Edmund Morris, Produced by Jules Schermer, Director of Photography: Roger Shearman, Art Director: Howard Campbell, Supervising Film Editor: James Moore, Film Editor: Marsh Hendry, Music Supervision: Paul Sawtell and Bert Shefter, Music Editor: Sam E. Levin, Sound: Francis E. Stahl, Set Decorator: Frank M. Miller, Production Manager: Oren W. Haglund, Assistant Director: William Lasky.

Synopsis: Troop, Johnny, and their prisoner are caught in a storm and seek shelter in an isolated cabin occupied by a man with a checkered past.

Commentary: This is one of many episodes when Troop and/or Johnny are confronted with obstacles while attempting to bring an outlaw to prison. It's also another storyline involving a young woman forced to live a subservient life. The fist fight is one of the longest of the series; usually Troop and Johnny dispose of their opponents in one or two punches. Peggie Castle does not appear in this episode, and is not listed in the credits.

Trivia: John Alderson played scores of western outlaws, but also co-starred as Sgt. Bullock in the western syndicated series, *Boots and Saddles* (1957-58) and portrayed Wyatt Earp in four 1966 *Dr. Who* episodes. He also played Alfred P. Doolittle's buddy in *My Fair Lady* (1964). Perhaps his most famous role was the gum chewer in *Blazing Saddles* (1974).

Episode 52: "Last Stop" January 3, 1960.
Starring John Russell, Peter Brown, and Peggie Castle. Featuring Richard Arlen (Bill Jennings), Rita Lynn (Amie), Johnathan Gilmore (Gabe Jennings), Clancy Cooper (Timmo).

Directed by Robert T. Sparr, Written by Clair Huffaker, Produced by Jules Schermer, Director of Photography: Ellis W. Carter, Art Director: Carl Macauley, Supervising Film Editor: James Moore, Film Editor: Lloyd Nosler, Music Supervision: Paul Sawtell and Bert Shefter, Music Editor: Theo W. Sebern, Sound: Charles Althouse, Set Decorator: Glenn P. Thompson, Production Manager: Oren W. Haglund, Assistant Director: James T. Vaughn.

Synopsis: A soon-to-be rancher is challenged to a gunfight by his long-lost son.

Commentary: Troop once again intervenes in a potential lethal confrontation between a father and son. Lily shows off another of her gorgeous hats. It's mentioned that Laramie's population is 1,720. What's not emphasized very often is the significance of Fort Laramie. As Michael Crichton wrote in his novel, *Dragon Teeth*, "Fort Laramie was an army outpost that had grown into a frontier town, but the army garrison still set the mood." Several episodes involve the military including "The Runaway" (1959), "The Last Man" (1959), "The Robbery" (1961), and "The Appointment" (1961)," but for the most part, the influence of the fort is downplayed.

Trivia: This was the second of three *Lawman* appearances for silent screen star Richard Arlen. In each, he played a man followed by trouble.

Episode 53: "The Showdown" January 10, 1960.
Starring John Russell, Peter Brown, and Peggie Castle. Featuring John Howard (Lance Creedy), James Coburn (Blake Carr), Roberta Haynes (Mattie Creedy), Jim Hayward (Hartwell).

Directed by Robert T. Sparr, Written by William F. Leicester, Produced by Jules Schermer, Director of Photography: Warren Lynch, Art Director: Carl Macauley, Supervising Film Editor: James Moore, Film Editor: Noel L. Scott, Music Supervision: Paul Sawtell and Bert Shefter, Music Editor: Joe Inge, Sound: Eugene Irvine, Set Decorator: Gene Redd, Production Manager: Oren W. Haglund, Assistant Director: James T. Vaughn.

Synopsis: A pardoned, former gunfighter is confronted by an old partner.

Commentary: This is another *Lawman* episode in which a man attempts to move on from his violent past. Troop explains why he doesn't believe in deadlines (setting up a ruling that men can't wear guns in town): "If men are going to fight, they'll fight. Now you check their guns, they'll think that you're afraid of them... These men aren't riff-raff. They're honest men. If you go telling them they can't be trusted, things'll get way out of hand." Jim Hayward's Hartwell is another of the show's instigating townsmen/barflies who hunger to witness the violence of a gunfight. Coburn makes an excellent villain with his sneering smile and authoritative voice.

Trivia: John Howard was one of the first well-known Hollywood actors to work in television. His best known film roles were Ronald

Colman's younger brother in *Lost Horizon* (1937) and Katherine Hepburn's fiancé in *The Philadelphia Story* (1940), but western fans will remember his Blake Randolph in John Wayne's *The Fighting Kentuckian* (1949). James Coburn had a long career in and out of the West and on either side of the law, but his seminal role was Britt in *The Magnificent Seven* (1960) even though he only had eleven lines of dialogue. He won a Best Supporting Actor Oscar for playing Nick Nolte's father in *Affliction* in 1997. Coburn always maintained that his favorite role was Pat Garrett in Sam Peckinpah's *Pat Garrett and Billy the Kid* (1973).

Episode 54: "The Stranger" January 17, 1960.
Starring John Russell, Peter Brown, and Peggie Castle. Featuring Ian Wolfe (Jason Smith), Clancy Cooper (Timmo), Roscoe Ates (Ike Jenkins), Brad Weston (Jack Edwards), Larry Blake (Chuck Slade).

Directed by Robert T. Sparr, Written by Clair Huffaker, Produced by Jules Schermer, Director of Photography: Ray Fernstrom, Art Director: Carl Macauley, Supervising Film Editor: James Moore, Film Editor: Edgar Zane, Music Supervision: Paul Sawtell and Bert Shefter, Music Editor: George W. Korngold, Sound: M.A. Merrick, Set Decorator: Glenn P. Thompson, Production Manager: Oren W. Haglund, Assistant Director: Don Blair.

Synopsis: After Troop is forced to kill a drunken stranger, he begins to receive unsigned, threatening letters.

Commentary: Johnny shows growth in both his maturity and in his detective skills as he, not the marshal, discovers the identity of the potential killer in this episode. Troop is continuously confronted by angry, strong-willed antagonists who dislike him and what he stands for. Larry Blake does an excellent job portraying one of these characters in this episode.

Trivia: Blake played the saloon owner in *High Noon* (1952). The music editor of this episode was George W. Korngold, the son of Eric Wolfgang Korngold, the renowned composer of the Oscar-winning scores of *Anthony Adverse* (1936) and *The Adventures of Robin Hood* (1938).

Episode 55: "The Wolfer" January 24, 1960.
Starring John Russell, Peter Brown, and Peggie Castle. Featuring Archie Duncan (Pike Reese), Jack Mather (Carl Haydn), Spencer Carlisle (Alf Betts), Gilman W. Rankin (Ed Fuller).

Directed by Robert T. Sparr, Written by Ric Hardman, Produced by Jules Schermer, Director of Photography: Warren Lynch, Art Director: Carl Macauley, Supervising Film Editor: James Moore, Film Editor: Elbert K. Hollingsworth, Music Supervision: Paul Sawtell and Bert Shefter, Music Editor: Joe Inge, Sound: Frank Webster, Set Decorator: Gene Redd, Production Manager: Oren W. Haglund, Assistant Director: James T. Vaughn.

Synopsis: An expert outdoorsman skilled at killing wolves is accused of murder.

Commentary: Troop demonstrates great empathy when he is forced to arrest a fiercely independent man with whom the marshal strongly identifies. The banter between Troop and Johnny concerning their romantic lives at the beginning of the show indicates a growing friendship of equals. Peggie Castle is in the credits but does not appear in this episode.

Trivia: Archie Duncan played Little John in 100 episodes of Richard Greene's *The Adventures of Robin Hood* television series (1955-60), and the bumbling Inspector Lestrade and other policemen in thirty-one episodes of the series, *Sherlock Holmes* (1954-55).

Episode 56: "The Hardcase" January 31, 1960.
Starring John Russell, Peter Brown, and Peggie Castle. Featuring Dody Heath (Beth Denning), Robert Armstrong (Lacey Grant), Paul Carr (Gilly Stuart), William Challee (Nat Denning), Tom Palmer (Doctor), Jack Shea (Miner), Don Drysdale (Roy Grant).

Directed by Robert T. Sparr, Written by William F. Leicester, Produced by Jules Schermer, Director of Photography: Warren Lynch, Art Director: Carl Macauley, Supervising Film Editor: James Moore,

Film Editor: Milt Kleinberg, Music Supervision: Paul Sawtell and Bert Shefter, Music Editor: George E. Marsh, Sound: Donald McKay, Set Decorator: Gene Redd, Production Manager: Oren W. Haglund, Assistant Director: Eddie Prinz.

Synopsis: After a flirtatious farm girl is seriously hurt, the son of a cattle baron is arrested as the primary suspect.

Commentary: Troop and Johnny are forced to stand up to yet another armed mob attacking the jail. Troop's philosophy of marshalling is summed up in the six words he tells the leader of the mob, "I don't take my job lightly." The closing credits end with "And Don Drysdale as Roy Grant."

Trivia: Don Drysdale was the Hall of Fame Dodger pitcher who dabbled in acting. Robert Armstrong played dozens of uncompromising "hardcases" for over thirty years; his most memorable role was as Carl Denham in the original *King Kong* (1933).

Episode 57: "To Capture the West" February 7, 1960.
Starring John Russell, Peter Brown, and Peggie Castle. Featuring Warren Stevens (Frederick Jameson), Henry Brandon (Tall Horse), Clancy Cooper (Timmo McQueen), Mickey Simpson (Connors), George Kennedy (Burt).

Directed by Robert T. Sparr, Written by Clair Huffaker, Produced by Jules Schermer, Director of Photography: Warren Lynch, Art Director: Carl Macauley, Supervising Film Editor: James Moore, Film Editor: Robert B. Warwick Jr., Music Supervision: Paul Sawtell and Bert Shefter, Music Editor: Charles Paley, Sound: Eugene H. Irvine, Set Decorator: Gene S. Redd, Production Manager: Oren W. Haglund, Assistant Director: Eddie Prinz.

Synopsis: Troop attempts to protect a talented painter from a gang of outlaws.

Commentary: Another example of Troop and Johnny helping out an underdog. The episode ends with a strongly photographed doorway conclusion. Henry Brandon is excellent in an emotional role as the artist's loyal Indian friend who utters the telling observation, "He'll never die; he'll live forever."

Trivia: The most famous artist of the West was Frederic Remington, who shared the same first name as Stevens' fictional character in this episode. This was one of George Kennedy's early roles; he has a bit as a loud barfly who challenged the artist to arm-wrestle.

Episode 58: "The Ugly Man" February 14, 1960.
Starring John Russell, Peter Brown, and Peggie Castle. Featuring Eve McVeagh (Josie), Ted Knight, (The Ugly Man), Clancy Cooper (Timmo), Mina Vaughn (Delores), Joyce Otis (Annette).

Directed by Robert T. Sparr, Written by Clair Huffaker, Produced by Jules Schermer, Director of Photography: Warren Lynch, Art Director: Carl Macauley, Supervising Film Editor: James Moore, Film Editor: Milt Kleinberg, Music Supervision: Paul Sawtell and Bert Shefter, Music Editor: Donald K. Harris, Sound: Ross Owen, Set Decorator: Gene S. Redd, Production Manager: Oren W. Haglund, Assistant Director: Eddie Prinz.

Synopsis: A man thinks Lily has rejected him and is determined to kill her.

Commentary: This mystery regarding the unknown stalker is developed well. Using a decoy to catch a criminal and other mistaken identity scenarios occur occasionally in *Lawman*. The sedate painting of Lily from the previous episode is displayed behind the bar.

Trivia: Mina Vaughn played a dancehall girl at "The Birdcage Saloon" five times. This was one of Ted Knight's early roles; he later achieved fame as Ted Baxter on *The Mary Tyler Moore Show* (1970-77) and as Judge Elihu Smails in *Caddyshack* (1980).

Episode 59: "The Kids" February 21, 1960.
Starring John Russell, Peter Brown, and Peggie Castle. Featuring Tom Drake (Lou Evans), Bart Bradley (Dennis Deaver), Ric Roman (George Deaver), Ron Anton (Chuck Deaver), Frank Watkins (Spade), Mina Vaughn (Sue), Ginger Dubberly (Anne), Evelyn Rudie (Dodie Deaver).

Directed by Robert T. Sparr, Written by Ric Hardman, Produced by Jules Schermer, Director of Photography: Warren Lynch, Art Director: Carl Macauley, Supervising Film Editor: James Moore, Film Editor: Michael Luciano, Music Supervision: Paul Sawtell and Bert Shefter, Music Editor: John Allyn, Jr., Sound: John Jensen, Set Decorator: Gene S. Redd, Production Manager: Oren W. Haglund, Assistant Director: Eddie Prinz.

Synopsis: Three unruly youngsters, a girl and her two brothers, arrive in Laramie hoping to join up with their outlaw father.

Commentary: Although there is some peripheral violence, "The Kids" is basically an enjoyable romp. Troop and Johnny's amused reactions, the banter between the marshal and Lily, and the comical musical score filled with clarinets and oboes result in a genuinely amusing episode. The dialogue is funny: "I want a turn," one kid mutters as she tries to grab the rifle and shoot at the lawmen; Drake's character attempts to explain "Quakers not Quackers" to his niece; the conversation between Dodie and her father, "I'll write, Pa, once I learn to write reading" –"I'll read what you write, Dodie, once I learn how to read writing;" and the conclusion with Troop talking about his future kids, and Lily and Johnny smiling, wisecracking, and making faces. The closing acting credits end with "And Evelyn Rudie as Dodie Deaver."

Trivia: Precocious Evelyn Rudie was a popular child actress in the late 1950s and early 1960s; one of her most memorable appearances was on Groucho Marx's *You Bet Your Life* in 1959.

Episode 60: "The Thimblerigger" February 28, 1960.
Starring John Russell, Peter Brown, and Peggie Castle. Featuring Gerald

Mohr (The Thimblerigger), DeForest Kelley (Sam White), Richard Reeves (Ed Shafter), Fred Sherman (Bill), Doodles Weaver (Jack Stiles).

Directed by Robert T. Sparr, Written by Ric Hardman, Produced by Jules Schermer, Director of Photography: Warren Lynch, Art Director: Carl Macauley, Supervising Film Editor: James Moore, Film Editor: Clarence Kolster, Music Supervision: Paul Sawtell and Bert Shefter, Music Editor: Robert Phillips, Sound: J. Earl Snyder, Set Decorator: Gene S. Redd, Production Manager: Oren W. Haglund, Assistant Director: Eddie Prinz.

Synopsis: A newcomer to Laramie intends to expose a coward and kill him without using a weapon.

Commentary: This suspenseful mystery successfully builds its tension before the climax which answers the "who" and "why" questions. Troop effectively thwarts potential mob violence by dealing with it directly.

Trivia: A thimblerigger is someone who runs a gambling game involving sleight of hand in which three inverted thimbles or nutshells are moved about and a player attempts to locate the pea underneath. Gerald Mohr, with his resemblance to Humphrey Bogart, played dozens of cocky scoundrels on both sides of the law on television and in the movies. He and Fred Foy were the only narrators of the introduction to the 1949-57 television western classic, *The Lone Ranger*. Richard Reeves played in just about every television western during the 1950s and 1960s, usually as a gruff, bullying henchman.

Episode 61: "The Truce" March 6, 1960.
Starring John Russell, Peter Brown, and Peggie Castle. Featuring Robert McQueeney (O.C. Coulsen), Don O'Kelly (Jess Hahn), Ed Prentiss (Governor), Pierce Lyden (Posse Member).

Directed by Robert T. Sparr, Written by Ric Hardman, Produced by Jules Schermer, Director of Photography: Warren Lynch, Art Director: Carl Macauley, Supervising Film Editor: James Moore, Film Editor: Elbert K. Hollingsworth, Music Supervision: Paul Sawtell and Bert

Shefter, Music Editor: Louis W. Gordon, Sound: M.A. Merrick, Set Decorator: Gene S. Redd, Production Manager: Oren W. Haglund, Assistant Director: Eddie Prinz.

Synopsis: Troop attempts to bring a wounded, notorious outlaw to meet with the governor to discuss possible clemency, but another lawman is determined to get credit for bringing the man in himself.

Commentary: This is one of many narratives that feature other lawmen who do not have Troop's moral fiber. Troop once again demonstrates his creativity with his use of a decoy. There appears to be a discrepancy with dates; this episode would have taken place around 1880 but one of the characters mentions the Civil War (which ended in 1865) being ten years before. Johnny's hair appears darker.

Trivia: Don O'Kelly changed his name to Don Kelly in 1960. Kelly played arrogant individuals on both sides of the law in numerous television and movie dramas.

Episode 62: "Reunion in Laramie" March 13, 1960.
Starring John Russell, Peter Brown, and Peggie Castle. Featuring William Schallert (Reed Smith), Murvyn Vye (Vint Fell), Bill Mims (Eph), I. Stanford Jolley (Willie), Craig Duncan (Soldier).

Directed by Robert T. Sparr, Written by William F. Leicester, Produced by Jules Schermer, Director of Photography: Ellis W. Carter, Art Director: Carl Macauley, Supervising Film Editor: James Moore, Film Editor: Jim Faris, Music Supervision: Paul Sawtell and Bert Shefter, Music Editor: Jack B. Wadsworth, Sound: Ross Owen, Set Decorator: Edward M. Parker, Production Manager: Oren W. Haglund, Assistant Director: Eddie Prinz.

Synopsis: Troop attempts to protect a depressed, talented pianist from a revengeful former soldier.

Commentary: Like the episode, "To Capture the West," Troop and Lily admire an artist and are willing to fight for his safety. And like the previous episode, "The Truce," repercussions of the Civil War are woven into this drama. Troop recalls the Civil War, "It was a long, bloody mess," and maintains that when he took off his uniform, the war was over for him. This is yet occasion in which Troop fights mob mentality.

Trivia: William Schallert played Patty Duke's dad on *The Patty Duke Show* (1963-66). Bill Mims portrayed scores of scoundrels on various television programs. His portrayal of the banker father, Ebenezer Dorset, in the 1977 television movie, *The Ransom of Red Chief* with Jack Elam and Strother Martin, was particularly memorable.

Episode 63: "Thirty Minutes" March 20, 1960.
Starring John Russell, Peter Brown, and Peggie Castle. Featuring Jack Elam (Jake Wilson), John Clarke (Len Eaton), Clancy Cooper (Timmo), Ted White (Joe), Gene Roth (Will Kelsey), Kathryn Harte (Louise Kelsey), Carolyn Komant (Dolores).

Directed by Robert T. Sparr, Written by Richard Matheson, Produced by Jules Schermer, Director of Photography: Ralph Woolsey, Art Director: Carl Macauley, Supervising Film Editor: James Moore, Film Editor: Elbert K. Hollingsworth, Music Supervision: Paul Sawtell and Bert Shefter, Music Editor: Erma E. Levin, Sound: Harold Hanks, Set Decorator: Ben Bone, Production Manager: Oren W. Haglund, Assistant Director: Eddie Prinz.

Synopsis: A crazed killer takes five hostages in "The Birdcage Saloon" including Lily and Johnny.

Commentary: It seems that whenever Johnny complains that nothing is happening, something does. There's good visual and musical foreshadowing when the marshal opens an envelope and peers at a wanted posture of Jake Wilson. The conversation between Johnny and Lily – "Johnny: "You and Mr. Troop; you're two of a kind." Lily: "You tell him that sometime." – reveals Lily's frustration with Troop's indecisiveness about their relationship. The time deadline and the shots of a ticking clock are reminiscent of *High Noon* (1952). Elam is excellent here as a despicable psychopath.

Trivia: After years as a villain, often in westerns, Elam later demonstrated his range and versatility with a pair of comic roles in *Support Your Local Sheriff* (1969) and *Support Your Local Gunfighter* (1971). He also played Deputy J.D. Smith in 1963's *The Dakotas* series, U.S. Marshal George Taggart in *Temple Houston* (1963-64) with Jeffrey Hunter, and Zach in *The Texas Wheelers* sitcom (1974-75) with Mark Hamill and Gary Busey.

Episode 64: "Left Hand of the Law" March 27, 1960.
Starring John Russell, Peter Brown, and Peggie Castle. Featuring John Anderson (Lloyd Malone), Regis Tooney (Jubal Malone), Robert Reed (Jim Malone), Clancy Cooper (Timmo), Frank Richards (Claypool).

Directed by Robert T. Sparr, Teleplay by Edmund Morris, Story by Margaret Armen, Produced by Jules Schermer, Director of Photography: Ralph Woolsey, Art Director: Carl Macauley, Supervising Film Editor: James Moore, Film Editor: George C. Shrader, Music Supervision: Paul Sawtell and Bert Shefter, Music Editor: Joe Inge, Sound: Harold Hanks, Set Decorator: Ben Bone, Production Manager: Oren W. Haglund, Assistant Director: Eddie Prinz.

Synopsis: After losing the use of his gun arm when Troop shot him in Wichita, an ex-con pressures his son to kill the marshal.

Commentary: This is another story of a vindictive father using his son to seek revenge against Troop. The lack of music toward the end builds up the dramatic tension. The episode features an unusual gunfight in the rain.

Trivia: Over his fifty-year career, Regis Tooney made over 270 appearances in a variety of roles. His friendly Uncle Arvide of the Salvation Army in *Guys and Dolls* (1955) is typical of his later work. Robert Reed is best known for starring in *The Defenders* (1961-65) and *The Brady Bunch* (1969-74 and various reunion sequels and spin-offs). He rarely made westerns, but he did portray "The Pathfinder," John C. Fremont, in the 1977 television movie, *Kit Carson and the Mountain Men*.

Episode 65: "Belding's Girl" April 3, 1960.
Starring John Russell, Peter Brown, and Peggie Castle. Featuring Susan Morrow (Meg Belding), Emile Meyer (Ben Belding), Donald Barry (Jim Gaylord), Dermot Cronin (Tip White), Rush Williams (Frank Gaylord), Doodles Weaver (Jack), Cecil Smith (Judge).

Directed by Robert T. Sparr, Written by William F. Leicester, Produced by Jules Schermer, Director of Photography: Ralph Woolsey, Art Director: Carl Macauley, Supervising Film Editor: James Moore, Film Editor: Fred M. Bohanan, Music Supervision: Paul Sawtell and Bert Shefter, Music Editor: Sam E. Levin, Sound: Karl E. Zint, Set Decorator: Ben Bone, Production Manager: Oren W. Haglund, Assistant Director: Eddie Prinz.

Synopsis: A cattleman refuses to allow his twenty-two year-old daughter any freedom so she runs away to work at Lily's saloon.

Commentary: Another episode with an uncompromising, overly-protective father refusing to allow his daughter to live her own life. Troop and Lily aid yet another couple to find happiness. When wide-eyed Lily asks the marshal, "You want the course of young love to run smooth, don't you?" he responds with the telling response, "I like to see the course of any love to run smooth."

Trivia: Dermot Cronin looked very much like Anthony Perkins. Character actor Doodles Weaver played the hotel clerk in four *Lawman* episodes. He was the uncle of actress Sigourney Weaver. Emile Meyer played harsh and heartless villains throughout his long career; perhaps his most infamous role was as one of the Ryker brothers in *Shane* (1953). This was Susan Morrow's last acting credit; she had been Charlton Heston's love interest in *The Savage* (1952).

Episode 66: "Girl from Grantsville" April 10, 1960.
Starring John Russell, Peter Brown, and Peggie Castle. Featuring Suzanne Lloyd (Jenny Miles), Burt Douglas (Jeff Hacker), Roy Barcroft (Stagecoach Driver), William Leicester (Stagecoach Guard).

Directed by Robert T. Sparr, Written by Clair Huffaker, Produced by Jules Schermer, Director of Photography: Ralph Woolsey, Art Director: Carl Macauley, Supervising Film Editor: James Moore, Film Editor: Holbrook N. Todd, Music Supervision: Paul Sawtell and Bert Shefter, Music Editor: George E. Marsh, Sound: Donald McKay, Set Decorator: William L. Kuehl, Production Manager: Oren W. Haglund, Assistant Director: Eddie Prinz.

Synopsis: Johnny falls in love with the new girl in town.

Commentary: In this episode as in others, Troop and Lily demonstrate their parental concern for Johnny. The poignant ending, complete with the orchestrations of violins, clearly depicts their love and concern for him.

Trivia: William Leicester wrote twenty-one *Lawman* scripts and also penned stories for numerous television western series during the 1950s and 1960s. He also acted, and was in this episode, one other *Lawman*, and forty-seven other movie and television productions. Burt Douglas resembled actor-writer Tom Tryon.

Episode 67: "The Surface of Truth" April 17, 1960.
Starring John Russell, Peter Brown, and Peggie Castle. Featuring Peter Whitney (Lucas Beyer), Richard Hale (Washita), Maurice Jara (Tonkawa), Millicent Patrick (Mary Beyer).

Directed by Robert T. Sparr, Written by Ric Hardman, Produced by Jules Schermer, Director of Photography: Robert Hoffman, Art Director: Carl Macauley, Supervising Film Editor: James Moore, Film Editor: David Wages, Music Supervision: Paul Sawtell and Bert Shefter, Music Editor: Charles Paley, Sound: Ross Owen, Set Decorator: William L. Kuehl, Production Manager: Oren W. Haglund, Assistant Director: Eddie Prinz.

Synopsis: Troop must decide what to do with a trapper who is accused of killing his Indian wife.

Commentary: As in other *Lawman* scenarios, Troop is respectful and fair with Native Americans and doesn't have a problem abiding by tribal judgement. This is one of several episodes that features some sort of test to determine guilt or innocence. The ending provides a satisfactory hook.

Trivia: The heavy-set, bellicose Peter Whitney was memorable in this episode and in another *Lawman*, "The Stalker" (1961). Whitney co-starred with Kent Taylor and Jan Merlin in *The Rough Riders* (1958-59). Richard Hale, who played an Indian in this episode, was an angry-looking character actor who played a variety of ethnic roles. He was Nathan Radley in *To Kill a Mockingbird* (1962).

Episode 68: "The Salvation of Owny O'Reilly" April 24, 1960.
Starring John Russell, Peter Brown, and Peggie Castle. Featuring Joel Grey (Owny O'Reilly), Donald Murphy (Jack O'Reilly), Clancy Cooper (Timmo McQueen), Bill Leicester (Samson).

Directed by Robert T. Sparr, Written by Ric Hardman, Produced by Jules Schermer, Director of Photography: Walter Castle, Art Director: Carl Macauley, Supervising Film Editor: James Moore, Film Editor: Robert B. Warwick Jr., Music Supervision: Paul Sawtell and Bert Shefter, Music Editor: Donald K. Harris, Sound: Dean Thomas, Set Decorator: Ralph S. Hurst, Production Manager: Oren W. Haglund, Assistant Director: Eddie Prinz.

Synopsis: A youngster is torn between following the path of his outlaw brother or doing the right thing.

Commentary: This is one of many *Lawman* episodes featuring a young character wavering between following the outlaw trail or the law. Johnny displays his growing maturity when he declares, "Kids! I don't know what gets into 'em today." Later, he asks Troop, "How do you straighten out a kid like O'Reilly?" Troop's response is revealing: "Johnny, there's an answer for each one of them." At the episode's conclusion, Lily makes this observation about the tough-minded marshal: "Dan, sometimes I believe beneath that rough exterior there beats a heart."

Trivia: This was the first of three episodes featuring Joel Grey as the diminutive Owny O'Reilly. The other two were "The Return of Owny O'Reilly" (1960) and "Owny O'Reilly, Esquire" (1961). Grey won a Tony in 1967 and an Oscar in 1973 for his stage and film portrayals of the master of ceremonies in the musical, *Cabaret*.

<u>Episode 69</u>: "The Lady Belle" May 1, 1960.
Starring John Russell, Peter Brown, and Peggie Castle. Featuring Joan Marshall (Lady Belle Smythe), Vinton Hayworth (Oren Slauson), Doodles Weaver (Jack Stoles), Bob Morgan (Al Miner), Slim Pickens (Cal), Orville Sherman (Bank Clerk), Bill Catching (Evans).

Directed by Robert T. Sparr, Written by Ric Hardman, Produced by Jules Schermer, Director of Photography: Walter Castle, Art Director: Carl Macauley, Supervising Film Editor: James Moore, Film Editor: Stefan Arnsten, Music Supervision: Paul Sawtell and Bert Shefter, Music Editor: John Allyn, Jr., Sound: Harold F. Hanks, Set Decorator: Ben Bone, Production Manager: Oren W. Haglund, Assistant Director: Eddie Prinz.

Synopsis: A beautiful woman arrives in Laramie and charms the marshal while annoying Lily.

Commentary: In a rare occurrence – similar to the actual events in Northfield, Minnesota on September 7, 1876 when citizens thwarted an attempted bank robbery by the James-Younger gang –Troop gets help from Laramie residents to halt a bank robbery. Troop attempts to share the little he knows about women with Johnny: "If a woman ever apologizes to you, Johnny, you're sunk. They'll never forgive you for it" and "I'll tell you, boy, hell hath no fury like a woman whose dress has been scorned." The serious and courageous marshal shows great wisdom and a sly sense of humor when he tells Lily at the end of the episode, "I like the dress."

Trivia: Slim Pickens' most memorable role was Major King Kong in *Dr. Strangelove: or How I Learned to Stop Worrying and Love the Bomb*

(1964), but his comical Taggart in *Blazing Saddles* (1974) and his Hollis P. Woods in Steven Spielberg's *1941* (1979) were also unforgettable. Pickens' first of many credited roles in westerns was in Errol Flynn's *Rocky Mountain* (1950). As a youth, Peter Brown's family rented Pickens' ranch in Coarsegold, California. Joan Marshall, a stunning Julie London-lookalike, co-starred in the 1958-59 television series, *Bold Venture*, with Dane Clark. Marshall was briefly married to director Hal Ashby; several of her life experiences were allegedly used in his 1975 film, *Shampoo*.

Episode 70: "The Payment" May 8, 1960.
Starring John Russell, Peter Brown, Peggie Castle, and Troy Donahue (David Manning). Featuring Robert McQueeney (Ron Fallon), Catherine McLeod (Judith Manning), Allan Lane (Joe Hoyt), Clancy Cooper (Timmo), Mickey Simpson (Lew), Rummy Bishop (Monk).

Directed by Robert T. Sparr, Teleplay by Berne Giler, Story by Lewis Reed and Harry Franklin, Produced by Jules Schermer, Director of Photography: Walter Castle, Art Director: Carl Macauley, Supervising Film Editor: James Moore, Film Editor: Robert Crawford, Music Supervision: Paul Sawtell and Bert Shefter, Music Editor: Lewis W. Gordon, Sound: Don McKay, Set Decorator: Ben Bone, Production Manager: Oren W. Haglund, Assistant Director: Eddie Prinz.

Synopsis: The son of an outlaw seeks revenge against his father's old partner.

Commentary: Another story of a son seeking revenge and Troop's reticence to share the truth in an attempt to prevent further bloodshed and calamity. The plot here is similar to the *Cheyenne* episode, "The Empty Gun," in which John Russell plays the gunfighter. Troy Donahue receives starring billing in this episode's credits.

Trivia: Fifties' teen heartthrob Troy Donahue co-starred in *A Summer Place* (1959), (1961), forty-seven episodes of *SurfSide 6* (1960-62) and thirty-two of *Hawaiian Eye* (1959-63). He was married to actress Suzanne Pleshette for eight months in 1964. Hollywood press agent

Henry Willson gave him his stage name, as he also did for Rock Hudson and Tab Hunter. Beautiful, sad-faced Catherine McLeod, who resembled Theresa Wright, starred in the 1946 romance, *I'll Always Love You*, and numerous television dramas including four *Lawman* episodes. Allan Lane was remembered for his *King of the Royal Mounted* (1940), his seven *Red Ryder* films in 1946 and 1947, and his numerous Allan "Rocky" Lane B-westerns during the late 1940s and early 1950s. Lane was also the voice of television's *Mr. Ed* (1958-66).

Episode 71: "The Judge" May 15, 1960.
Starring John Russell and Peter Brown, Featuring Randy Stuart (Rose Grant), John Hoyt (Judge Loren Grant), Diane McBain (Lilac).

Directed by Robert T. Sparr, Teleplay by Montgomery Pittman and W. Hermanos, Story by Montgomery Pittman, Produced by Jules Schermer, Director of Photography: Walter Castle, Art Director: Carl Macauley, Supervising Film Editor: James Moore, Film Editor: Elbert K. Hollingsworth, Music Supervision: Paul Sawtell and Bert Shefter, Music Editor: Robert Phillips, Sound: Ross Owen, Set Decorator: Ben Bone, Production Manager: Oren W. Haglund, Assistant Director: Eddie Prinz.

Synopsis: After Troop is bushwhacked in an ambush, two women who live with a cynical judge in an isolated setting nurse him back to health.

Commentary: The cat and mouse battle of wits between Troop and his antagonist demonstrates the marshal's intelligence and ingenuity. This is one of many episodes where Troop is wounded and then tended to by someone who has an outlaw family member who wants the marshal dead. Peggie Castle is not in the credits and does not appear in this episode. In several scenes, Russell, with his collar up, resembles John Wayne's Captain Nathan Brittles in *She Wore a Yellow Ribbon* (1949). The plot here is similar to the *Cheyenne* story, "The Angry Sky" (1958), featuring Andrew Duggan as the judge.

Trivia: During a writers' strike, Warner Bros. took several older episodes from one series and rewrote them for other shows. The producers used the nom de plume, "W. Hermanos," for the name of the episode's writer. The W stood for Warner Bros. and Hermanos is Spanish for brothers. Diane McBain appeared in most of the Warner Bros. television series and in forty-four episodes of *SurfSide 6* (1960-62). She also co-starred with Troy Donahue and Suzanne Pleshette in the cavalry western, *A Distant Trumpet* (1961).

Episode 72: "Man on a Wire" May 22, 1960.
Starring John Russell, Peter Brown, and Peggie Castle. Featuring Gustavo Rojo (Guiseppe Soldano), Karen Steele (Laura Soldano), Clancy Cooper (Timmo).

Directed by Robert T. Sparr, Written by W. Hermanos, Produced by Jules Schermer, Director of Photography: Wesley Anderson, Art Director: Carl Macauley, Supervising Film Editor: James Moore, Film Editor: Elbert K. Hollingsworth, Music Supervision: Paul Sawtell and Bert Shefter, Music Editor: Jack B. Wadsworth, Sound: John K. Kean, Set Decorator: Ben Bone, Production Manager: Oren W. Haglund, Assistant Director: Eddie Prinz.

Synopsis: A highwire act's Italian headliner is the target of "Black Hand" gangsters.

Commentary: This is another episode revolving around Troop's concern, empathy, and protection of an outsider.

Trivia: W. Hermanos was the alleged author of this episode. The 1960 *Maverick* episode, "Mano Nera," also dealt with an assassin from "The Black Hand." Throughout the 1950s and 1960s, the statuesque Karen Steele appeared in scores of television dramas; she also co-starred with Randolph Scott in *Decision at Sundown* (1957). Gustavo Rojo resembled Donna Reed's television husband, Carl Betz.

Episode 73: "The Parting" May 29, 1960.
Starring John Russell, Peter Brown, and Peggie Castle. Featuring Kenneth Tobey (Tom Bishop), Nancy Valentine (Jennie), Mike Road (Bluel), Doodles Weaver (Jack), Ollie O'Toole (Peddler).

Directed by Robert T. Sparr, Written by David Lang, Produced by Jules Schermer, Director of Photography: Ralph Woolsey, Art Director: Carl Macauley, Supervising Film Editor: James Moore, Film Editor: George E. Luckenbacher, Music Supervision: Paul Sawtell and Bert Shefter, Music Editor: Erma E. Levin, Sound: Samuel F. Goode, Set Decorator: Ben Bone, Production Manager: Oren W. Haglund, Assistant Director: Eddie Prinz.

Synopsis: An escaped convict agrees to surrender to Troop if the marshal will promise the reward money to the outlaw's lady fair.

Commentary: Troop becomes embroiled in another complex romantic relationship and embellishes the truth again to prevent undue sorrow. The marshal actually laughs at the end of this show.

Trivia: Kenneth Tobey starred in the television series, *Whirlybirds* (1957-60), portrayed Bat Masterson in *Gunfight at the O.K. Corral* (1957), and played Jim Bowie in Disney's *Davy Crockett at the Alamo* (1955). Cinematographer Ralph Woolsey photographed twenty-six *Lawman* episodes, worked on numerous other Warner Bros. television productions, and won an Emmy for his work on the 1968 program, *To Catch a Thief*. He lived to the age of 104.

Episode 74: "The Swamper" June 5, 1960.
Starring John Russell and Peter Brown. Featuring Luana Anders (Ellie Phelan), J. Pat O'Malley (Jim Phelan), Emory Parnell (Hank), Ken Becker (Greg Thatcher), Don Wilbanks (Chad Walters), Donald Elson (Mr. Oliver).

Directed by Mark Sandwich, Jr., Teleplay by Edmund Morris, Story by Finlay McDermid, Produced by Jules Schermer, Director of Photography: Harold Stine, Art Director: Howard Campbell, Supervising Film Editor:

James Moore, Film Editor: Clarence Kolster, Sound: B.F. Ryan, Set Decorator: William Wallace, Production Manager: Oren W. Haglund, Assistant Director: Claude E. Archer.

Synopsis: The town drunk is suddenly flush with money.

Commentary: Peggie Castle does not appear in this episode. As in the previous episode, Troop withholds the truth to prevent undue pain and sorrow. The theme of a weak innocent falling to temptation is repeated numerous times in this series. Johnny falls for and loses another pretty young lady. A swamper is an unskilled worker who does odds and ends; in the West, he often cleaned up after the patrons in a saloon. Although listed in the credits, Emory Parnell does not appear in this episode.

Trivia: Character actor J. Pat O'Malley had over 230 acting credits. He played a judge in seven episodes of *Black Saddle* (1959-60) and the butler/cook in Disney's *Spin and Marty* series (1955-57). The music supervisors and the music editor were no longer listed in the credits.

Episode 75: "Man on a Mountain" June 12, 1960.
Starring John Russell and Peter Brown. Featuring Lee Van Cleef (Clyde Wilson), Richard Garland (Ben Jaegers), Roscoe Ates (Jenkins), Dick Rich (Joe Perell), Steve Pendleton (Kelsey), Forrest Taylor (Sheriff Dawson), Dee Carroll (Molly Jaegers), Chris Essay (Durey), Rodney Bell (Drummer).

Directed by Paul Guilfoyle, Written by Clair Huffaker, Produced by Jules Schermer, Director of Photography: Perry Finnerman, Art Director: LeRoy Deane, Supervising Film Editor: James Moore, Film Editor: James W. Graham, Music Supervision: Paul Sawtell and Bert Shefter, Music Editor: Theo W. Sebern, Sound: Theodore B. Hoffman, Set Decorator: Steve Potter, Production Manager: Oren W. Haglund, Assistant Director: William Lasky.

Synopsis: A callous deputy kills innocents in his quest to punish a friend of Marshal Troop.

Commentary: This is another instance in which Troop defeats a posse's vigilante mentality by using both his gun and his ingenuity to save a prisoner. Peggie Castle does not appear in this episode, the second in a row.

Trivia: Forrest Taylor had over 400 acting credits between 1915 and 1963; he appeared with Rex Reason in the television western series, *Man Without a Gun* (1957-59), as Doc Brannon. Steve Pendleton played the posse member who was wounded. Two of Pendleton's more memorable film roles were as the rich young snob who played patty cake, patty cake with Bob Hope and Bing Crosby in *Road to Singapore* (1940), and as the army officer who mistook Maureen O'Hara for the wife of a supply wagon driver in John Ford's *Rio Grande* (1950). Arthur Lubin did some uncredited direction of several scenes in this episode.

Episode 76: "Fast Trip to Cheyenne" June 19, 1960.
Starring John Russell, Peter Brown, and Peggie Castle. Featuring Suzanne Storrs (Amy Saunders), Clancy Cooper (Timmo), William Fawcett (Charlie Greer), Pitt Herbert (Pittsford), King Calder (Frank Saunders), Larry Hudson (Ritt Ketchum), Bill Dolan (Pete Barton).

Directed by Robert Sparr, Teleplay by W. Hermanos, Story by Jules Schermer, Produced by Jules Schermer, Director of Photography: Robert Hoffman, Art Director: Carl Macauley, Supervising Film Editor: James Moore, Film Editor: Milt Kleinberg, Music Supervision: Paul Sawtell and Bert Shefter, Music Editor: Joe Inge, Sound: Samuel F. Goode, Production Manager: Oren W. Haglund, Set Decorator: Ben Bone Assistant Director: Eddie Prinz, Supervising Hair Stylist: Jean Burt Reilly.

Synopsis: Troop must overcome a variety of obstacles to get to Cheyenne and prevent the hanging of an innocent man.

Commentary: The storyline has an excellent surprise hook as to who's responsible for blocking Troop's attempts to stop the hanging.

Trivia: This is another episode with the teleplay allegedly written by W. Hermanos (and the story credited to producer Jules Schermer). Schermer co-wrote the World War II drama, *The Fighting Sullivans* (1944), which received an Academy Award nomination for best story. Jean Burt Reilly, the supervising hair stylist, was listed in the credits for the first of eighty-one times. Reilly was involved in most of the Warner Bros. television productions and in such films as *Sunrise at Campobello* (1960), *Parrish* (1961), and *Gypsy* (1962).

Season Three

Episode 77: "The Town Boys" September 18, 1960.
Starring John Russell, Peter Brown, and Peggie Castle. Featuring Tommy Rettig (Dean Bailer), Richard Evans (Pete Goff), Hank Patterson (Harrison Lester), Dick Rich (Matt Hodges), Terry Rangno (Herbie), Rickey Sorenson (Chuck), Phil Chambers (Sam Jowett).

Directed by Robert Sparr, Teleplay by George Lairden, Story by Jules Schermer, Produced by Jules Schermer, Director of Photography: Edwin DuPar, Art Director: Carl Macauley, Supervising Film Editor: James Moore, Film Editor: James W. Graham, Music Supervision: Paul Sawtell and Bert Shefter, Music Editor: Joe Inge, Sound: Samuel F. Goode, Set Decorator: Jerry Welch, Production Manager: Oren W. Haglund, Assistant Director: Eddie Prinz, Supervising Hair Stylist: Jean Burt Reilly.

Synopsis: Johnny attempts to save four delinquents.

Commentary: To open the third season, Marshal Troop gives Johnny significant latitude to follow his own instincts. Johnny identifies with the boys: "It's like looking into an old mirror, Mr. Troop, and seeing an old reflection. I wasn't much older than they are when you took me in." The episode ends lightly to the sound of oboes honking the *Lawman* theme song and Troop uncharacteristically winking and laughing.

Trivia: James Moore was the supervising film editor for eighty-six *Lawman* episodes and was also involved with all the other Warner Bros. television productions of the late 1950s and early 1960s. This was George

Lairden's only writing credit. Tommy Rettig played Robert Mitchum's son in *River of No Return* (1954) and then co-starred as Jeff Miller on the *Lassie* show from 1954 to 1957. After two years and seventy-six listings in the credits, production manager Oren W. Haglund was no longer listed.

Episode 78: "The Go-Between" September 25, 1960.
Starring John Russell, Peter Brown, and Peggie Castle. Featuring Paul Comi (Cole Reese), Tom Gilson (Charlie Dane), Larry Blake (Jennings), Lane Bradford (Link Barker), Charles Fredericks (Kelly), Gary Conway (Sam Carter).

Directed by Stuart Heisler, Teleplay by Thomas Hyatt, Story by Jules Schermer, Produced by Jules Schermer, Director of Photography: Ralph Woolsey, Art Director: Carl Macauley, Supervising Film Editor: James Moore, Film Editor: John M. Haffen, Music Supervision: Paul Sawtell and Bert Shefter, Music Editor: Erma E. Levin, Sound: John K. Kean, Set Decorator: Hal Overell, Assistant Director: James T. Vaughn, Supervising Hair Stylist: Jean Burt Reilly.

Synopsis: Lily and Johnny are kidnapped and held for ransom.

Commentary: This is another kidnapping scenario when Troop is forced to follow instructions to protect Lily's life. Troop's feelings for Lily are apparent at this episode's conclusion.

Trivia: The acclaimed British film, *The Go-Between* (1971) was an Edwardian romantic drama that starred Margaret Leighton, Julie Christie, and Alan Bates.

Episode 79: "The Mad Bunch" October 2, 1960.
Starring John Russell, Peter Brown, Peggie Castle, and Edward Byrnes (Joe Knox). Featuring Asa Maynor (Dory), Harry Antrim (Doc Shea), Frank Ferguson (Uncle Ben), Jack Hogan (Duke Janks), Nick Dennis (Skitter), James Stapleton (Bob Terry), Frederick Crane (Larrabee).

Directed by Robert Sparr, Teleplay by Ric Hardman, Produced by Jules Schermer, Director of Photography: Bert Glennon, Art Director:

Carl Macauley, Supervising Film Editor: James Moore, Film Editor: Elbert K. Hollingsworth, Music Supervision: Paul Sawtell and Bert Shefter, Music Editor: Charles Paley, Sound: B.F. Ryan, Set Decorator: Ben Bone, Assistant Director: Eddie Prinz, Supervising Hair Stylist: Jean Burt Reilly.

Synopsis: A gang member quits a murderous gang of outlaws and attempts to go straight.

Commentary: For the second episode in a row, Troop and Johnny combat a cruel gang of killers. This is another storyline of an outlaw developing a conscience. It's also another episode involving a character posing as someone else. The repeated introductory scene, with the *Lawman* song sung in the background and Troop and his deputy in the jail in the marshal's office, is shortened with Johnny no longer aiming the rifle twice. Starring credits list Edward Byrnes.

Trivia: Byrnes, who was then playing Gerald Lloyd "Kookie" Kookson on *77 Sunset Strip* (1958-64), later married Asa Maynor, his love-interest in this episode. Byrnes portrayed an outlaw in the first *Lawman* episode. Before photographing thirty-four episodes of *Lawman* and numerous other television series, Bert Glennon had a distinguished motion picture career; among his accomplishments were filming John Ford's *Young Mr. Lincoln* (1939), *Stagecoach* (1939), *Drums Along the Mohawk* (1939), *Wagon Master* (1950), *Rio Grande* (1950), and *Sergeant Rutledge* (1960).

Episode 80: "The Old War Horse" October 9, 1960.
Starring John Russell, Peter Brown, and Peggie Castle. Featuring Lee Patrick (Bess Harper), Arch Johnson (Jason McQuade), Vinton Hayworth (Oren Slauson), Dan Sheridan (Jake), Grady Sutton (Stiles), Jim Hayward (First Man), Charles Alvin Bell (Second Man).

Directed by Robert Sparr, Teleplay by Ric Hardman, Produced by Jules Schermer, Director of Photography: Bert Glennon, Art Director: Carl Macauley, Supervising Film Editor: James Moore, Film Editor: Robert Jahns, Music Supervision: Paul Sawtell and Bert Shefter, Music

Editor: George E. Marsh, Sound: Samuel F. Goode, Set Decorator: Ben Bone, Assistant Director: Eddie Prinz, Supervising Hair Stylist: Jean Burt Reilly.

Synopsis: Troop and Lily attempt to undermine a scam involving Lily's dancehall mentor.

Commentary: Troop, Lily, and Johnny combat another swindling scam while aiding Lily's friend. More of Lily's back story is revealed. Arch Johnson's character has advice for Troop: "If you're smart, marshal, you'll never tie up with any dancehall dancer."

Trivia: This was Dan Sheridan's initial appearances as Jake, Lily's loyal bartender. He remained in the role until the series ended. Arch Johnson's villains made formidable antagonists for the marshal; in his three *Lawman* appearances, he played a master scammer in this episode, a relentless rancher in "The Lords of Darkness" (1961), and a power-hungry gangster in "The Hold-Out" (1962).

Episode 81: "The Return of Owny O'Reilly" October 16, 1960.
Starring John Russell, Peter Brown, and Peggie Castle. Featuring Joel Grey (Owny O'Reilly), Lee Van Cleef (Jack Sanders), William Fawcett (Jenkins), Bill Forster (Ed Wrangel).

Directed by Stuart Heisler, Written by Ric Hardman, Produced by Jules Schermer, Director of Photography: Bert Glennon, Art Director: Carl Macauley, Supervising Film Editor: James Moore, Film Editor: Jim Faris, Music Supervision: Paul Sawtell and Bert Shefter, Music Editor: Sam E. Levin, Sound: Samuel F. Goode, Set Decorator: Ben Bone, Assistant Director: Dick L'Estrange, Supervising Hair Stylist: Jean Burt Reilly.

Synopsis: Marshal Troop appoints a youngster as a special deputy.

Commentary: This is one of the funniest episodes of the entire series ranking with "Gun-Shy," *Maverick*'s 1959 spoof of *Gunsmoke*. Lots of squealing clarinets and honking oboes in the background add to the comical nature of the story. This is not quite a spoof, but when Joel Grey's diminutive character dresses up like a midget Marshal Troop, one can see that John Russell's marshal is having a difficult time keeping a straight face.

Trivia: Between them, Sam and Erma Levin edited music for twenty-five *Lawman* episodes. William Fawcett, who played dozens of crusty old-timers and shopkeepers during his long career, had a Ph.D. in theater from Michigan State University. He made six appearances on *Lawman*.

Episode 82: "Yawkey" October 23, 1960.
Starring John Russell, Peter Brown, Peggie Castle, and Ray Danton (Yawkey). Featuring Dan Sheridan (Jake), David McMahon, (Thompson), John Eimen (Young Boy), Martin Eric, (George Birdwell), Ben Erway (Waterman), George Selk (Editor), Mina Vaughn (Dolores), Sailor Vincent (Jim Foster).

Directed by Stuart Heisler, Written by Richard Matheson, Produced by Jules Schermer, Director of Photography: Bert Glennon, Art Director: Carl Macauley, Supervising Film Editor: James Moore, Film Editor: Robert B. Warwick Jr., Music Supervision: Paul Sawtell and Bert Shefter, Music Editor: John Allyn, Jr., Sound: Joseph T. Wissmann, Set Decorator: Ben Bone, Assistant Director: Eddie Prinz, Supervising Hair Stylist: Jean Burt Reilly.

Synopsis: A notorious gunman with a secret arrives in Laramie and challenges Troop to a gunfight.

Commentary: Ray Danton is given fourth star billing in the opening credits. Danton's character is well drawn: hard, cold, and, ultimately, quite human. Lily's feelings for the marshal are obvious during the gunfight.

Trivia: Although Richard Matheson wrote six episodes for *Lawman*, scripted for various television western series, and authored several western novels, his fame revolves around his science fiction including his classic 1954 novel, *I Am Legend* (1954), which was adapted into films on three separate occasions; *The Last Man on Earth* (1964), *The Omega Man* (1971), and *I Am Legend* (2007). He also wrote the 1975 book (*Bid Time*

Return) and script for the science fiction romantic movie *Somewhere in Time* (1980) and sixteen memorable *Twilight Zone* screenplays between 1959 and 1964. Uncredited Milton Parsons was a serious-looking actor who usually played creepy undertakers and frightened citizens. His most memorial role was as the political hack reading the Election Day results in William Powell's *The Senator was Indiscrete* (1947).

Episode 83: "Dilemma" October 30, 1960.
Starring John Russell, Peter Brown, and Peggie Castle. Featuring Tom Drake (Dr. Sam Burbage), John Beradino (Walt Carmody), James Anderson (Harry Carmody), Harry Antrim (Doc Shea), Percy Helton (Ellery Pervy), John McCann (Fen Carmody).

Directed by Robert B. Sinclair, Written by William F. Leicester, Produced by Jules Schermer, Director of Photography: Bert Glennon, Art Director: Carl Macauley, Supervising Film Editor: James Moore, Film Editor: Holbrook N. Todd, Music Supervision: Paul Sawtell and Bert Shefter, Music Editor: Donald K. Harris, Sound: B.F. Ryan, Set Decorator: Ben Bone, Assistant Director: Victor Vallejo, Supervising Hair Stylist: Jean Burt Reilly.

Synopsis: Lily's handyman is much more than he appears to be.

Commentary: Another storyline about a man running from his past who is forced to confront his fears.

Trivia: James Anderson played outlaws in more than 100 television westerns and feature films including *Little Big Man* (1970) and *The Ballad of Cable Hogue* (1970). His most memorable role was evil Bob Ewell in *To Kill a Mockingbird* (1962).

Episode 84: "The Post" November 6, 1960.
Starring John Russell, Peter Brown, and Peggie Castle. Featuring Don Megowan (Rafe), Bernie Fein (Sheriff Sabin), Saundra Edwards (Leora),

Directed by Marc Lawrence, Written by Ric Hardman, Produced by Jules Schermer, Director of Photography: Bert Glennon, Art Director:

Carl Macauley, Film Editor, Music Supervision: Paul Sawtell and Bert Shefter, Music Editor: Joe Inge, Sound: B.F. Ryan, Set Decorator: Ben Bone, Assistant Director: Eddie Prinz, Supervising Hair Stylist: Jean Burt Reilly.

Synopsis: Troop returns a fugitive to New Mexico where trouble awaits the marshal.

Commentary: One of the few storylines that takes place mainly outside of Laramie. Another episode involving a corrupt lawman and the rehabilitation of a wanted man. This episode features Troop uncharacteristically unkempt. Bernie Fein's portrayal of the episode's villain is the worst overacting in the series.

Trivia: Six-foot-six Don Megowan appeared in most of the Warner Bros. westerns and dramas; he also co-starred as Captain Huckabee in the 1962 series, *The Beachcomber*, with Cameron Mitchell. Bernie Fein played Private Gomez in 138 episodes of *The Phil Silvers Show* (1955-59) and later co-created and co-produced *Hogan's Heroes* (1965-71).

Episode 85: "Chantay" November 13, 1960.
Starring John Russell, Peter Brown, and Peggie Castle. Featuring Sharon Hugueny, Dean Fredericks (Great Bear), Milton Parsons (Grimshaw), Dan Sheridan (Jake Summers), Jan Arvan (Captain Weil), Edith Leslie (Mrs. Grimshaw), Barbara Luddy (Mrs. Gaddis), Stella Garcia (Indian Girl).

Directed by Robert B. Sinclair, Written by Ric Hardman, Produced by Jules Schermer, Director of Photography: Bert Glennon, Art Director: Carl Macauley, Film Editor: Jim Faris, Music Supervision: Paul Sawtell and Bert Shefter, Music Editor: Norman Bennett, Sound: Ross Owen, Set Decorator: Ben Bone, Assistant Director: Eddie Prinz, Supervising Hair Stylist: Jean Burt Reilly.

Synopsis: A pretty Indian girl who is infatuated with Johnny is accused of murder.

Commentary: Another example of Troop and Johnny's respect and compassion for Native Americans. In a reversal of roles, Johnny is the one being chased.

Trivia: Lovely Sharon Hugueny signed a seven year contract with Warner Bros. at the age of sixteen. She was under the personal supervision of Jack L. Warner and there were high hopes for her career after her appearances in most of Warner Bros. television series and the movie *Parrish* (1961). However, a marriage to producer Robert Evans didn't work out and soon her acting career was over.

Episode 86: "Samson the Great" November 20, 1960.
Starring John Russell, Peter Brown, and Peggie Castle. Featuring Walter Burke (Jimmy Fresco), Mickey Simpson (Samson the Great), Dan Sheridan (Jake), Charles Horvath (Pat Cassidy), Mina Vaughn (Dolores).

Directed by Stuart Heisler, Written by Richard Matheson, Produced by Jules Schermer, Director of Photography: Bert Glennon, Art Director: Carl Macauley, Film Editor: Noel L. Scott, Music Supervision: Paul Sawtell and Bert Shefter, Music Editor: Erma E. Levin, Sound: Ross Owen, Set Decorator: Ben Bone, Assistant Director: Eddie Prinz, Supervising Hair Stylist: Jean Burt Reilly.

Synopsis: Troop is forced into the ring to fight a gigantic and belligerent professional boxer.

Commentary: Mickey Simpson makes an excellent antagonist for Troop. The episode is filled with excellent dialogue. For example, when Samson wakes up after the fistfight, he asks. "What hit me?" His manager replies, "Justice, my boy. Justice." The final scene with the mashed-up Troop, Lily, and Johnny discussing how it's been "a slow month" is quite funny.

Trivia: Paul Sawtell and Bert Shefter were classically trained musicians and composers. Together they supervised the music for most of the Warner Bros. television productions during the late 1950s and early 1960s including sixty-four *Lawman* episodes. One of their most well-known collaborations was the music to the 1961 movie, *Voyage to the Bottom of the Sea*.

Episode 87: "The Second Son" November 27, 1960.
Starring John Russell, Peter Brown, and Peggie Castle. Featuring Harry Shannon (Carl May), Kimm Charney (Charlie May), Warren Oates (Al May), Harry Cheshire (Judge Trager), Fred Crane (Lawyer).

Directed by Robert B. Sinclair, Written by Ric Hardman, Produced by Jules Schermer, Director of Photography: Bert Glennon, Art Director: Carl Macauley, Film Editor: William W. Moore, Music Supervision: Paul Sawtell and Bert Shefter, Music Editor: Robert Phillips, Sound: Ross Owen, Set Decorator: Ben Bone, Assistant Director: Dick Landry, Supervising Hair Stylist: Jean Burt Reilly.

Synopsis: A youngster confesses to a murder but Lily is skeptical.

Commentary: Troop intervenes in another father-son relationship and again manipulates the facts to force the truth to come out.

Trivia: Warren Oates had a successful career playing weak, unreliable, violent outlaws. He acted in most of the television westerns beginning in *The Adventures of Rin Tin Tin* in 1958, was a regular in the television rodeo series *Stoney Burke* from 1962 to 1963, and was a member of Sam Peckinpah's stock company with roles in *Ride the High Country* (1962), *Major Dundee* (1965), and *The Wild Bunch* (1969). Kim (or Kimm) Charney was a popular child actor during the 1950s and early 1960s. He appeared in numerous western series including this episode and "The Hunch" (1960). He played the younger doomed brother of Debbie Reynolds and Carroll Baker in *How the West Was Won* (1962). After his acting career ended, he became a surgeon.

Episode 88: "The Catcher" December 4, 1960.
Starring John Russell, Peter Brown, and Peggie Castle. Featuring James Coburn (Lank Bailey), Robert Armstrong (Frank Fenway), Med Flory

(Catcher), Claudia Barrett (Missie Fenway), Don Wilbanks (Till Foley), Steve Mitchell (Ory Task).

Directed by Marc Lawrence, Written by William Leicester, Produced by Jules Schermer, Director of Photography: Bert Glennon, Art Director: Carl Macauley, Film Editor: Noel L. Scott, Music Supervision: Paul Sawtell and Bert Shefter, Music Editor: Sam E. Levin, Sound: Samuel F. Goode, Set Decorator: Fay C. Babcock, Assistant Director: Eddie Prinz, Supervising Hair Stylist: Jean Burt Reilly.

Synopsis: A gentle sheep drover named Catcher is accused of murder.

Commentary: This is one of several storylines that involves an intoxicated man who may or may not have committed murder. It's also an episode that features mob rage. Catcher's real name is Molly.

Trivia: In addition to acting in numerous motion pictures and television series (including three notable roles in *Lawman* episodes), tall, lanky Flory, a young Henry Fonda look-alike, was also an accomplished musician. He played saxophone with Woody Herman's band in the early 1950s then organized his own. He appeared as himself in twenty-three *The Ray Anthony Shows* in 1956 and 1957 and his "SuperSax," an ensemble devoted to Charlie Parker's music, won a Grammy for its debut album in 1974.

Episode 89: "Cornered" December 11, 1960.
Starring John Russell, Peter Brown, and Peggie Castle. Featuring Frank de Kova (Jed Barker), Tom Troupe (Jim Barker), Dan Sheridan (Jake), Harrison Lewis (Blake), Guy Wilkerson (Phillips), Frank Krieg (Waters).

Directed by Marc Lawrence, Written by Richard Matheson, Produced by Jules Schermer, Director of Photography: Bert Glennon, Art Director: Carl Macauley, Film Editor: Cliff Bell, Music Supervision: Paul Sawtell and Bert Shefter, Music Editor: George E. Marsh, Sound: Ross Owen, Set Decorator: William L. Kreig, Assistant Director: Eddie Prinz, Supervising Hair Stylist: Jean Burt Reilly.

Synopsis: After Johnny luckily kills a gunman renowned for his quick draw, he waits for the man's son to seek vengeance.

Commentary: This episode begins lightheartedly and then soon builds toward the confrontations between Johnny and the notorious outlaw and, eventually, with the outlaw's son. The screenplay provides Johnny with the ultimate test as he must go into a gunfight against someone faster than himself. Troop has some important words for Johnny: "There's one thing you gotta avoid on this job. Worrying before it's time to worry. It's nerve that counts, not speed." The trio of blood-thirsty barflies enamored with gunplay are three of many seen throughout the series. The wide-angled shots expand the sense of time and place. The look of pride on Troop's face at the end of the show is telling.

Trivia: Tom Troupe, who closely resembled actor Paul Richards, was Corporal Job in Clint Eastwood's *Kelly's Heroes* (1970). Although Frank de Kova played scores of menacing outlaws and hoodlums in his long career, his most famous role, as Chief Wild Eagle in sixty-three episodes of *F Troop* from 1965 to 1967, was comic.

Episode 90: "The Escape of Joe Kilmer" December 18, 1960.
Starring John Russell, Peter Brown, and Peggie Castle. Featuring Lenore Roberts (Donna Kilmer), Wynn Pearce (Joe Kilmer), Ken Lynch (Al Kilmer), Joseph Ruskin (Reed Benton).

Directed by Robert Sparr, Teleplay by James Pitts, Story by Jules Schermer, Produced by Jules Schermer, Director of Photography: Ray Fernstrom, Art Director: Carl Macauley, Supervising Film Editor: James Moore, Film Editor: Elbert K. Hollingsworth, Music Supervision: Paul Sawtell and Bert Shefter, Music Editor: Theo W. Sebern, Sound: Theodore B. Hoffman, Set Decorator: Ralph S. Hurst, Assistant Director: Richard Mayberry, Supervising Hair Stylist: Jean Burt Reilly.

Synopsis: The wife of an outlaw turns him in to Troop and demands the reward money.

Commentary: Another scenario involving outlaws intimidating an innocent and a brother vs. brother conflict. Once again, Lily's intervention helps someone see the light.

Trivia: Ken Lynch played tough guys on both sides of the law in over 190 television and movie productions. He starred in an early television series, *The Plainclothesman* (1950-53), and had a recurring role as the policeman, Grover, on *McCloud* between 1972 and 1975.

Episode 91: "Old Stefano" December 25, 1960.
Starring John Russell, Peter Brown, and Peggie Castle. Featuring Vladimir Sokoloff (Old Stefano), Gregg Palmer (Tracy McNeil), John Qualen (Doc Shannon), Frank Mitchell (Hank Buel), Jim Galante (Boy).

Directed by Robert B. Sinclair, Written by Ric Hardman, Produced by Jules Schermer, Director of Photography: Bert Glennon, Art Director: Carl Macauley, Supervising Film Editor: James Moore, Film Editor: Robert B. Warwick Jr., Music Supervision: Paul Sawtell and Bert Shefter, Music Editor: Jack B. Wadsworth, Sound: Gilbert Plenty, Set Decorator: Ben Bone, Assistant Director: Eddie Prinz, Supervising Hair Stylist: Jean Burt Reilly.

Synopsis: A suave rancher with ambitions to take over Laramie woos Lily.

Commentary: Troop's antagonist here is a bit different than most, outwardly charming and debonair, but still filled with hate for the marshal. As usual, Troop wears the whitest of hats. The argument between the marshal and Lily after the accident in the street demonstrates her frustration with his "denseness." The rich rancher has some choice words for Troop: "Your craw's so full of envy you can't even swallow. You know, when the chips are down, Lily's not about to move in with a sixty dollar-a-month marshal." Vladimir Sokoloff brings immense pathos to his old loner character whenever he's on the screen. The difference between explaining and telling is discussed several times. From the initial "Tally

Ho!" to the lines "Ring when you want me" and "I just might do that," the episode displays a range of emotions and feelings.

Trivia: Russian-born Vladimir Sokoloff played scores of characters of diverse nationalities; his most memorable role was the wise Mexican elder in *The Magnificent Seven* (1960).

Episode 92: "The Robbery" January 1, 1961.
Starring John Russell, Peter Brown, and Peggie Castle. Featuring) Hal Torey (Sam Deever), Warren Kemmerling (Tay Roach), Peter Miller (Lutie Roach), Robert Ridgely (Lt. Davidson), Lee Turnbull (Sgt. Dooley).

Directed by Robert Altman, Written by Dean Riesner, Produced by Jules Schermer, Director of Photography: Bert Glennon, Art Director: Carl Macauley, Supervising Film Editor: James Moore, Film Editor: Harry Reynolds, Music Supervision: Paul Sawtell and Bert Shefter, Music Editor: Louis W. Gordon, Sound: B.F. Ryan, Set Decorator: Ben Bone, Assistant Director: Eddie Prinz, Supervising Hair Stylist: Jean Burt Reilly.

Synopsis: A trio of outlaws intends to rob a huge army payroll.

Commentary: This is the one of several episodes involving Troop coming into conflict with a pompous and egotistical character, "a little man with big ideas." It's also another storyline involving the marshal with a former mentor, "an old style lawman." Although director Robert Altman's distinctive style of overlapping dialogue and satirical comedy are not present in "The Robbery," his anti-authoritarianism is displayed with the way the army officer is pictured. Also, Altman's ability to personalize relationships is illustrated in the bond between Troop and his old friend.

Trivia: Before becoming a prominent motion picture director of such films as *MASH* (1970), *McCabe and Mrs. Miller* (1971), *Nashville* (1975), and *The Player* (1992), Altman spent most of the 1950s and 1960s directing a diverse number of television productions including *The Gale Storm Show* (1956-60), *Alfred Hitchcock Presents* (1955-65), *The Roaring*

Twenties (1960-61) and numerous western series including this one *Lawman* episode.

Episode 93: "Firehouse Lil" January 8, 1961.
Starring John Russell, Peter Brown, and Peggie Castle. Featuring Vinton Hayworth (Oren Slauson), Dan Sheridan (Jake), Sheldon Allman (Ed Dirckes), Louis Vestuto (Beefheart Simpson), I. Stanford Jolley (Wampus Jack), Jan Stine (Little Britches), Ray Reese (Fire Runner).

Directed by Leslie H. Martinson, Written by Ric Hardman, Produced by Jules Schermer, Director of Photography: Bert Glennon, Art Director: Carl Macauley, Film Editor: Robert Watts, Music Supervision: Paul Sawtell and Bert Shefter, Music Editor: Charles Paley, Sound: Robert B. Lee, Set Decorator: William L. Kuehl, Assistant Director: John F. Murphy, Supervising Hair Stylist: Jean Burt Reilly.

Synopsis: Bandits plan to take advantage of Laramie's fascination with their fire department by starting a fire to serve as a diversion while they rob the bank.

Commentary: There is a good balance between humor and drama in this episode. The script offers a unique solution to preventing the bad guys from getting away. This may be Lily's most memorable hat.

Trivia: Vinton Hayworth was the slightly dim-witted Laramie townsman Slauson in ten *Lawman* episodes. He played the magistrate Galindo in thirteen episodes of the television series *Zorro* in 1958. His sister was actress Rita Hayworth's mother. Actor Louis Vestuto resembled Hershel Bernardi from the private eye series, *Peter Gunn* (1958-61).

Episode 94: "The Frame-Up" January 15, 1961.
Starring John Russell, Peter Brown, and Peggie Castle. Featuring Randy Stuart (Jessica Kindle), Dabbs Greer (Les Courtney), Ric Roman (Chares Belmont), William Mims (Rich Mathews), Dan Sheridan (Jake), Harry Cheshire (Judge Trager), Grady Sutton (Ben Toomey), Bo Lee (Gambler).

Directed by Marc Lawrence, Written by John Tomerlin, Produced by Jules Schermer, Director of Photography: Bert Glennon, Art Director: Carl Macauley, Film Editor: Lloyd Nosler, Music Supervision: Paul Sawtell and Bert Shefter, Music Editor: John Allyn, Jr., Sound: Samuel F. Goode, Set Decorator: Gene Redd, Assistant Director: Rex Bailey, Supervising Hair Stylist: Jean Burt Reilly.

Synopsis: The wife of a man hanged for murder announces that she was the killer.

Commentary: This episode examines the complexities of peacekeeping and doing the right thing. The story also illustrates the way a corrupt and manipulative voice can sway a community. After some of Laramie's citizens begin to question Troop's competence, he tells Johnny, "As long a man wears one of these," as he stares at the marshal's badge in his hand, "folks expect him to be right." Johnny replies, "Can't be right all the time," and Troop responds, "I know, but they expect it; they've got a right to it." Dabbs Greer is excellent as the corrupt, well-spoken lawyer.

Trivia: Most of Dabbs Greer's characters were not as despicable as Les Courtney. He played Mr. Jonas in forty-three episodes of *Gunsmoke* between 1956 and 1974, Reverend Alden on *Little House on the Prairie* between 1974 and 1983, and the clergymen who married both Laura and Rob Petrie on *The Dick Van Dyke Show* in 1962 and Carol and Mike Brady on *The Brady Bunch* in 1969. Randy Stuart was Anne Baxter's conniving roommate in *All About Eve* (1950), the female lead with George Montgomery in the film *Man from God's Country* (1958), and Nellie Cashman in eighteen episodes of *The Life and Legend of Wyatt Earp* in 1959-60.

Episode 95: "The Marked Man" January 22, 1961.
Starring John Russell, Peter Brown, Peggie Castle, and Andrew Duggan (Tod Larson). Featuring Miranda Jones (Muriel Hanley), Dan Sheridan (Jake), Jedd DeBenning (Ross Darby), Douglas Odney (Arnie Steele).

Directed by Marc Lawrence, Teleplay by Paul Savage and Bronson Howitzer, Story by Victoria and Peter Schermer, Produced by Jules Schermer, Director of Photography: Bert Glennon, Art Director: Carl Macauley, Film Editor: Jim Faris, Music Supervision: Paul Sawtell and Bert Shefter, Music Editor: Louis W. Gordon, Sound: Samuel F. Goode, Set Decorator: Gene Redd, Assistant Director: Eddie Prinz, Supervising Hair Stylist: Jean Burt Reilly.

Synopsis: A killer is hired to murder Troop.

Commentary: This is another storyline in which an old crony of Troop's has turned to crime and must make a difficult decision. It's also an example of the degree to which a corrupt individual will go in order to defeat law and order in Laramie. The marshal and his deputy continue to bond and think alike: Troop: "Pay good money for watered whiskey and throw away what's left on crooked games." Johnny: "And then they get angry at us for trying to protect them. I guess what that's called is human nature." Lily has a great closing line. Andrew Duggan is listed in the opening starring credits.

Trivia: Between 1949 and 1987, Duggan made over 180 appearances in films and television shows. He was featured in two *Lawman* episodes, played General Britt in seventeen *Twelve O' Clock High* television shows (1965-67), and starred in the western series *Lancer* (1968-70).

Episode 96: "The Squatters" January 29, 1961.
Starring John Russell, Peter Brown, and Peggie Castle. Featuring DeForest Kelley (Bent Carr), Nina Shipman (Molly Prentice), Tom Gilson (Stape), King Calder (Ad Prentice), Hal K, Dawson (Fane), Stephen Ellsworth (Doctor), Robert C. Ross (Albie).

Directed by Marc Lawrence, Written by William Leicester, Produced by Jules Schermer, Director of Photography: Bert Glennon, Art Director: Carl Macauley, Film Editor: Cliff Bell, Music Supervision: Paul Sawtell and Bert Shefter, Music Editor: Robert Phillips, Sound: Stanley Jones,

Set Decorator: Gene Redd, Assistant Director: Eddie Prinz, Supervising Hair Stylist: Jean Burt Reilly.

Synopsis: A foreman will do anything to take over a 30,000 acre ranch.

Commentary: Troop finds himself forced to follow the law – "Rotten as it is" – and not do what he knows is just. Once again, Troop sets up a murderer by embellishing the truth. Kelley does an excellent job playing a deceitful scoundrel. The episode ends with an upbeat surprise.

Trivia: Jerry Livingston wrote the music and Mack David wrote the lyrics to *Lawman's* theme song. The two collaborated on many motion pictures and television productions; they were nominated for Academy Awards for three movie songs: *Cinderella's* "Bibbidi-Bobbidi-Boo" (1950), "The Hanging Tree" (1959) and "The Ballad of Cat Ballou" (1965). Separately, Livingston co-wrote the novelty song, "Mairzy Doates" (1944) and the Johnny Mathis hit "The Twelfth of Never" (1956)," while David co-wrote the Shirelles' "Baby It's You" (1961) and Vicki Carr's "It Must Be Him" (1967).

Episode 97: "Homecoming" February 5, 1961.
Starring John Russell, Peter Brown, and Peggie Castle. Featuring Marc Lawrence (Frank Walker), Ray Stricklyn (Eddy Walker), Adrienne Marden (Mary Walker), Freeman Lusk (Warden), James Parnell (Guard).

Directed by Robert B. Sinclair, Written by Richard Matheson, Produced by Jules Schermer, Director of Photography: Bert Glennon, Art Director: Carl Macauley, Film Editor: Victor C. Lewis, Jr., Music Supervision: Paul Sawtell and Bert Shefter, Music Editor: Theo W. Sebern, Sound: B.F. Ryan, Set Decorator: Ben Bone, Assistant Director: Eddie Prinz, Supervising Hair Stylist: Jean Burt Reilly.

Synopsis: An outlaw who has sworn revenge against Troop escapes from prison.

Commentary: The storyline is similar to another *Lawman* episode, "Cornered," but this time it's the marshal, not Johnny, who is awaiting a revengeful gunman. This is one of the rare times when Troop appears vulnerable. As he has done before, at the end of the show Troop compassionately bends the truth to do the right thing.

Trivia: Marc Lawrence had more than 200 acting credits, usually as vicious and crafty criminals. He also directed several Warner Bros. series including sixteen *Lawman* episodes. Adrienne Marden was married to actor Whit Bissell who appeared in four *Lawman* shows.

Episode 98: "Hassayampa" February 12, 1961.
Starring John Russell, Peter Brown, and Peggie Castle. Featuring John Anderson (Hassayampa Edwards), George Wallace (Clyde Morton), Donald Barry (Dusty McCade), Dan Sheridan (Jake), Harry Cheshire (Judge), Gail Bonney (Woman), Charles Horvath (Bouncer #1), Chuck Hicks (Bouncer #2).

Directed by Marc Lawrence, Ric Hardman, Produced by Jules Schermer, Director of Photography: Bert Glennon, Art Director: Carl Macauley, Film Editor: Jim Faris, Music Supervision: Paul Sawtell and Bert Shefter, Music Editor: Sam E. Levin, Sound: Eugene Irvine, Set Decorator: Morris Hoffman, Assistant Director: Eddie Prinz, Supervising Hair Stylist: Jean Burt Reilly.

Synopsis: A crusading anti-saloon zealot arrives in Laramie.

Commentary: John Anderson, as the reformer Hassayampa, resembles a combination of John Brown and Abraham Lincoln. He makes a great entrance, and milks every scene he's in: "I stand for the sanctity of the home. Down with saloons and rot-gut booze!" This is one of the most comical episodes, with the sound of many background oboes and lines like Lily's "What is he – a Pasha from Bagdad?" Lily dons different attire with her woolen pillbox hat and matching mini shawl and muff. Anderson's over-acted Hassayampa is such an obvious fake that Troop, Johnny, Jake, and Lily are laughing when he makes his hasty departure, especially when Lily discovers that the teetotaler's tea cup is filled with whiskey.

Trivia: Except for his comedic role in this episode and in *The Hallelujah Trail* (1965), John Anderson usually played austere men of authority. He was Virgil Earp six times in *The Life and Legend of Wyatt Earp* (1960-61), Lincoln three times, and also portrayed Andrew Jackson, Franklin Roosevelt, and baseball commissioner Kennesaw Mountain Landis.

Episode 99: "The Promoter" February 19, 1961.
Starring John Russell, Peter Brown, and Peggie Castle. Featuring John Van Dreelen (Malcolm Tyler DeVries), Frank Gerstle (David Ferris), Don Beddoe (Simon Rodgers), J. Edward McKinley (Clifford North), Dan Sheridan (Jake), Grady Sutton (Ben Toomey), Lee Sands (Adolph Hagan), Ann Loos (Mrs. Ferris), Doug Carlson (Hank).

Directed by Leslie H. Martinson, Written by Howard Browne, Produced by Jules Schermer, Director of Photography: Bert Glennon, Art Director: Carl Macauley, Film Editor: Robert Jahns, Music Supervision: Paul Sawtell and Bert Shefter, Music Editor: Norman Bennett, Sound: B.F. Ryan, Set Decorator: Gene Redd, Assistant Director: Sam Schneider, Supervising Hair Stylist: Jean Burt Reilly.

Synopsis: An Englishman attempts to buy up all of Laramie's saloons.

Commentary: Troop is confronted by a duo of dangerous antagonists: a smooth talker and a silent killer. Shadows and darkness aid in building tension at the conclusion of the show. Troop's quip, "He bought his last saloon," is *Maverickesque*.

Trivia: Carl Macauley was the art director for 107 *Lawman* episodes and also worked on most of the other Warner Bros. series. He began his career with the 1950 television show, *Space Patrol*, and ended with the original Jack Lord *Hawaii Five-O* (1968-80). Dutch-born actor John Van Dreelen escaped from a World War II concentration camp by disguising himself as a Nazi officer. Later, he played high-ranking wartime Germans in such films as Van Johnson's *The Enemy General* (1960) and Frank Sinatra's *Von Ryan's Express* (1965).

Episode 100: "Detweiler's Kid" February 26, 1961.
Starring John Russell, Peter Brown, and Peggie Castle. Featuring Joyce Meadows (Elfreida Detweiler), Otto Waldis (Old Man Detweiler), Chad York (Jim Austin), Dan Sheridan (Jake), Harry Cheshire (Judge Trager), Harrison Lewis (Blake).

Directed by Marc Lawrence, Written by Ric Hardman, Produced by Jules Schermer, Director of Photography: Bert Glennon, Art Director: Carl Macauley, Film Editor: Lloyd Nosler, Music Supervision: Paul Sawtell and Bert Shefter, Music Editor: Erma E. Levin, Sound: Charles Althouse, Set Decorator: Gene Redd, Assistant Director: Eddie Prinz, Supervising Hair Stylist: Jean Burt Reilly.

Synopsis: A father's anger at everything and everyone incites his daughter to threaten Johnny.

Commentary: This is another episode involving a young adult dealing with an overbearing father. Chad (Everett) York's character is quite affable as the young cowboy. It's also another ugly-duckling-grows-into-a-beautiful-swan scenario – thanks to Lily. Otto Waldis plays a memorable Paul Muni-type.

Trivia: Lovely, feisty Joyce Meadows was in this *Lawman* episode and in "The Cold One (1961). She also made numerous Warner Bros. series appearances, and co-starred in the cult science fiction movie, *The Brain from Planet Arous* (1957) and the western television show, *Two Faces West* (1960-61). Chad Everett starred in *Medical Center* (1969-76) and, in the western world, co-starred as Deputy Del Stark in the television series in *The Dakotas* (1962-63), the movie *Return of the Gunfighter* (1967), and the mini-series, *Centennial* (1978-79).

Episode 101: "The Inheritance" March 5, 1961.
Starring John Russell, Peter Brown, and Peggie Castle. Featuring Will Wright (Tecumsah Pruitt), Rex Holman (Owlie Pruitt), Lurene Tuttle (Mrs. Pruitt), Fuzzy Knight (Mr. Morris), Guy Wilkinson (Slim), Harrison Lewis (Luke Blake).

Directed by Marc Lawrence, Written by John Tomerlin, Produced by Jules Schermer, Director of Photography: Bert Glennon, Art Director: Carl Macauley, Film Editor: Robert Crawford, Music Supervision: Paul Sawtell and Bert Shefter, Music Editor: Joe Inge, Sound: Samuel F. Goode, Set Decorator: Tom Oliphant, Assistant Director: Eddie Prinz, Supervising Hair Stylist: Jean Burt Reilly.

Synopsis: A son is convinced his father has hidden a huge fortune.

Commentary: Troop and Johnny again become involved in a father-son dispute. The black boots motif arises throughout the episode. Deceiving appearances and a lack of honesty bring about conflict, but Troop, Johnny, and Lily show compassion and restraint in resolving the trouble. The marshal's job is summed up in three words: "Rounding up strays." Great lighting enhances Lily's beauty and character.

Trivia: Except for Rex Holman's appearances in the *Lawman* episode, "The Ring," in the 1960 *Gunsmoke* episode, "No Chip" and the 1968 *Star Trek* episode, "Spectre of the Gun" (as Virgil Earp), he usually portrayed despicable outlaws and criminals. Fuzzy Knight played scores of comic cowboy sidekicks to the likes of Roy Rogers, Tex Ritter, Gene Autry, and Johnny Mack Brown, and also appeared as Private Fuzzy Knight in Buster Crabbe's television adventure series, *Captain Gallant of the Foreign Legion* (1955-57).

Episode 102: "Blue Boss and Willie Shay" March 12, 1961.
Starring John Russell, Peter Brown, Peggie Castle, and Sammy Davis, Jr. (Willie Shay). Featuring Richard Jaeckel (Al Janaker), James Waters (James Waters).

Directed by Stuart Heisler, Written by Ric Hardman, Produced by Jules Schermer, Director of Photography: Bert Glennon, Art Director: Carl Macauley, Film Editor: Robert B. Warwick Jr., Music Supervision: Paul Sawtell and Bert Shefter, Music Editor: Donald K. Harris, Sound: Stanley Jones, Set Decorator: George James Hopkins, Assistant Director: Eddie Prinz, Supervising Hair Stylist: Jean Burt Reilly.

Synopsis: A trail boss dislikes one of his cowboys and the cowboy's pet lead steer.

Commentary: A lonely man's love for an animal is highlighted here as well as in "The Wolfer" (1960) and "Old Stefano" (1960). Troop, Lily, and Johnny again treat an outsider as an equal. Richard Jaeckel does a good job depicting an odious character. The opening credits list Sammy Davis, Jr. as a guest star.

Trivia: Davis' western credits included television's *Frontier Circus* (1962), *The Rifleman* (1962), and *The Wild Wild West* (1966); he also co-starred in the Rat Pack's remake of 1939's *Gunga Din*, *Sergeants 3* (1962). Richard Jaeckel began his career in the 1943 WWII film, *Guadalcanal Diary*, and ended it forty years later with *Baywatch*. In between, he made dozens of appearances in western films including *The Gunfighter* (1950), *Flaming Star* (1960), *Ulzana's Raid* (1972), *Chisum* (1970), and *Pat Garrett and Billy the Kid* (1973).

Episode 103: "The Man from New York" March 19, 1961.
Starring John Russell, Peter Brown, Peggie Castle, and Mike Road (Police Lt. Foster). Featuring Richard Arlen (Fred Stiles), Sheila Bromley (Winnie Stiles), John Cliff (Dawson), James Waters (Pres Baker), Douglas Carlson (Waddie).

Directed by Jim Faris, Written by Rik Vollaerts, Produced by Jules Schermer, Director of Photography: Bert Glennon, Art Director: Carl Macauley, Film Editor: Byron Chudnow, Music Supervision: Paul Sawtell and Bert Shefter, Music Editor: Theo W. Sebern, Sound: Francis E. Stahl, Set Decorator: Tom Oliphant, Assistant Director: Eddie Prinz, Supervising Hair Stylist: Jean Burt Reilly.

Synopsis: An arrogant, know-it-all New York City police detective arrives in Laramie.

Commentary: This is another screenplay dealing with Troop helping an uncompromising man become less rigid. It also includes Troop stating one of the codes of the West: "The only thing we're interested in is what a man is now." Johnny's hair is lighter. Road's moustache gives him a much different, less suave look than he had in his three other *Lawman* episodes. His character's eastern perspective of Laramie is revealing: "Animals walking the streets." The pursued helping the pursuer scenario is done well, as is the episode's believable resolution. Opening starring credits include Mike Road.

Trivia: Jim Faris, the director of this episode, was primarily a television film editor; he edited over 100 television episodes including seven *Lawman* shows, many of the Warner Bros. series, and thirty-four episodes of *The Adventures of Ozzie and Harriet* between 1955 and 1960. This was his only directing credit. John Cliff played more than 100 outlaws and thugs from an appearance in Randolph Scott's western, *Fighting Man of the Plains* in 1949 to the television eastern western, *Kung Fu* in 1973. Perhaps his most memorable role was masquerading as the Lone Ranger in *The Lone Ranger* episode, "Counterfeit Mask" (1956).

Episode 104: "Mark of Cain" March 26, 1961.
Starring John Russell, Peter Brown, and Peggie Castle. Featuring Coleen Gray (Rena Kennedy), John Kellogg (Chad Kennedy), Theodore Newton (Aaron Kennedy), Dan Sheridan (Jake), James Waters (Bates), Fred Sherman (Streeter), Bruce MacFarland (Cooper).

Directed by Marc Lawrence, Written by Paul Savage, Produced by Jules Schermer, Director of Photography: Bert Glennon, Art Director: Carl Macauley, Film Editor: Harry Reynolds, Music Supervision: Paul Sawtell and Bert Shefter, Music Editor: George E. Marsh, Sound: Eugene Irvine, Set Decorator: Morris Hoffman, Assistant Director: Richard Landry, Supervising Hair Stylist: Jean Burt Reilly.

Synopsis: The widow of a man shot to death is convinced her brother-in-law is the killer.

Commentary: This episode depicts another family feud that Troop, Lily, and Johnny attempt to resolve. Troop again does his job protecting a man he doesn't like and facing down an angry mob. The wind and cold are used as symbols for turmoil, isolation, and despair. Gray overacts.

Trivia: Coleen Gray was the girl John Wayne left behind in *Red River* (1948). Her other westerns included *Fury at Furnace Creek* (1948) with Victor Mature, *The Vanquished* (1953) with John Payne, and *Arrow in the Dust* (1954) with Sterling Hayden. John Kellogg played henchmen and villains for fifty years; one of his most memorable movie hoodlums was the midway cheater in *The Greatest Show on Earth* (1952).

Episode 105: "Fugitive" April 2, 1961.
Starring John Russell, Peter Brown, and Peggie Castle. Featuring Catherine McLeod (Cormack), Keith Richards (Casey Cormack), Dorothy Konrad (Mrs. Fields), Baynes Barron (Carver), Michael Davis (Joey), Dan Sheridan (Jake).

Directed by Marc Lawrence, Teleplay by John Downing and Bronson Howitzer, Story by John Downing, Produced by Jules Schermer, Director of Photography: Bert Glennon, Art Director: Carl Macauley, Film Editor: Jim Faris, Music Supervision: Paul Sawtell and Bert Shefter, Music Editor: Charles Paley, Sound: B.F. Ryan, Set Decorator: Gene Redd, Assistant Director: Eddie Prinz, Supervising Hair Stylist: Jean Burt Reilly.

Synopsis: A man involved in a stagecoach robbery escalating into a killing is on the run.

Commentary: This episode revolves around the decision to abandon a child and a criminal's move toward redemption. The marshal giving someone "a decent break" occurs again as Troop, Lily, and Johnny help direct a man who made bad decisions to take responsibility for his actions. In this and three other *Lawman* episodes, "Battle Scar," (1959), "The Payment" (1960), and "The Prodigal Mother" (1961), Catherine McLeod demonstrates her ability to project emotional pain and anguish.

Trivia: Bronson Howitzer was the pseudonym of writer Ric Hardman. Throughout the four years of *Lawman*, producers and writers often used pseudonyms when they rewrote scripts for the series.

THE EPISODES

Episode 106: "The Persecuted" April 9, 1961.
Starring John Russell and Peggie Castle. Featuring Adam Williams (Burley Keller), Jean Willes (Annie), Evan McCord (Roy), Dan Sheridan (Jake), Jeffrey Morris (Bob Turner), Sandy Kevin. (Ted Turner), Fred Crane, (Jury Foreman).

Directed by Richard C. Sarafian, Written by Leonard Paul Smith, Produced by Jules Schermer, Director of Photography: Bert Glennon, Art Director: Carl Macauley, Film Editor: Robert L. Wolfe, Music Supervision: Paul Sawtell and Bert Shefter, Music Editor: Theo W. Sebern, Sound: Francis E. Stahl, Set Decorator: Gene Redd, Assistant Director: Eddie Prinz, Supervising Hair Stylist: Jean Burt Reilly.

Synopsis: A gunfighter who likes to kill swears he wants to go straight.

Commentary: Troop again must follow the letter of the law and protect someone found innocent whom he knows is not. The gunfighter tells Lily, "You're the marshal's private stock." In this storyline, Troop shows he can goad just as well as the killer. The evil shootist here is similar to John Doucette's in *Lawman's* second episode, "The Prisoner" (1958). Peter Brown is not in this episode.

Trivia: Adam Williams, who resembled comedian Gabe Kaplan, appeared as scores of heavies on television and in the movies. One of his memorable roles was as the menacing Valerian in *North by Northwest* (1959). Jean Willes' Annie in this episode was much more vulnerable than the strong woman she usually played. Jeffrey Morris played "Cowboy" in Clint Eastwood's *Kelly's Heroes* (1970).

Episode 107: "The Grubstake" April 16, 1961.
Starring John Russell, Peter Brown, and Peggie Castle. Featuring Heather Angel (Stephanie Collins), Frank Ferguson (Rainbow Jack/A. J. Rambeau), Philip Terry (Clayton Rambeau), Robert Cornthwaite (Edward Coughill), Dan Sheridan (Jake Summers), Diana Darrin (Girl), Jud Beaumont (Miner).

Directed by Robert B. Sinclair, Written by Bronson Howitzer and Marc McCarty, Produced by Jules Schermer, Director of Photography: Bert Glennon, Art Director: Carl Macauley, Film Editor: Robert Jahns, Music Supervision: Paul Sawtell and Bert Shefter, Music Editor: John Allyn, Jr., Sound: Tom R. Ashton, Set Decorator: Jack H. Ahearn, Assistant Director: Eddie Prinz, Supervising Hair Stylist: Jean Burt Reilly.

Synopsis: A prospector comes to Laramie looking for a partner who will gamble on a dream.

Commentary: The hopes and aspirations of many who came west are depicted here. Ferguson as Rainbow Jack is an excellent feisty old-timer and Heather Angel as an older saloon girl captures the poignancy of aging. When Rainbow Jack attempts to get a grubstake, he tells everyone different locations of his strike: Medicine Bow, Powder Mountains, Soda Mountains, and Black Butte Canyon.

Trivia: Heather Angel played many ingénues and refined ladies in 1930s and 1940s films such as the 1931 version of *The Hound of the Baskervilles*, *The Informer* (1935), *Kitty Foyle* (1940), *Pride and Prejudice* (1940), and *Lifeboat* (1944). She tested for the part of Melanie in *Gone With the Wind* (1939). Her first husband was Robert B. Sinclair, who directed this *Lawman* episode and fourteen others. She witnessed his stabbing murder by an intruder in their home in 1970. Frank Ferguson appeared in numerous western films and television productions. He was in *Rancho Notorious* (1952) and *Johnny Guitar* (1954), played Gus in thirty-nine *My Friend Flicka* television episodes (1955-56), and had a memorable bit as the reporter at the end of John Ford's *Fort Apache* (1948).

Episode 108: "Whiphand" April 23, 1961.
Starring John Russell, Peter Brown, Peggie Castle, and Peggy McCay (Cassie Nickerson). Featuring Med Flory (Jed Pennyman), Leo Gordon (Bull Nickerson), Dan Sheridan (Jake), Jack Beutel (Ryder), Duane Grey (Slate), James Galante (First Man), James Horan (Second Man).

Directed by Marc Lawrence, Written by Sheldon Stark, Produced by Jules Schermer, Director of Photography: Bert Glennon, Art Director: Carl Macauley, Film Editor: Robert B. Warwick, Jr., Music Supervision: Paul Sawtell and Bert Shefter, Music Editor: Louis W. Gordon, Sound: Tom R. Ashton, Set Decorator: Gene Redd, Assistant Director: Eddie Prinz, Supervising Hair Stylist: Jean Burt Reilly.

Synopsis: A woman decides to leave her abusive husband.

Commentary: This episode balances evil and innocence, and also shows why it's an adult western in the way it deals with complex problems and the possible choices that arise from them. Troop tells Johnny, "There's one thing you have to learn. You can't help people solve problems. They've gotta face up to them themselves one way or another." Johnny's quick appraisal of a situation and his quick draw again prevents bloodshed. At the end of the episode, the marshal again avoids discussing romance with Lily. Peggy McCay is listed in the opening starring credits.

Trivia: Peggy McCay had a career that lasted almost seventy years, culminating in over three decades playing Caroline Brady on the soap, *Days of Our Lives* between 1983 and 2017. She won an Emmy for her work in *The Trials of Rosie O'Neil's* episode, "State of Mind" (1991). Jack Buetel, who co-starred with Jane Russell in Howard Hughes' *The Outlaw* (1943), has a bit as a henchman. Leo Gordon played menacing, ornery outlaws throughout his long career, although his last credit was portraying Wyatt Earp in the television movie, *The Adventures of Young Indiana Jones: Hollywood Follies* (1994). He scripted one *Lawman* episode, "Get Out of Town" (1962), and also wrote thirty other television screenplays. His confrontations with John Wayne in the films *Hondo* (1953) and *McLintock!* (1962) were memorable.

Episode 109: "The Threat" April 30, 1961.
Starring John Russell and Peggie Castle. Featuring Whit Bissell (Edgar Chase), Don O'Kelly, (Kurt Swan), Russ Conway (Herm Villiers), Walter Reed (James Chase), Dan Sheridan (Jake), Grady Sutton (Ben Toomey).

Directed by Richard C Sarafian, Written by John Tomerlin, Produced by Jules Schermer, Director of Photography: Bert Glennon, Art Director: Carl Macauley, Film Editor: Robert Jahns, Music Supervision: Paul Sawtell and Bert Shefter, Music Editor: Sam E. Levin, Sound: Franklin Hansen, Set Decorator: Gene Redd, Assistant Director: Eddie Prinz, Supervising Hair Stylist: Jean Burt Reilly.

Synopsis: The non-violent brother of a murdered man vows revenge against the killer.

Commentary: Troop's conversation at the end of the episode is revealing: "Fear can be a weapon, Lily. Most people forget that. It spreads faster than typhoid and is more deadly than all the guns and bullets ever made. The worst thing about it, no one is immune." This storyline features an ironic, if not a surprise, ending. Peter Brown does not appear in the episode.

Trivia: John Tomerlin wrote eleven *Lawman* storylines. Although he also wrote scripts for such television westerns as *U.S. Marshal* (1958) and *Wanted Dead or Alive* (1959-60), his preference was writing science fiction and thrillers.

Episode 110: "The Trial" May 7, 1961.
Starring John Russell, Peter Brown, and Peggie Castle. Featuring Shirley Knight (Tandis Weston), Ray Teal (Judge Whitehall), Richard Sakal (Dexter Weston), Tim Graham (Charlie Weston), Claudia Bryar (Clara Weston), Don Wilbanks (Ed Pender), Grady Sutton (Ben Toomey), Slim Pickens (Barney).

Directed by Marc Lawrence, Written by John Tomerlin, Produced by Jules Schermer, Director of Photography: Harold Stine, Art Director: Carl Macauley, Film Editor: Basil Wrangell, Music Supervision: Paul Sawtell and Bert Shefter, Music Editor: Donald K. Harris, Sound: Robert B. Lee, Samuel F. Goode, Set Decorator: Jack H. Ahearn, Assistant Director: Eddie Prinz, Supervising Hair Stylist: Jean Burt Reilly.

Synopsis: The son of a man whom a judge hanged puts the judge on trial.

Commentary: Troop's intuition about the good in a man turns out to be accurate again. The concept and cost of revenge is examined in this episode: "An eye for an eye – that is not the way. That leaves only the blind untouched." When Troop is asked, "How many men have you killed?" he responds, "I don't keep score." Ray Teal, who usually played villains, is good here as a decent man with strong convictions mixed with regrets.

Trivia: The kangaroo court with a jury of outlaws was reminiscent of the trial in *The Devil and Daniel Webster* (1941). Richard Sakal resembled a young Montgomery Clift. At the same time she was appearing in many of the Warner Bros. television series such as this *Lawman* episode, Shirley Knight was doing exceptional film work in *The Dark at the Head of the Stairs* (1960) and *Sweet Bird of Youth* (1962), for which she received Academy Award nominations. In her sixty-year career, Knight won Emmys for her work in *Thirtysomething* (1988), *NYPD Blue* (1995), and *Indictment: The McMartin Trial* (1995), as well as one Tony Award for *Kennedy's Children* (1976).

Episode 111: "Blind Hate" May 14, 1961.
Starring John Russell, Peter Brown, and Peggie Castle. Featuring Mala Powers (Lucy Pastor), Jason Evers (Shag Warner), Ted de Corsia (Lem Pastor), John Qualen (Doc Shea), Craig Marshall (Lorman Pastor), Cherrill Lynn, (Deborah Pastor).

Directed by Marc Lawrence, Written by Rik Vollaerts, Produced by Jules Schermer, Director of Photography: Bert Glennon, Art Director: Carl Macauley, Film Editor: John Joyce, Music Supervision: Paul Sawtell and Bert Shefter, Music Editor: Robert Phillips, Sound: Samuel F. Goode, Set Decorator: Gene Redd, Assistant Director: Eddie Prinz, Supervising Hair Stylist: Jean Burt Reilly.

Synopsis: A possessive father horsewhips a cowboy enamored with his daughter.

Commentary: This storyline is similar to the *Lawman* episodes, "The Return," "The Hardcase," and "Detweiler's Kid;" each depicts a headstrong, possessive father. De Corsia's character declares, "She's my daughter and I'll be deciding who's good enough to marry her," refusing for selfish reasons to allow his daughter the freedom to grow and be independent. Once again, Troop and Lily intercede. De Corsia makes an excellent antagonist for Troop and sad-eyed Powers performs well in the climactic scene. The dramatic tension is aided by apt music and photography. The cowboy character makes a revealing observation about Troop: "I know about you and the law. You don't do anything that isn't exactly right."

Trivia: After initial striking performances in 1950 in *Outrage* and as Roxanne in *Cyrano de Bergerac*, Maya Powers co-starred in such westerns as Lex Baxter's *The Yellow Mountain* (1954), Randolph Scott's *Rage at Dawn* (1955), and Scott Brady's *The Storm Rider* (1957) before becoming a staple in television westerns and dramatic series.

Episode 112: "The Break-In" May 21, 1961.
Starring John Russell and Peggie Castle. Featuring Sheldon Allman (Walt Hudson), Maurice Manson (Harold G. Berliner), Chubby Johnson (Cactus Gates). James Anderson (Ed Hill), Grady Sutton (Ben Toomey).

Directed by Richard C. Sarafian, Written by Montgomery Pittman, Produced by Coles Trapnell, Supervising Producer: Jules Schermer, Director of Photography: Bert Glennon, Art Director: Carl Macauley, Film Editor: Stefan Arnsten, Sound: Samuel F. Goode, Music Editor: George E. Marsh, Set Decorator: Gene Redd, Assistant Director: Eddie Prinz, Supervising Hair Stylist: Jean Burt Reilly.

Synopsis: An outlaw wants to turn himself in so he can have the $1,000.00 reward after he serves his time in prison.

Commentary: An outlaw's perception of Troop: "You are the most suspicious man I ever did meet." Peter Brown does not appear in this episode.

Trivia: Sheldon Allman resembled actor MacDonald Carey. Chubby Johnson was a journalist before turning to acting in his 40s. His debut was in Errol Flynn's *Rocky Mountain* (1950). Johnson alternated between television and films throughout the 1950s and 1960s; he had memorable roles in such western movies as *Bend of the River* (1952), *The Far Country* (1954), *Tribute to a Bad Man* (1956), and *The Fastest Gun Alive* (1956). He had a wonderful bit as Rattlesnake in *Calamity Jane* (1953).

Episode 113: "Conditional Surrender" May 28, 1961.
Starring John Russell, Peter Brown, and Peggie Castle. Featuring Claire Griswold (Iona Beason), Robert F. Simon (Pa Beason), Hampton Fancher (Lester Beason), Tyler MacDuff (Ernie Beason), Grady Sutton (Ben Toomey).

Directed by Marc Lawrence, Written by Walter Wagner, Produced by Jules Schermer, Director of Photography: Bert Glennon, Art Director: Carl Macauley, Film Editor: John Hall, Sound: Lincoln Lyons, Music Editor: Norman Bennett, Set Decorator: Gene Redd, Assistant Director: Eddie Prinz, Supervising Hair Stylist: Jean Burt Reilly.

Synopsis: An old outlaw will confess to all of his crimes if Troop meets certain demands.

Commentary: Lily once again transforms a tomboy into a dazzling beauty who then infatuates Johnny. This is a departure from many of the family feuds depicted in *Lawman*; in this episode, it's the father who wants to make his peace with the law while it is his sons who fail to see the light. The parasol is a nice touch.

Trivia: Lovely Claire Griswold was a popular television actress in the late 1950s and early 1960s. She wed her former acting teacher, Sydney Pollack, in 1958. She retired from acting in 1963 to devote herself to her family and was married for fifty years until Pollack's death in a plane crash in 2008. Pollack, who won an Oscar for directing *Out of Africa* (1985), also helmed *Jeremiah Johnson* (1972), *The Way We Were* (1973), and *Tootsie* (1982).

Episode 114: "Cold Fear" June 4, 1961.
Starring John Russell and Peggie Castle. Featuring Frank Overton (Brad Turner), Maggie Mahoney (Ann Turner), Chris Alcaide (Lou Quade), Jerry Barclay (Bert Quade), Dan Sheridan (Jake).

Directed by Richard C. Sarafian, Written by Rik Vollaerts, Produced by Coles Trapnell, Supervising Producer: Jules Schermer, Director of Photography Bert Glennon, Art Director: Carl Macauley, Film Editor: John Hall, Sound: Ralph Butler, Music Editor: Charles Paley, Set Decorator: Gene Redd, Assistant Director: Eddie Prinz, Supervising Hair Stylist: Jean Burt Reilly.

Synopsis: Gunmen brothers vow revenge against a retired marshal.

Commentary: Troop again gets involved attempting to thwart revengeful outlaws. A wound to a man's gun hand is again a significant part of the plot. Windy weather helps build up the suspense. The reason the marshal is hesitant about a relationship with Lily is explained in the words of an ex-lawman's wife: "The whole town depended on him. And then you add a woman to that, someone he loved. Now everything's changed." Lily tells Troop that he's got a case of "Lawman's Complaint." When he asks what that is, she replies, "Seeing trouble when there isn't any." Peter Brown is not listed in the credits and does not appear in this show. John Russell is in every *Lawman* episode.

Trivia: Serious-looking Frank Overton was the sheriff in *To Kill a Mockingbird* (1962), General Brogan in *Fail Safe* (1964), and Major Stovell in the *Twelve O' Clock High* television series (1964-67).

Episode 115: "The Promise" June 11, 1961.
Starring John Russell, Peter Brown, and Peggie Castle. Featuring Don Haggerty (Simm Bracque), Ken Lynch (Jed Barrister), Carolyn Komant (Nancy Fuller), Dan Sheridan (Jake), Robert Palmer (Geoff Washburn), Stuart Randall (Colonel Strappin), Charles Tannen (Hardy Albrecht), Harry Woods (Charley Hames), Ed Faulkner (Corporal Hayden).

Directed by Irving J. Moore, Written by John D.F. Black, Producer: Jules Schermer, Director of Photography: Bert Glennon, Art Director: Carl Macauley, Film Editor: Harry Reynolds, Sound: Ross Owen, Music Editor: Erma E. Levin, Set Decorator: Gene Redd, Assistant Director: Richard Mayberry, Supervising Hair Stylist: Jean Burt Reilly.

Synopsis: An outlaw about to be hanged offers a reward for anyone who kills Troop.

Commentary: Johnny shows his mettle in the way he attempts to protect his marshal from unknown vengeful killers. Troop talks about awaiting trouble: "I can't hide my head in the sand every time someone decides to threaten me." This episode features a good use of shadows and lighting as well as music to build up the tension. Johnny's mistaken opinion about a possible killer is a lesson for him. Lily's dress is the least attractive she's worn in the series. Troop's words of wisdom to Johnny: "Johnny, you're letting this bother you too much. You know better than to let a threat or a thousand threats get to you. You can't afford that moment to think. There's too much to lose." At the end of the episode, Troop's affectionate fatherly appraisal of Johnny and the way the marshal and his deputy walk across the street together symbolizes their mutual respect and friendship.

Trivia: A former ladies' hats salesman, Harry Woods played vicious outlaws and hoodlums in most of his 250 credits ranging from the 1920s to the 1960s. His George Clew in John Wayne's *Tall in the Saddle* (1944) was a typically, menacing Woods desperado. Don Haggerty was often confused with Dan Haggerty, television's Grizzly Adams. Don Haggerty was a television and movie character actor who usually played secondary cavalry and lawmen in westerns. He appeared twenty-one times as newspaper editor Marsh Murdock in *The Life and Legend of Wyatt Earp* (1955-61).

Season Four

Episode 116: "Trapped" September 17, 1961.
Starring John Russell, Peter Brown, and Peggie Castle. Featuring Peter Breck (Hale Connors), Vinton Hayworth (Oren Slauson), House Peters Jr., (Joe Poole), Grady Sutton (Ben Toomey), Maxine Wagner (Mrs. Willock).

Directed by Richard Safarian, Written by Walter Wagner, Producer: Coles Trapnell, Supervising Producer: Jules Schermer, Director of Photography: Bert Glennon, Art Director: Carl Macauley, Film Editor: Cliff Bell, Sound: Tom R. Ashton, Music Editor: Donald K. Harris, Set Decorator: Alfred E. Kegerris, Assistant Director: Richard Mayberry, Supervising Hair Stylist: Jean Burt Reilly.

Synopsis: A stranger announces to Troop that the incoming stagecoach's passengers have been taken hostage and will be killed unless he is given all of the money in Laramie's bank.

Commentary: The tone of the entire storyline is lighter than usual. Breck makes an excellent foil for the marshal; his jolly sarcasm plays well off of Troop's sternness. The clever scheme almost works except for one slipup. Peter Brown is in the starring credits but never appears in this episode.

Trivia: House Peters Jr. portrayed the telegraph operator who punched Breck's character. Peters Jr. was a serious-looking character actor who was the son of House Peters, a silent movie actor known as "The Star of a Thousand Emotions." Peters Jr. was active in television westerns and dramas throughout the 1950s and had a recurring role in the television series *Lassie* (1956-66) as the sheriff. In 1957, he was the original Mr. Clean.

Episode 117: "The Juror" September 24, 1961.
Starring John Russell, Peter Brown, and Peggie Castle. Featuring Harry Cheshire (Judge Traeger), Jack Hogan (Bob Cawley), Dan Sheridan

(Jake), Larry Blake (Mister Parker), Jim Hayward (Adam Larkin), Karl Davis (Gang Member), Bruce MacFarland (First Man).

Directed by Marc Lawrence, Written by Ric Hardman, Producer: Jules Schermer, Director of Photography: Bert Glennon, Art Director: Carl Macauley, Film Editor: Cliff Bell, Sound: Eugene Irvine, Music Editor: Joe Inge, Set Decorator: Gene Redd, Assistant Director: Eddie Prinz, Supervising Hair Stylist: Jean Burt Reilly.

Synopsis: After a member of a murderous gang is arrested, the remaining outlaws terrorize the citizens of Laramie so much that no one is willing to serve as a juror – except Lily.

Commentary: This episode's framework is similar to the plot of *High Noon* (1952) with fear dominating the town's residents and nobody offering to help the marshal oppose the bad guys. Troop describes the citizens succinctly: "This whole town is locked up with terror" and then adds, "Now the Lord destroyed Sodom and Gomorrah for the want of ten good men and I tell you Laramie will not be spared either. I'm not the law here, you are. This badge rests on you; I only wear it." Lily once again displays her courage and determination not only in being willing to serve as a juror but by picking up a gun to take on the outlaws ala Grace Kelly in *High Noon* (1952). She certainly looks captivating holding the rifle. The marshal's uttering, "Ha-hmm!" is reminiscent of Gregory Peck's Horatio Hornblower. Larry Blake and Jim Hayward are excellent in their depictions of loudmouthed cowards.

Trivia: The credits at the end of each episode varied considerably; there was no consistency. For the fourth season, the musical supervisors, Paul Sawtell and Bert Shefter, were no longer listed, the order of the crew changed, and middle initials were sometimes used and sometimes omitted. For example, Dan Sheridan's recurring character, bartender Jake Summers, is listed in the credits as Jake after one episode and as Jake Summers after another. Jack Hogan, who played the jailed outlaw, resembled actor Don Gordon, Steve McQueen's police partner in *Bullitt* (1968).

Episode 118: "The Four" October 1, 1961.
Starring John Russell, Peggie Castle, and Evan McCord (Lee Darragh). Featuring Jack Elam (Herm Forrest), Norm Alden (Charlie), Dan Sheridan (Jake), Grady Sutton (Ben Tooney), Dorothy Konrad (Mrs. Bangle), Richard Gardner (Frank), Johnny Weissmuller, Jr. (Willy).

Directed by Richard Safarian, Written by John D.F. Black, Producer: Coles Trapnell, Supervising Producer: Jules Schermer, Director of Photography: Ralph Woolsey, Art Director: William Campbell, Film Editor: Noel L. Scott, Sound: Everett A. Hughes, Music Editor: John Allyn, Jr., Set Decorator: Albert E. Kegerris, Assistant Director: John F. Murphy, Supervising Hair Stylist: Jean Burt Reilly.

Synopsis: A good looking youngster turns out to be a vicious killer.

Commentary: This is a very strong storyline filled with surprising hooks. It features a powerful opening with Elam's typically menacing character in the marshal's office and ends unexpectedly with a very different Jack Elam. The photography is vivid and clean, and helps build up the dramatic tension. As in other episodes, Troop knows his limitations and has no problem asking for help when needed. Peter Brown is not in the starring credits and does not appear in this show. Evan McCord is listed under the starring credits.

Trivia: McCord had significant roles in his three *Lawman* episodes; the other two were "The Persecuted" (1961) and "The Youngest" (1962). He was in many of the other Warner Bros. westerns and dramas, and under his real name, Joseph Gallison, played Dr. Neil Curtis for seventeen years on the daytime soap, *Days of Our Lives,* from 1974 to 1991. Johnny Weissmuller, Jr., the son of the most famous Tarzan, played one of the brothers, Willy.

Episode 119: "The Son" October 8, 1961.
Starring John Russell, Peter Brown, Peggie Castle, and Chad Everett (Cole Herod), Featuring James Westerfield (Zacharia Herod), Tom Reese (Bob Mengis), Dan Sheridan (Jake), Charles Irving (Eugene Thomas).

Directed by Richard C. Sarafian, Written by John D.F. Black, Producer: Coles Trapnell, Supervising Producer: Jules Schermer, Director of Photography: Bert Glennon, Art Director: Carl Macauley, Film Editor: Robert Crawford, Sound: B. F. Ryan, Music Editor: Norman Bennett, Set Decorator: Hoyle Barrett, Assistant Director: Eddie Prinz, Supervising Hair Stylist: Jean Burt Reilly.

Synopsis: A blind man, the only witness to a killing, arrives in Laramie with his father, both searching for the murderer.

Commentary: With the marshal forced out of town, Johnny takes charge and demonstrates he is an apt substitute. The extremely windy, wintry weather adds to the dramatic tension regarding the identity of the murderer. Chad Everett is excellent as the blind son trying to protect his father. The early scene with the men in the saloon being eliminated from suspicion by listening to their voices is reminiscent of a similar scene (searching for muddy boots) in *Rio Bravo* (1958). At the end of the episode, Troop tells an emotional Johnny, who is worrying about his new blind friend, "The only way you lose hope, is if you let go of it. Cole won't. He'll be alright." Since appearing in the *Lawman* episode, "Detweiler's Kid," eight months previously, Chad Everett changed his name from Chad York and gained star billing in this show.

Trivia: Tom Reese played dozens of hard and harsh men in the movies and on television for over fifty years. His first film was John Cassavetes' *Shadows* (1958) and his first western was Elvis Presley's *Flaming Star* (1960). Reese was featured as Sergeant Velie in twenty-two episodes of Jim Hutton's *Ellery Queen* series (1975-76).

Episode 120: "Owny O'Reilly, Esquire" October 15, 1961.
Starring John Russell, Peter Brown, and Peggie Castle. Featuring Joel Grey (Owny O'Reilly), Roberta Shore (Millie Cotton), Mort Mills (Jack Saunders), Barry Kelley (Governor Johnson), Grady Sutton (Ben Toomey).

Directed by Leslie H. Martinson, Written by Ric Hardman, Producer: Coles Trapnell, Supervising Producer: Jules Schermer, Director of Photography: Bert Glennon, Art Director: Carl Macauley, Film Editor: Noel L. Scott, Sound: Everett A. Hughes, Music Editor: Robert Phillips, Set Decorator: Gene Redd, Assistant Director: Eddie Prinz, Supervising Hair Stylist: Jean Burt Reilly.

Synopsis: Owny O'Reilly gets held up by a runaway teenager.

Commentary: Troop again confronts a domineering father while Lily continues to take in strays. In his final appearance as Owny, Joel Grey, for the third time, adds humor and poignancy to the storyline. Mort Mills makes an excellent villain. Owny collected the $150.00 reward for capturing the outlaw Jack Saunders played by Lee Van Cleef in the earlier episode, "The Return of Owny O'Reilly" and portrayed by Mills in this story. "A girl is a man's best friend" is the closing motto verbalized by Owny, and approved both by a smirking Lily and an appeasing marshal.

Trivia: After appearances in such television shows as *Annette* (1958), *Father Knows Best* (1959), and *The Adventures of Ozzie and Harriet* (1960-62), Roberta Shore played Betsy Garth in the first three seasons of *The Virginian* from 1962 to 1965. It's her voice yodeling in the song "It's a Small World" in the Disneyland and Disneyworld amusement parks. Solemn-faced Mort Mills played either vicious outlaws or tough lawman. He had recurring roles as Marshal Frank Tallman in the *Man Without a Gun* series (1957-59), the sheriff in *The Big Valley* (1965-66), and Sgt. Ben Landro in *Perry Mason* (1961-65). He also portrayed the suspicious highway patrolman in Hitchcock's *Psycho* (1960), and a spy in *Torn Curtain* (1966).

Episode 121: "The Substitute" October 22, 1961.
Starring John Russell, Peter Brown, and Peggie Castle. Featuring Whit Bissell (Al Skinner), Kathleen Freeman (Mavis Martingale), Jan Arvan (Homer Martingale), Dan Sheridan (Jake), Dee Carroll (Trilby Johnson),

Almira Sessions (First Lady), Ann Blake (Second Lady), Hank Stanton (Bobby Martingale), Anjo Stanton (Edith Martingale).

Directed by Robert B. Sinclair, Teleplay by Bronson Howitzer, Story by Robert Palmer, Producer: Coles Trapnell, Supervising Producer: Jules Schermer, Director of Photography: Bert Glennon, Art Director: Carl Macauley, Film Editor: Robert Jahns, Sound: Robert B. Lee, Music Editor: Joe Inge, Set Decorator: Hoyle Barrett, Assistant Director: C. Carter Gibson, Supervising Hair Stylist: Jean Burt Reilly.

Synopsis: Laramie's spinster teacher has a marriage offer she can't resist, so the town must find a replacement.

Commentary: This storyline is a *Lawman* rarity as it features no crime, although Troop does use a jail cell to help solve a dilemma. The marshal is forced to take on a different sort of bias in this episode. Lily demonstrates enormous class and self-restraint when she rejects an opportunity to get back at a hurtful snob. Bissell as the intellectual town drunk, Arvan as the henpecked husband, and Freeman as the pompous busybody are perfectly cast.

Trivia: Kathleen Freeman had a long career playing town gossips and meddlers. She was in eleven Jerry Lewis comedies, played the voice tutor in *Singin' in the Rain* (1952), and voiced Al Bundy's mother-in-law nemesis in *Married with Children* (1987-97). One of her most memorable western bits was in James Garner's *Support Your Local Sheriff* (1969).

Episode 122: "The Stalker" October 29, 1961.
Starring John Russell, Peter Brown, and Peggie Castle. Featuring Peter Whitney (Alteeka McClintoch), Harry Lauter (Compton Schaeffer), Don Barry (Jess Schaeffer), Dan Sheridan (Jake), Bob Gunderson (Masten).

Directed by Richard C. Sarafian, Written by John Tomerlin, Producer: Coles Trapnell, Supervising Producer: Jules Schermer, Director of Photography: Ralph Woolsey, Art Director: Carl Macauley, Film Editor: John Joyce, Sound: Ross Owen, Music Editor: Sam E. Levin,

Set Decorator: Jerry Welch, Assistant Director: Eddie Prinz, Supervising Hair Stylist: Jean Burt Reilly.

Synopsis: After a trapper accidently kills a man in Laramie, his brother vows revenge.

Commentary: Troop is forced to deal with familial revenge almost as often as famous gunfighters. The photography and sound effects (particularly the wind) help make the exterior scenes believable. Barry is a convincing bully and Whitney is excellent as the skilled outdoorsman who is unschooled in the rules and regulations of civilization. One of several *Lawman* scenarios involving accidental deaths.

Trivia: Harry Lauter played dozens of outlaws in a thirty-year-long movie and television career. Two exceptions were when he played the hero in the twelve-part Republic adventure serial, *Trader Tom of the China Seas* (1954), and Ranger Clay Morgan in the western television series, *Tales of the Texas Rangers* (1955-59).

Episode 123: "The Catalog Woman" November 5, 1961.
Starring John Russell, Peter Brown, and Peggie Castle. Featuring Richard Carlyle (Agatha Wingate/o Ida Creevey), Vinton Hayworth (Oren Slauson), Herb Vigran (Walt Perkins), William Fawcett (John), Charles Alvin Bell (Passenger), Lester Miller (Man).

Directed by Leslie H. Martinson, Written by Ric Hardman, Producer: Coles Trapnell, Supervising Producer: Jules Schermer, Director of Photography: Bert Glennon, Art Director: Carl Macauley, Film Editor: John Joyce, Sound: Francis E. Stahl, Music Editor: Charles Paley, Set Decorator: Gene Redd, Assistant Director: Eddie Prinz, Supervising Hair Stylist: Jean Burt Reilly.

Synopsis: Troop investigates a mail-order bride scam and murder by posing as a rich, lonely bachelor.

Commentary: Russell looks so different in a black hat and gray suit. Lily demonstrates her pent-up feelings for the marshal when she exclaims, "If that woman so much as touches you, I will scratch her eyes out!" Troop later declares to Lily, "There's only one woman in this world who scares me... you!" The ending echoes with the obvious emotions shared by Lily and the marshal. Lily displays one of her most lavish outfits in her visit to Cheyenne.

Trivia: Heavyset, genial Herb Vigran resembled Johnny Carson's buddy Ed McMahon and had over 370 acting credits during his fifty-year career. Between 1970 and 1975, he played Judge Brooker eleven times on *Gunsmoke*.

Episode 124: "The Cold One" November 12, 1961.
Starring John Russell, Peter Brown, and Peggie Castle. Featuring Joyce Meadows (Barbara Harris), Michael Pate (King Harris), Tom Gilson (Rio), Ric Morrow (Willis), Percy Helton (Thatcher), I. Stanford Jolley (Tom Carver), Sandy Kevin (Ed Lane), Dick Winslow (Bartender), Emile Avery (Stage Coach Driver).

Directed by Richard C. Sarafian, Written by Mark Rodgers, Producer: Coles Trapnell, Supervising Producer: Jules Schermer, Director of Photography: Bert Glennon, Art Director: Carl Macauley, Film Editor: Richard Jahns, Sound: Francis E. Stahl, Music Editor: Louis W. Gordon, Set Decorator: Gene Redd, Assistant Director: Robert Templeton, Supervising Hair Stylist: Jean Burt Reilly.

Synopsis: A killer escapes from prison and plans to murder his wife who he feels betrayed him.

Commentary: There are two "Cold Ones" in the story, the killer and his wife. Joyce Meadows is exceptional as a woman accepting her impending doom. The episode is excellent at building up tension. Although Peter Brown was known to be one of Hollywood's fastest pistol-drawing actors, in the early scene when Troop and Johnny draw at the same time, it appears that the marshal is quicker. Troop's words here sum up his view of his job: "A peace officer can't look at another life and decide because that life has been lived badly, that he has no duty to protect it. It's the sacredness of all human life that the law establishes." The ending is satisfactory as it enables Meadows' character to actually smile.

Trivia: Australian-born Michael Pate portrayed numerous Native American leaders in his long career, including Vittorio in the *Hondo* film (1953) and in the *Hondo* television series (1967). He also played Geronimo in *The Zane Grey Theater* 1960 episode, "The Last Bugle," Sitting Bull in *The Great Sioux Massacre* (1965), and Crazy Horse in three 1966 *Branded* shows. Pate also did turns as depraved outlaws such as King Harris in dozens of westerns.

Episode 125: "Porphyria's Lover" November 19, 1961.
Starring John Russell, Peter Brown, and Peggie Castle. Featuring Lance Fuller (Galt Stevens), Benny Baker (Dave), Jeanne Vaughn (Eve).

Directed by Richard C. Sarafian, Written by Margaret Armen, Producer: Coles Trapnell, Supervising Producer: Jules Schermer, Director of Photography: Ralph Woolsey, Art Director: Carl Macauley, Film Editor: Jim Faris, Sound: Ross Owen, Music Editor: Erma E. Levin, Set Decorator: Gene Redd, Assistant Director: Eddie Prinz, Supervising Hair Stylist: Jean Burt Reilly.

Synopsis: Lily is stalked by an obsessed killer.

Commentary: Two storylines in a row involve killers who have escaped from prison seeking revenge against women whose testimony convicted them. The stormy weather – "even the ducks are hiding" – adds to the episode's sense of ominous tension. Fuller's characterization is over-the-top; his performance (and makeup) are like a silent movie villain's. Troop's intelligence is reflected in how he breaks the case: "He used that poem as a weapon; maybe we can use it as a map." At the end of the episode, the marshal actually recites poetry to Lily.

Trivia: "Porphyria's Lover" was a Robert Browning poem first published in 1836 that describes an obsessive lover strangling a golden-haired beauty. Lance Fuller co-starred in the westerns *Cattle Queen of Montana* (1954) with Barbara Stanwyck and Ronald Reagan, and also

THE EPISODES

Roger Corman's *Apache Woman* (1955) with Lloyd Bridges. Fuller was married to the statuesque beauty Joi Lansing.

Episode 126: "The Appointment" November 26, 1961.
Starring John Russell, Peter Brown, and Peggie Castle. Featuring Kent Smith (Major Jason Leeds), John Kellogg (Bern Lochard), Dan Sheridan (Jake), Grady Sutton (Ben Toomey), Tom London (Pete), Zach Foster (Lieutenant).

Directed by Dick Benedict, Written by John D.F. Black, Producer: Coles Trapnell, Supervising Producer: Jules Schermer, Director of Photography: Bert Glennon, Art Director: Carl Macauley, Film Editor: Noel L. Scott, Sound: Ross Owen, Music Editor: Erma E. Levin, Set Decorator: Alfred E. Kegerris, Assistant Director: Eddie Prinz, Supervising Hair Stylist: Jean Burt Reilly.

Synopsis: Johnny is offered an appointment to West Point.

Commentary: The storyline focuses on Johnny choosing between two very different futures: the perilous life of a western lawman or a career as an officer and a gentleman in the army. It also depicts the complex reactions of the men Johnny respects the most and how they affect Johnny's decision. The parental pride on the Troop and Lily's faces when Johnny reads his appointment letter is memorable. The symbolism with the sword is outstanding.

Trivia: The director, Dick Benedict, also helmed the *Lawman* episode, "Get Out of Town" (1962) as well as over fifty movie and television shows. Benedict was also an actor with over 125 credits. His most notable character was Leo Minosa, the miner used by Kirk Douglas' reporter in *Ace in the Hole* (1951). Benedict had a part as Lou Silk in the *Lawman* episode, "By the Book (1961)."

Episode 127: "The Lords of Darkness" December 3, 1961.
Starring John Russell, Peter Brown, and Peggie Castle. Featuring Arch Johnson (Andrew Lord), Elen Willard (Caroline Lord), Dan Sheridan

(Jake), Corey Allen (William Lord), Jim DeClose (Robert Lord), Damian O'Flynn (Sutter), Owen Bush (Bartender), Charles Maxwell (Marshal).

Directed by Richard C. Sarafian, Written by Mark Rodgers, Producer: Coles Trapnell, Supervising Producer: Jules Schermer, Director of Photography: Bert Glennon, Art Director: Carl Macauley, Film Editor: Harry Reynolds, Sound: Francis E. Stahl, Music Editor: Donald K. Harris, Set Decorator: Hoyle Barrett, Assistant Director: Eddie Prinz, Supervising Hair Stylist: Jean Burt Reilly.

Synopsis: Troop trails two killer brothers back to their rich, haughty father's ranch.

Commentary: The marshal confronts yet another overbearing father, whose daughter describes as being such a know-it-all that "Not God himself could make you listen." Troop meets another lawman who has sold out. The original senseless killing is described but not shown. Arch Johnson again creates a formable adversary for Troop.

Trivia: Corey Allen, who played William Lord, was the son of legendary Las Vegas casino owner and bookie, Carl Cohen, who famously punched out Frank Sinatra. Allen split his time between acting (fifty-seven credits) and directing (seventy-nine credits). He played the teen, Buzz Gunderson, who raced against James Dean in *Rebel Without a Cause* (1955) and won an Emmy for his direction on *Hill Street Blues* in 1984.

<u>Episode 128</u>: "Tarot" December 10, 1961.
Starring John Russell, Peter Brown, and Peggie Castle. Featuring Robert McQueeney (Joe Wyatt), Dan Sheridan (Jake), Bill Zuckert (Luther), K.L. Smith (Jess), Fred Sherman (Line Agent), Bruce MacFarland (Ike Buford), Nick Pawl (Third Gunman), Emile Avery (Stage Coach Driver).

Directed by Robert B. Sinclair, Written by Mark Rodgers, Producer: Coles Trapnell, Supervising Producer: Jules Schermer, Director of Photography: Bert Glennon, Art Director: Carl Macauley, Film Editor: Robert Jahns, Sound: M.A. Merrick, Music Editor: Erma E. Levin, Set

Decorator: Hal Overell, Assistant Director: Eddie Prinz, Supervising Hair Stylist: Jean Burt Reilly.

Synopsis: Lily's childhood acquaintance arrives in Laramie and maintains that his tarot cards will predict the future for Troop, Johnny, Lily, and himself.

Commentary: This episode's plot, like "The Thimblerigger," revolves around a game of chance. Another instance when there are repercussions for cowardice. McQueeney is intriguing as the mysterious stranger in town with an agenda. Lily's bonnet is ready for Easter.

Trivia: Emile Avery appeared as a barfly, townsman, or stage coach driver in ninety-seven *Lawman* episodes. Between 1947's *Jesse James Rides Again* starring Clayton Moore and 1969's *The Great Bank Robbery* with Clint Walker, Avery had over ninety appearances in mostly uncredited roles.

Episode 129: "The Prodigal Mother" December 17, 1961.
Starring John Russell, Peter Brown, and Peggie Castle. Featuring Catherine McLeod (Margaret Coleson), Billy Booth (Tad McCallan), Mina Brown (Ella McCallan), King Calder (Dave McCallan).

Director: Robert B. Sinclair, Teleplay by Paul Savage, Story by Fanya Lawrence, Producer: Coles Trapnell, Supervising Producer: Jules Schermer, Director of Photography: Bert Glennon, Art Director: Carl Macauley, Film Editor: Milt Kleinberg, Sound: Francis E. Stahl, Music Editor: Theo W. Sebern, Set Decorator: Gene Redd, Assistant Director: Eddie Prinz, Supervising Hair Stylist: Jean Burt Reilly.

Synopsis: A mother, who had abandoned her son nine years before, wants to take him away from his adoptive parents.

Commentary: As in the episode "The Squatters," Troop is forced to use a court order to do what he knows is wrong. Johnny mentions meeting the dime novelist, Ned Buntline, who wants to write a book about the marshal and his deputy titled, *The Law Comes to the Wild West*. Troop explains to Johnny how Buntline embellishes the truth, which turns Johnny off. Johnny's hair has a blondish tint. There's a bit of a time discrepancy in the storyline. Nine years before, Troop was involved in getting Tad adopted, but he had only been in Laramie for a few years. Two powerful scenes: When his friends who had adopted the boy want to flee with him, Troop declares, "It's the law and I can't let you do it." Tad to his birth mother: "You're my mother; you could never be my maw." The episode ends with Troop telling Johnny, "There's some things that only a woman can understand."

Trivia: Billy Booth played Dennis' best friend, Tommy Anderson, in the *Dennis the Menace* show for 111 episodes from 1959 to 1963. After his acting career ended in the mid-1960s, Booth focused on school and became an attorney. Paul Savage was an actor who switched to writing. He had a successful thirty-five-year career, including his work on twenty-seven episodes of *Gunsmoke* between 1963 and 1975. Peter Brown's mother Mina who had been the "Dragon Lady" on the *Terry and the Pirates* radio show during the 1940s portrayed Ella "Maw" McCallan in this episode.

Episode 130: "By the Book" December 24, 1961.
Starring John Russell, Peter Brown, and Peggie Castle. Featuring Lyle Talbot (Orville Luster), Walter Burke (Ernie), Sheldon Allman (Teakwood), Dan Sheridan (Jake), Dick Benedict (Lou Silk), John Cason (Brad Oliver), James Waters (Mr. Friendly).

Directed by Irving J. Moore, Written by John Tomerlin, Producer: Coles Trapnell, Supervising Producer: Jules Schermer, Director of Photography: Bert Glennon, Art Director: Carl Macauley, Film Editor: John Joyce, Sound: Francis E. Stahl, Music Editor: John Allyn, Jr., Set Decorator: Hoyle Barrett, Assistant Director: Eddie Prinz, Supervising Hair Stylist: Jean Burt Reilly.

Synopsis: An investigator from the territorial marshal's office disapproves of Troop's flexible methods of law enforcement.

Commentary: Troop is confronted by another authoritarian figure who cannot grasp the difference between "bad men" and "boisterous men." Troop shares his view of the law with Johnny: "[Law] books like this are fine, Johnny, as long as you remember they're only the road maps to the law. The real law is in men's minds." Burke and Allman make entertaining drunks.

Trivia: Lyle Talbot had a long acting career that lasted from the Warner Bros. pre-code dramas of the early 1930s to a *Newhart* in 1987. He played Paul Fonda in twenty-two episodes of *The Bob Cummings Show* between 1955 and 1959, and was Ozzie's buddy, Joe Randolph, in ninety episodes of *The Adventures of Ozzie and Harriet* between 1955 and 1966.

Episode 131: "Trojan Horse" December 31, 1961.
Starring John Russell, Peter Brown, and Peggie Castle. Featuring Ken Tobey (Clooney), Richard Bakalyan (Eggers), Charles Briggs (Falk), Emile Avery (Man).

Directed by Richard C. Sarafian, Written by John Tomerlin, Producer: Coles Trapnell, Supervising Producer: Jules Schermer, Director of Photography: Ralph Woolsey, Art Director: Carl Macauley, Film Editor: Milt Kleinberg, Sound: Everett A. Hughes, Music Editor: George E. Marsh, Set Decorator: Gene Redd, Assistant Director: Eddie Prinz, Supervising Hair Stylist: Jean Burt Reilly.

Synopsis: After Laramie is evacuated so nitroglycerine can be brought through the town, two opportunists plan to use the explosives to rob the bank.

Commentary: The episode introduces modern weaponry, first with an examination of a high powered rifle, and then with a discussion of nitroglycerin. "Nitro" is described as being "touchier than a sick bobcat" and "the work of the devil." This second description is followed by the remark, "it seems to me that men do that work." The storyline depicts another outlaw who pulls away from crime at a crucial moment. When

Johnny declares, "This business of ours is getting more dangerous all the time," Troop responds, "That's progress."

Trivia: Coles Trapnell, who was listed as the *Lawman* producer thirty-one times, also produced numerous other television series. Moreover, he was the story editor and story writer for such shows as *Yancy Derringer* in 1959 and *Maverick* from 1959 to 1961, and the author of *Teleplay*, a 1966 book for television writers.

Episode 132: "The Locket" January 7, 1962.
Starring John Russell, Peter Brown, Peggie Castle, and Robert Colbert (Breen). Featuring Julie Van Zandt (Marcia), Boyd "Red" Morgan (Scar).

Directed by Robert B. Sinclair, Written by Margaret Armen, Producer: Coles Trapnell, Supervising Producer: Jules Schermer, Director of Photography: Bert Glennon, Art Director: Carl Macauley, Film Editor: Bill Wiard, Sound: Everett A. Hughes, Music Editor: Lewis W. Gordon, Set Decorator: Mowbray F. Berkeley, Assistant Director: Eddie Prinz, Supervising Hair Stylist: Jean Burt Reilly.

Synopsis: An old friend of Lily's arrives in Laramie mysteriously unconscious on a driverless stage.

Commentary: Troop's hunches keep him delving into the episode's mysteries. He is wounded, and saved by Johnny's quick actions. Shadows build up the tension, especially in the stairway scene. The locket serves as the key to revealing the outlaw's true identity and intentions. Robert Colbert receives starring billing in the opening credits.

Trivia: In additional to numerous appearances on multiple Warner Bros. television series of the early 1960s, Colbert played the third Maverick brother, Brent, in two 1961 *Maverick* episodes, "The Forbidden City" and "Benefit of Doubt," co-starred in the 1966-67 *Time Tunnel* series, and played Stuart Brooks on the daytime soap, *The Young and the Reckless*, for ten years from 1973 to 1983. From the mid-1950s to the mid-1960s, striking Julie Van Zandt was active on numerous television series including five episodes of *77 Sunset Strip* in 1961-63 and *The Twilight Zone* in 1962.

She was also an avid fisherman and artist; she held the world record for landing the largest needlefish ever caught and one of her murals of the Chumash Indians is displayed in the Malibu Lagoon Museum.

Episode 133: "A Friend of the Family" January 14, 1962.
Starring John Russell and Peter Brown. Featuring Frank Ferguson (Joe Henry), Vinton Hayworth (Oren Slouson) Don O'Kelly (Grat), Gertrude Flynn (Miss Selma), Ted Quillin (Gus Baker).

Directed by Richard C. Sarafian, Written by John Tomerlin, Producer: Coles Trapnell, Supervising Producer: Jules Schermer, Director of Photography: Ralph Woolsey, Art Director: Carl Macauley, Film Editor: William W. Moore, Sound: Robert B. Lee, Music Editor: Robert Phillips, Set Decorator: Jack H. Ahearn, Assistant Director: Eddie Prinz, Supervising Hair Stylist: Jean Burt Reilly.

Synopsis: A captured bank robber turns out to be a man who helped raise Johnny.

Commentary: This is one of several storylines involving someone from Johnny's childhood. The episode features another trio of outlaws. This is one of the rare times Johnny disappoints Troop, and the marshal lets him know it. The ending amid the storm with the barn's barred window and the final compliment is filled with sadness and irony. Peggie Castle is not in the credits and does not appear in this episode.

Trivia: Executive Producer William/Wm. T. Orr was the head of Warner Bros. television productions for nine years beginning in 1955, eventually overseeing twenty-four different shows. Orr's ability to assembly-line the movie production process into weekly television series and to find new stars like Clint Walker, James Garner, Will Hutchins, Edd Byrnes, and Peter Brown for these programs elevated ABC-TV to compete with NBC-TV and CBS-TV. Orr was married to Jack L. Warner's step-daughter, actress Joy Page.

Episode 134: "The Vintage" January 21, 1962.
Starring John Russell, Peter Brown, and Peggie Castle. Featuring Ernest

Sarracino (Lazaro Lazarino), Kevin Hagen (Kulp), Armand Alzamora (Antonio Lazarino), Richard Reeves (Joe), Dan Sheridan (Jake), Harry Cheshire (Judge Traeger).

Directed by Richard C. Sarafian, Written by John D.F. Black, Producer: Coles Trapnell, Supervising Producer: Jules Schermer, Director of Photography: Bert Glennon, Art Director: Carl Macauley, Film Editor: Harry Reynolds, Sound: Robert B. Lee, Music Editor: Joe Inge, Set Decorator: Bertram C. Granger, Assistant Director: Eddie Prinz, Supervising Hair Stylist: Jean Burt Reilly.

Synopsis: A fight in the street between two drunken buddies results in the trampling of priceless grapevines.

Commentary: Foreshadowing the episode's events, the initial scene has Troop commenting to Johnny on the extremely hot weather: "Heat does peculiar things to people. Tempers run short, dry up, snap." Reeves and Hagen make up an engaging pair of cowboy buddies. The screenplay features an uplifting ending revolving around taking responsibility for one's actions.

Trivia: Kevin Hagen played both evil villains and kindly townsmen during his thirty-year acting career. His most famous role was as Dr. Hiram Baker in 113 episodes of *Little House on the Prairie* (1974-83).

Episode 135: "The Tarnished Badge" January 28, 1962.
Starring John Russell and Peter Brown. Featuring Lon Chaney (Jess Bridges), Jack Searl (Slick), Marshal Reed (Jake), Rex Devereaux (Posse Member),

Directed by Richard C. Sarafian, Written Margaret Armen, Producer: Coles Trapnell, Supervising Producer: Jules Schermer, Director of Photography: Bert Glennon, Art Director: Carl Macauley, Film Editor: Milt Kleinberg, Sound: Ross Owen, Music Editor: Sam E. Levin, Set Decorator: Hal Overell, Assistant Director: Eddie Prinz, Supervising Hair Stylist: Jean Burt Reilly.

Synopsis: An ex-lawman attempts to rob the Laramie stage while disguised as a marshal bringing in two prisoners.

Commentary: Good, suspenseful opening scene. Johnny shows increased maturity. As in several other episodes, Troop encounters an older mentor (and Johnny's idol), Chaney's Jess Bridges, who has turned bad. Johnny gets captured again. There's a revealing interchange between Bridges and Johnny: Bridges: "A man that's dreaming is half asleep." Johnny: "A man that doesn't dream is half dead." When the old outlaw says, "You think a lot of Troop," Johnny replies, "He gives me a lot to reach for." At one point, Johnny is given a foreboding choice by the ex-marshal when the posse approaches: "You're either with us or you're dead." Peggie Castle is not in the credits and does not appear in this episode.

Trivia: Lon Chaney Jr. was the son of silent film star Lon Chaney and had a long career playing burly villains and monsters. He (the son) was listed in the episode's credits as Lon Chaney. There was also a 1974 *Gunsmoke* episode titled "The Tarnished Badge," with Victor French as the dirty lawman.

Episode 136: "No Contest" February 4, 1962.
Starring John Russell, Peter Brown, and Peggie Castle. Featuring Richard Rogers (Jeff Allen), Dawn Wells (Elaine [Elly] Stratton), Guy Stockwell (Jib), Frank Watkins (Ames).

Directed by Irving J. Moore, Written by Berne Giler, Producer: Coles Trapnell, Supervising Producer: Jules Schermer, Director of Photography: Ralph Woolsey, Art Director: Carl Macauley, Film Editor: Robert B. Warwick, Jr., Sound: Everett A. Hughes, Music Editor: Theo W. Sebern, Set Decorator: Gene Redd, Assistant Director: Sam Schneider, Supervising Hair Stylist: Jean Burt Reilly.

Synopsis: Johnny's cousin from Boston visits Laramie; he looks like Billy the Kid.

Commentary: When the stage is arriving with the first kin Johnny has ever met as an adult, the marshal and Lily look very parental. Johnny sounds like his mentor when he speaks to his cousin about carrying a gun. Troop uses harsh physical tactics to teach the cousin a lesson, a lesson approved by Johnny.

Trivia: After playing parts in most of the Warner Bros. western and dramatic television series of the early 1960s, Dawn Wells had her most memorable role as Mary Ann Summers in *Gilligan's Island* (1964-67). Guy Stockwell, the brother of Dean Stockwell, was in over thirty movies and two hundred television productions. He co-starred in the television series *Adventures in Paradise* during its first season (1961-62), and had significant movie roles in remakes of Gary Cooper's *Beau Geste* (1966) and *The Plainsman* (1966).

Episode 137: "Change of Venue" February 7, 1962.
Starring John Russell, Peter Brown, and Philip Carey (Barron Shaw). Featuring Jan Shepard (Madelyn Chase), Robert Adler (Stagecoach Driver), Roy Barcroft (Luke Tennant). Larry Blake (Parker), Jack Williams (Clay).

Directed by Richard C. Sarafian, Written by Mark Rodgers, Producer: Coles Trapnell, Supervising Producer: Jules Schermer, Director of Photography: Bert Glennon, Art Director: Carl Macauley, Film Editor: Cliff Bell, Sound: Ross Owen, Music Editor: George E. Marsh, Set Decorator: Hoyle Barrett, Assistant Director: Eddie Prinz, Supervising Hair Stylist: Jean Burt Reilly.

Synopsis: Troop guards a remorseless killer being transported by stagecoach.

Commentary: Philip Carey is listed in the starring credits. He makes a memorable, jovial outlaw with no sense of decency. His philosophy is, "Cut down the odds, one by one, then sweep over what's left." For the first time since Lily became a part of his life, Troop is tempted by another woman. Peggie Castle is not listed in the credits and does not appear in this episode

Trivia: Carey played Captain Edward Parmalee in the series *Laredo*

(1965-67) co-starring Peter Brown. Before playing Texas tycoon Asa Buchanan on the daytime soap, *One Life to Live* (1984-2008), Carey acted in such westerns as *Springfield Rifle* (1952), *Calamity Jane* (1953), *The Man Behind the Gun* (1953), *Gun Fury* (1953), *The Nebraskan* (1953), and *Tonka* (1958). Jan Shepard guested on many television westerns during the late 1950s and early 1960s and appeared in two Elvis Presley movies, *King Creole* (1958) and *Paradise, Hawaiian Style* (1966). Dolores Hart, the Hollywood starlet who became a nun, is Shepard's goddaughter.

Episode 138: "The Hold-Out" February 18, 1962.
Starring John Russell, Peter Brown, and Peggie Castle. Featuring Arch Johnson (Logan), Larry Ward (Blake Stevens), Harry Cheshire (Judge Traeger), Addison Richards (Ben Thurston), Joseph Ruskin (Ed James), Tom Munroe (Bob Sherman).

Directed by Richard C. Sarafian, Teleplay by Anthony Spinner, Story by OCee Ritch, Producer: Jules Schermer, Director of Photography: Bert Glennon, Art Director: Carl Macauley, Film Editor: Harry Reynolds, Sound: Robert B. Lee, Music Editor: John Allyn, Jr., Set Decorator: Hal Overell, Assistant Director: Russ Saunders, Supervising Hair Stylist: Jean Burt Reilly.

Synopsis: An extortion gang in Laramie pressures the town council to fire Troop.

Commentary: A gang and its leader create a sinister threat for Troop's law and order regime in Laramie. Arch Johnson as the imposing Logan makes an excellent antagonist for Troop. Tension dominates this episode. Troop tells Logan, "I wear a star, not a halo. It's not inconceivable that I could be pushed into throwing that star away." Cheshire's judge again gives the marshal good advice. Peter Brown does well with perhaps his most dramatic scene in the series when he angrily attempts to persuade Ward's character to stand up against "The Vigilantes." The deputy is certainly now an adult. Peggie Castle is not listed in the credits and does not appear in this episode

Trivia: Larry Ward met producer Jules Schermer when he was attempting to sell Schermer a script. Schermer liked Ward's appearance and put him in this *Lawman* and then in the 1962 *Cheyenne* episode, "A Man Called Ragan," as a lawman named Marshal Frank Ragan. That worked out so well, Ward was soon staring in *The Dakotas* series (1963) as the same peace officer.

Episode 139: "The Barber" February 25, 1962.
Starring John Russell, Peter Brown, and Peggie Castle. Featuring Pitt Herbert (Sylvester [Sil] O'Toole), Wendell Holmes (Frank MacStrowd), Vinton Hayworth (Oren Slauson), Dan Sheridan (Jake), William Fawcett (Ed Carruthers), Gail Bonney (Mrs. Wilson), Owen Bush (Will Puffin), Frank Watkins (Hank Koop), George Greco (Ren Herbert).

Directed by Richard C. Sarafian, Written by John D.F. Black, Producer: Jules Schermer, Director of Photography: Bert Glennon, Art Director: Carl Macauley, Film Editor: Robert Jahns, Sound: Frank McWhorter, Music Editor: Charles Paley, Set Decorator: Hal Overell, Assistant Director: Russell Llewellyn, Supervising Hair Stylist: Jean Burt Reilly.

Synopsis: The new barber in town isn't exactly who he claims to be.

Commentary: The episode is perfectly balanced between a serious crime and "one of those days" silliness involving stolen long johns and toupees. Pitt Herbert's Sylvester O'Toole and his uniquely well-planned, ingenious heist offer a different type of antagonist and problem for Troop to contend with. Lily comes to the rescue again. Johnny's suspicions prove accurate. The episode features picturesque wide-angled, telescopic photography of Laramie when the barber opens his door. Johnny demonstrates his patented rolling dive move again.

Trivia: The new barber in town was played by Pitt Herbert, who resembled a cross between Arthur O'Connor, Jack Albertson, and Bob Hoskins. Herbert was a staple on television throughout the 1950s, 1960s, and 1970s, usually playing dapper little men who often stole his scenes.

THE EPISODES

Episode 140: "The Long Gun" March 4, 1962.
Starring John Russell, Peter Brown, Peggie Castle, and John Dehner (Ben Wyatt). Featuring George Dunn (Ed Love), Dan Sheridan (Jake), Grady Sutton (Ben Toomey), Buzz Henry (1st Bodeen Brother), Al Wyatt (2nd Bodeen Brother).

Written and Directed by Burt Kennedy, Producer: Jules Schermer, Director of Photography: Louis Jennings, Art Director: Carl Macauley, Film Editor: Robert B. Warwick, Jr., Sound: Robert B. Lee, Music Editor: Louis W. Gordon, Set Decorator: Hal Overell, Assistant Director: Eddie Prinz, Supervising Hair Stylist: Jean Burt Reilly.

Synopsis: A legendary marshal intends to ambush two outlaws whose brother he's killed.

Commentary: Troop again encounters a famous, veteran peacemaker who is having difficulty adjusting to growing old. The aged marshal's name is an obvious reference to Wyatt Earp. There's even an aside mentioning the Clantons, the cowboys Earp faced at the O.K. Corral: Troop: "Are you the same man who rode down the Clanton boys and faced them out one by one?" After Johnny sees a young outlaw buried, he states, "He was awfully young." Troop replies, "He was as old as his gun." The episode ends with perfect, terse dialogue between the two marshals, and a wonderful closing shot through the hotel window. John Dehner is listed under the starring credits for this episode.

Trivia: Dehner was an animator for the Walt Disney Studio and worked on *Fantasia* (1940) and *Bambi* (1942) before beginning his long acting career. For over forty years his tall stature and rich baritone voice added depth and emotions to the many good and bad men he portrayed in countless westerns, dramas, and comedies on the radio and on the big and small screens. Although his focus was more on serious roles, two of his most memorable contributions to westerns were his portrayal of the dishonest banker, John Bates, in *Maverick*'s classic 1958 episode, "Shady Deal at Sunny Acres," and his comedic narration of *The Hallelujah Trail* (1965). Burt Kennedy directed three other *Lawman* episodes during its final season, "The Wanted Man," "Sunday," and "Cort." Kennedy wrote the scripts for all of these episodes except "Cort." He penned the screenplays for several of the Budd Boetticher-Randolph Scott classic oaters, including *The Tall T*, (1957), *Ride Lonesome* (1959), and *Comanche Station* (1960). Kennedy then directed numerous notable westerns including *Welcome to Hard Times* (1967), *Support Your Local Sheriff* (1969), and *The War Wagon* (1967).

Episode 141: "Clootey Hutter" March 11, 1962.
Starring John Russell, Peter Brown, and Peggie Castle. Featuring Virginia Gregg (Clootey Hunter), Jack Elam (Paul Henry), Jack Hogan (Earl Henry), Justin Smith (Ed Cramer).

Directed by Richard C. Sarafian, Written by Robert Vincent Wright, Producer: Coles Trapnell, Supervising Producer: Jules Schermer, Director of Photography: Bert Glennon, Art Director: Carl Macauley, Film Editor: Noel L. Scott, Sound: B.F. Ryan, Music Editor: Donald K. Harris, Set Decorator: Hal Overell, Assistant Director: Eddie Prinz, Supervising Hair Stylist: Jean Burt Reilly.

Synopsis: A naive country woman who has a way with guns is accused of murder.

Commentary: Jack Elam is very endearing in this episode. Virginia Gregg is perfectly cast as the Calamity Jane-type frontierswoman. The rain adds to the dramatic tension. Justin Smith's Ed Cramer is an excellent blood-thirsty agitator. In his conversation with the deputy after Clootey demonstrates her way with guns, Cramer declares, "She ain't human." Johnny immediately replies, "How would you know?"

Trivia: Virginia Gregg was a radio and television character actress for over forty years. She was the voice of Mrs. Bates in *Psycho* (1960) and its two sequels. She could play all types of western women from dancehall girls to farmers' wives to outlaws. She was quoted in a 1959 newspaper interview, "When casting people have a call for a woman who looks like the wrath of God, I'm notified."

Episode 142: "Heritage of Hate" March 18 1962.
Starring John Russell, Peter Brown, and Peggie Castle. Featuring Kathie Browne (Laurie Kemper), Roy Roberts (John Kemper), William Joyce (Bill Fells), Frank Albertson (Henry Bildy), Harry Cheshire (Judge Traeger), Ken Mayer (Moss), Baynes Barron (Burns), Grace Albertson (Sarah Bildy), Jack Catron (Cowboy).

Directed by Robert B. Sinclair, Written by William Leicester, Producer: Coles Trapnell, Supervising Producer: Jules Schermer, Director of Photography: Bert Glennon, Art Director: Carl Macauley, Film Editor: Fred M. Bohanan, Sound: B.F. Ryan. Music Editor: Theo W. Sebern, Set Decorator: Hal Overell, Assistant Director: Eddie Prinz, Supervising Hair Stylist: Jean Burt Reilly.

Synopsis: A woman who killed her abusive husband and served a prison sentence for manslaughter is hounded by her former father-in-law.

Commentary: This is another storyline revolving around a stubborn, uncompromising father, in this case, Roberts' John Kemper, who refuses to recognize his son for what he actually was. In a conversation with the rigid, full-of-hate Kemper, Troop reveals his disdain for public opinion and his belief that some people change for the good: Kemper: "You know, people ain't going to like your attitude, marshal." Troop: "I'll take my chances." Kemper: "You know their kind; they never change." Troop: "They do if you give them a chance." The feel-good ending features the kindness of strangers and a husband reassuring his "chuckled headed wife who's pretty, awfully pretty."

Trivia: Handsome William Joyce looked like a thinner version of Clint Walker. Lovely Kathie Browne, who resembled Inge Stevens, guested in numerous television series during the 1960s and 1970s, and co-starred as Angie with Ralph Taeger in the series, *Hondo* (1967). She was married to actor Darren McGavin. The Bildy couple in the episode were a real life married couple, Frank and Grace Albertson.

Episode 143: "Mountain Man" March 25, 1962.
Starring John Russell, Peter Brown, and Peggie Castle. Featuring Med Flory (Lex Buckman). Dan Sheridan (Jake), William Fawcett (Barber), Rusty Wescoatt (Blacksmith), Emile Avery (Stage Coach Driver), Jack Shea (Wagoneer).

Director: Robert B. Sinclair, Written by Sheldon Stark, Producer: Coles Trapnell, Supervising Producer: Jules Schermer, Director of Photography: Bert Glennon, Art Director: Carl Macauley, Film Editor: Robert Jahns, Sound: M.A. Merrick, Music Editor: George E. Marsh, Set Decorator: Gene Redd, Assistant Director: Eddie Prinz, Supervising Hair Stylist: Jean Burt Reilly.

Synopsis: A mountain man arrives in Laramie and decides that he wants Lily for his bride.

Commentary: The plotline is similar to that of *Seven Brides for Seven Brothers* (1954) when Howard Keel's character goes to town in search of a wife. Peggie Castle has fun with Lily's reactions to the announcement that Buckner has decided to marry her: "Miss Lily, you're it!" and later, when he decides that the open spaces are more appealing than matrimony, "Don't you go grieving; you've still got him (gesturing toward the marshal)." In this, his third and last *Lawman* appearance, Med Flory is again extremely likeable and helps shape the storyline's lightness and warmth.

Trivia: In this episode, Johnny sang "The Streets of Laredo" while strumming on a guitar. Troop declared, "You have a good voice – for a deputy." Peter Brown was one of fifteen Warner Bros. television actors who performed on the 1959 album, *We Wish You a Merry Christmas*. Brown sang "Walking in a Winter Wonderland."

Episode 144: "The Bride" April 1, 1962.
Starring John Russell, Peter Brown, and Peggie Castle. Featuring Jo Morrow (Melanie Wells), William Mims (Frank Farnum), L.Q. Jones (Ollie Earnshaw), Dan Sheridan (Jake), Grady Sutton (Ben Toomey), Frank Scannell (Saul), Bob Terhune (Haw), Harry Strang (Ed Lecky).

THE EPISODES

Directed by Richard C. Sarafian, Teleplay by John Tomerlin, Story by Berne Giler, Producer: Jules Schermer, Director of Photography: Louis Jennings, Art Director: Carl Macauley, Film Editor: Harry Reynolds, Sound: Everett A. Hughes, Music Editor: Erma E. Levin. Set Decorator: Hal Overell, Assistant Director: Eddie Prinz, Supervising Hair Stylist: Jean Burt Reilly.

Synopsis: A rich, young rancher falls for a pretty newcomer to Laramie who isn't what she appears to be.

Commentary: The episode opens with uplifting music which is often played when the stagecoach rumbles into town. The scheme of bamboozling the rich rancher doesn't work out as planned. Mims makes a powerful adversary for the marshal. Grady Sutton is not in this episode even though he is listed in the credits.

Trivia: L.Q. Jones took his stage name from the character he played in his first movie, *Battle Cry* (1955). He was Cheyenne Bodie's partner Smitty in the first three *Cheyenne* episodes in 1955. Among his many movie and television appearances, Jones participated in five Sam Peckinpah westerns: *Ride the High Country* (1962), *Major Dundee* (1965), *The Wild Bunch* (1969), *The Ballad of Cable Hogue* (1970), and *Pat Garrett and Billy the Kid* (1973). Striking Jo Morrow co-starred with Michael Landon in *The Legend of Tom Dooley* (1959) and with Tony Young and Dan Duryea in *He Rides Tall* (1964). She stopped acting after the birth of a deaf daughter.

Episode 145: "The Wanted Man" April 8, 1962.
Starring John Russell and Peter Brown. Featuring Marie Windsor (Ann Jesse), Dick Foran (Frank Jesse), Alan Baxter (Joe Street), Jan Stine (Ben Jese), Ralph Moody (Doc Greer).

Written and Directed by Burt Kennedy. Producer: Jules Schermer, Director of Photography: Louis Jennings, Art Director: Carl Macauley, Film Editor: Noel L. Scott, Sound: Everett A. Hughes, Music

Editor: Charles Paley, Set Decorator: Gene Redd, Assistant Director: B.F. McEveety, Supervising Hair Stylist: Jean Burt Reilly.

Synopsis: A country woman about to give birth arrives in Laramie.

Commentary: Delivering the baby in a stable rings with symbolism. The rainy weather, resulting in mud everywhere, adds to the dark despondency of the production. Jan Stine does very well as the simple country boy who is wise in some ways: "Frank Jesse's wanted for a lot of things, Marshal, but there ain't none of them as bad as what he's done to his own." Troop's immaculate white hat gets dirty. The marshal displays two sides of his character in his angry, threatening interchange with the bounty hunter and his decision to look the other way to save two lives. Kudos to cinematographer Louis Jennings and director Burt Kennedy for the photography in this production. The shot of the livery from the viewpoint of the bounty hunter, the paralleled reaction shot of the father and son hearing the baby's cries, and the perfectly balanced, final shot of Troop, Johnny, and the doctor watching the wagon pull away are each memorable. Peggie Castle is not listed in the credits and does not appear in the episode.

Trivia: Marie Windsor played dozens of tough femme fatales, gun molls, and saloon gals; this softer and gentler role was a departure for her. Among the many westerns she co-starred in were John Wayne's *The Fighting Kentuckian* (1949), the cult *Outlaw Women* (1952), Lloyd Bridges' *The Tall Texan* (1953), and Randolph Scott's *The Bounty Hunter* (1954). This was the first *Lawman* episode aired at 10:30 to 11:00 on Sunday evenings.

Episode 146: "Sunday" April 15, 1962.
Starring John Russell, Peter Brown, Peggie Castle, and Andrew Duggan (Frank Boone). Featuring Richard Evans (Billy Deal), Greg Benedict (Jim Young), Dan Sheridan (Jake), Buzz Henry (Wid Young).

Written and Directed by Burt Kennedy, Producer: Jules Schermer,

Director of Photography: Bert Glennon, Art Director: Carl Macauley, Film Editor: Robert B. Warwick Jr., Sound: Everett A. Hughes, Music Editor: Theo W. Sebern, Set Decorator: John P. Austin, Assistant Director: B. F. McEveety, Supervising Hair Stylist: Jean Burt Reilly.

Synopsis: Frank Boone, an outlaw and old acquaintance of Troop, wants the marshal's prisoner so Boone can get amnesty in Montana.

Commentary: In the opening teaser, Troop is bringing a prisoner into the jail, shots are fired, and Troop declares, "Well, it's started," and the viewer is hooked. Johnny looks older. The tough conversation between Troop and Duggan's Boone, with the church organ's music in the background, is beautifully written and paced: "Short of it is, only thing that stands between me starting life clean over is you, Dan." The back story explains why the marshal will not compromise with Boone. As in *High Noon* (1952), the clock is another of the episode's characters. Andrew Duggan is listed under the starring credits for this episode

Trivia: In a career lasting over fifty years, Richard Evans usually portrayed men with either an attitude or a secret. He played an obnoxious juvenile delinquent in an earlier *Lawman*, "The Town Boys" (1960). He was the young college English professor, Paul Hanley, in twenty-six episodes of the television drama, *Peyton Place*, in 1965.

Episode 147: "The Youngest" April 22, 1962.
Starring John Russell, Peter Brown, and Peggie Castle, and Evan McCord (Jim Martin, Jr.). Featuring Olive Carey (Ma Martin), Tom Gilson (Sam Martin), Charlie Briggs (Darrel Martin), Dan Sheridan (Jake), Gene Roth (Jim Martin, Sr.).

Directed by Robert B. Sinclair, Teleplay by John Tomerlin and Eric Stone, Story by Eric Stone, Producer: Jules Schermer, Director of Photography: Louis Jennings, Art Director: Carl Macauley, Film Editor: Robert Jahns, Sound: Ross Owen, Music Editor: George E. Marsh, Set Decorator: Alfred E. Kegerris, Assistant Director: Dick L'Estrange, Supervising Hair Stylist: Jean Burt Reilly.

Synopsis: A forceful mother demands that her youngest son kill Marshal Troop.

Commentary: John Russell appears only in this episode briefly at the beginning and at the end, so Johnny is the one to confront the vengeful Martins. Johnny constantly demonstrates courage, resolve, and maturity. In his tough conversation with the youngest son revolving around who and what Ma Martin is, Johnny sounds like Marshal Dan Troop. In the final scene, Troop pays Johnny the ultimate compliment: "You did exactly right." Evan McCord is listed in the opening starring credits.

Trivia: Olive Carey, the widow of actor Harry Carey and the mother of Harry Carey Jr. gave up her acting career after she married in 1916 but later returned for a few movies in the 1930s including *Trader Horn* (1931). After her husband's death in 1947, she began playing strong-willed western woman like Mrs. Jorgensen in John Ford's *The Searchers* (1956) and Ma Clanton in Burt Lancaster's *Gunfight at the O.K. Corral* (1957).

Episode 148: "Cort" April 29, 1962.
Starring John Russell, Peter Brown, and Peggie Castle. Featuring Kevin Hagen (Cort Evers), Harry Carey, Jr. (Mitch Evers), Ralph Moody (Doc Jessup).

Directed by Burt Kennedy, Written by Anthony Spinner, Producer: Jules Schermer, Director of Photography: Willard Van der Veer, Art Director: Carl Macauley, Film Editor: Elbert K. Hollingsworth, Sound: Everett A. Hughes, Music Editor: John Allyn, Jr., Set Decorator: William L. Kuehl, Assistant Director: B.F. McEveety, Supervising Hair Stylist: Jean Burt Reilly.

Synopsis: A dying stranger intends to kill his brother to avenge the deaths of half a dozen soldiers during the Civil War.

Commentary: The six soldiers' deaths supposedly occurred ten years prior, but the Civil War ended in 1865, Troop became marshal of Laramie in 1879, and this is several years later. Excellent symbolic use of the church bells tolling as the stranger rides into town and the church's cross in the background at the climatic showdown. The ending is somehow both predictable and surprising.

Trivia: Harry Carey Jr. was a western fixture for over forty years, from *Red River* in 1948 to *Tombstone* in 1993. In between, he appeared in such John Ford classics as *3 Godfathers* (1948), *She Wore a Yellow Ribbon* (1949), *Wagon Master* (1950), *Rio Grande* (1950), and *The Searchers* (1956). The name Cort Evers is similar to Quirt Evans, John Wayne's character in *Angel and the Badman* (1947).

Episode 149: "The Doctor" May 6, 1962.
Starring John Russell and Peter Brown. Featuring Eloise Hardt (Cissy Lawson), Whit Bissell (Alexander Burrell), Charles Lane (Morris Weeks), Sherwood Price (Will Evans), I. Stanford Jolley (Ed Sims), Harry Strang (Randy Whedon), Lyle Latell (Sheriff Parker).

Directed by Gunther V. Fritsch, Teleplay by John D.F. Black and OCee Ritch, Story by OCee Ritch, Producer: Jules Schermer, Director of Photography: Bert Glennon, Art Director: Carl Macauley, Film Editor: Lloyd Nosler, Sound: Stanley Jones, Music Editor: Sam E. Levin Set Decorator: William L. Stevens, Assistant Director: B. F. McEveety, Supervising Hair Stylist: Jean Burt Reilly.

Synopsis: Taking a resistant material witness to trial by stagecoach, Troop comes across a variety of roadblocks.

Commentary: The storyline is reminiscent of John Ford's *Stagecoach* (1939), with a diverse group of passengers including an alcoholic doctor, an arrogant know-it-all, and a woman trying to get away from her past. The photography provides a sense of openness in the exterior stagecoach scenes. Peggie Castle is not in the credits and does not appear in this episode.

Trivia: Charles Lane played stern, uncompromising curmudgeons for almost seventy years. Two representative roles were his typing teacher, Mr. Woodruff, in Lucille Ball's *Miss Grant Takes Richmond* (1949) and his

Constable Locke in *The Music Man* (1962). Harry Strang, who played the stagecoach driver, was one of Hollywood's busiest bit players with over 500 acting credits, mostly uncredited, between 1930 and 1965. Perhaps his most memorable bit in movies was his tough trucker, Fred, who, touched by the kindness of a café waitress to the two Joad children, left her a generous tip in John Ford's *The Grapes of Wrath* (1940).

Episode 150: "The Man Behind the News" May 13. 1962.
Starring John Russell, Peter Brown, and Peggie Castle. Featuring Clinton Sundberg (Luther Boardman), Hal Baylor (Mort Peters), Harry Cheshire (Judge Traeger), Peggy Mondo (Flora), Bruce MacFarland (Townsman).

Directed by Robert B. Sinclair, Teleplay by John Tomerlin, Story by John Tomerlin and William Idelson, Producer: Coles Trapnell, Supervising Producer: Jules Schermer, Director of Photography: Bert Glennon, Art Director: Carl Macauley, Film Editor: Robert Crawford, Sound: Ross Owen, Music Editor: Norman Bennett, Set Decorator: Jack H. Ahearn, Assistant Director: Eddie Prinz, Supervising Hair Stylist: Jean Burt Reilly.

Synopsis: The new editor of the Laramie newspaper is stirring up trouble for Marshal Troop.

Commentary: An impressive, wide-angled opening scene of Laramie with the marshal walking across the street sets the stage for this episode. Troop comes into conflict with yet another editor of Laramie's "Free Press." Sundberg sounds like W.C. Fields. Johnny has a touch of lightness in his hair. Hal Baylor's Mort Peters, "a bear with a child's mind," is someone with whom the marshal exhibits great patience, a likeable fellow who turns deadly when drinking.

Trivia: Clinton Sundberg played courteous secondary characters who often had a hidden agenda and exhibited an attitude of superiority. A representative role was the suspicious Mike Fitzgerald in William Powell and Ann Blyth's *Mr. Peabody and the Mermaid* (1948).

THE EPISODES

Episode 151: "Get Out of Town" May 20, 1962.
Starring John Russell, Peter Brown, and Peggie Castle. Featuring Bill Williams (Jim Bushrod), Vinton Hayworth (Oren Slauson), Tim Graham (Amos Hall), Dan Sheridan (Jake), John Hubbard (Sy), Tom London (Pete), Art Stewart (Remmy).

Directed by Dick Benedict, Teleplay by John D.F. Black, Story by Leo Gordon and Paul Leslie Peil, Producer: Coles Trapnell, Supervising Producer: Jules Schermer, Director of Photography: Bert Glennon, Art Director: Carl Macauley, Film Editor: John Hall, Sound: B.F. Ryan, Music Editor: Sam E. Levin, Set Decorator: William L. Kuehl, Assistant Director: Eddie Prinz, Supervising Hair Stylist: Jean Burt Reilly.

Synopsis: A man with a shady past intends to open a saloon in Laramie.

Commentary: Tim Graham's character's fun-loving but extremely moral old-timer steals the show. Troop's nose for possible conflict and unrest – "Trouble's coming and I've got to head it off" – holds true. Amos's slant on Troop is accurate and succinct: "Dan, you're a good lawman. You're conscientious and you're fair." The final scene features Troop and Johnny walking the street as equals.

Trivia: Bill Williams played the title role in the western series, *The Adventures of Kit Carson* (1951-55). He was married to Barbara Hale, *Perry Mason's* Della Street, and was the father of William Katt, the star of television's *The Greatest American Hero* (1981-83).

Episode 152: "The Actor" May 27, 1962.
Starring John Russell, Peter Brown, and Peggie Castle. Featuring John Carradine (Geoffrey Hendon), Mary Anderson (Martha Carson), Dan Sheridan (Jake), Warren Kemmerling (Bill Carson), Harry Harvey Sr. (Dr. Wilson), Ray Mayo (George Carson), Harry Seymour (Piano Player).

Directed by Richard C. Sarafian, Written by Richard Matheson, Producer: Jules Schermer, Director of Photography: Robert Gough, Art Director: Carl Macauley, Film Editor: Lloyd Nosler, Sound: Gary Harris,

Music Editor: Joe Inge, Set Decorator: Hal Overell, Assistant Director: Sergei Petschnikoff, Supervising Hair Stylist: Jean Burt Reilly.

Synopsis: An old actor staggers into "The Birdcage Saloon" followed by trouble.

Commentary: Carradine plays himself, a veteran thespian using his charisma to entertain, to mesmerize, and to cause problems. Lily exhibits her usual beauty, charm, and kindness. The ending is as aptly dramatic as the player.

Trivia: John Carradine, with his powerful voice and presence, played countless villains in his long career but also was Jim Casey in *The Grapes of Wrath* (1940), the Mormon scout Porter in *Brigham Young – Frontiersman* (1940), and Bret Harte in *The Adventures of Mark Twain* (1944). He portrayed the gambler Hatfield in *Stagecoach* (1939) and fathered three acting sons: David, Keith, and Robert who were all in *The Long Riders* (1980).

Episode 153: "Explosion" June 3, 1962.
Starring John Russell, Peter Brown, Peggie Castle, and Gary Vinson (Jess Billings). Featuring Miranda Jones (Bobbie Desmond), Denver Pyle (Sam Brackett), John Qualen (Doc Shay), Milton Parsons (Mr. Murdock), Gil Rankin (Paul Dales), Blossom Rock (Mrs. Murdock).

Directed by Richard C. Sarafian, Written by Rik Vollaerts, Producer: Coles Trapnell, Supervising Producer: Jules Schermer, Director of Photography: Bert Glennon, Art Director: Carl Macauley, Film Editor: Lloyd Nostler, Sound: M.A. Merrick, Music Editor: Charles Paley, Set Decorator: Hoyle Barrett, Assistant Director: Eddie Prinz, Supervising Hair Stylist: Jean Burt Reilly.

Synopsis: A brain-injured cowboy murders the owners of the ranch he rides for.

Commentary: Troop, Johnny, and Lily show their sensitivity and compassion in this episode attempting to protect yet another outsider from mob violence. The doctor's diagnosis of brain-damage from a beating affecting behavior is novel for a television western of this time. Denver Pyle's character is another strong, driven adversary whom the marshal is forced to face. Gary Vinson is listed in the opening starring credits for this episode.

Trivia: Gary Vinson was a boyish-faced actor who was the son of talent scout Joe Vincent. Warner Bros. built up Vinson in the early 1960s, but he never made it as a leading man. He played the bumbling office boy, Chris Higbee, in Warner Bros. *The Roaring Twenties* (1960-61) and later, George Christopher, in all 138 *McHale's Navy* episodes (1962-66), and Sheriff Harold Sikes in *Pistols 'n' Petticoats* (1967-68). He committed suicide at the age of forty-seven in 1984.

Episode 154: "Jailbreak" June 10, 1962.
Starring John Russell, Peter Brown, and Peter Breck (Pete Bole), Featuring Pamela Austin (Little Britches), James Griffith (Heracles Snead), Frank Ferguson (Howard Callaghan), Mickey Simpson (Murph), Dee Woolem (Man of the Street).

Directed by Paul Landres, Teleplay by John D.F. Black and Wells Root, Story by Coles Trapnell and Don Tait. Producer: Coles Trapnell, Director of Photography: Bert Glennon, Art Director: Carl Macauley, Film Editor: Milt Kleinberg, Sound: B.F. Ryan, Music Editor: Erma E. Levin, Set Decorator: Hoyle Barrett, Assistant Director: B.F. McEveety, Supervising Hair Stylist: Jean Burt Reilly.

Synopsis: A young woman will stop at nothing to free her boyfriend from jail.

Commentary: Johnny is forced to deal with a whirlwind of a girl. Breck's outlaw has no redeeming traits. Griffith plays a different type of mastermind criminal who saves a sheriff's life and is rewarded in the script by escaping. Humor and drama are balanced throughout the episode with a comic scene at the end. Peggie Castle is not in the credits and does not appear in this episode. Peter Breck is in the opening starring credits.

Trivia: James Griffith was a multi-talented man. In addition to playing scores of villains in films and television, he played saxophone in the Spike Jones band and wrote the screenplays for the westerns *Shalako* (1968) and *Catlow* (1971).

Episode 155: "The Unmasked" June 17, 1962.
Starring John Russell, Peter Brown, and Peggie Castle. Featuring Angela Greene (Marian Brockwell), Dabbs Greer (Joe Brockwell), Jack Albertson (Doc Peters), Vinton Hayworth (Oren Slauson), Barry Atwater (Carter Banks), Charles Maxwell (Samuel Davidson), Dan Sheridan (Jake), Henry Rowland (Riggs), Ted White (Barton).

Directed by Robert B. Sinclair, Written by Charles B. Smith, Producer: Coles Trapnell, Director of Photography: Bert Glennon, Art Director: Carl Macauley, Film Editor: William W. Moore, Sound: B.F. Ryan, Music Editor: Louis W. Gordon, Set Decorator: William L. Kuehl, Assistant Director: Dick L'Estrange, Supervising Hair Stylist: Jean Burt Reilly.

Synopsis: Two tough southerners arrive in Laramie allegedly searching for a cousin.

Commentary: The musical background to this episode includes such standards as "Oh, Susanna," "The Big Rock Candy Mountain," "Little Brown Jug," and "Pop Goes the Weasel." The bad guys' plot involves a cunning and surprising hook. Excellent use of shadows in the photography. Another time discrepancy: Greer's character states that he shot John Wilkes Booth six years previously. Booth was shot (or burned to death) in 1865, and this episode of *Lawman* would have taken place in the early 1880s. When Johnny voices frustration due to not being able to comprehend one man hiring another man to kill someone, Troop replies, "You never will, Johnny, and that's part of the job. You can't understand them all. Sometimes it's better that way."

Trivia: Irish-born Angela Greene was a former "Miss Rheingold" and John Robert Powers model who had a thirty-year career in the movies and television. She played Tess Trueheart in seven 1950 episodes of the early television *Dick Tracy* series (1950-52) and had one of her biggest roles in Martin and Lewis' *At War with the Army* (1950).

Episode 156: "The Witness" June 24, 1962.
Starring John Russell, Peter Brown, and Peggie Castle. Featuring John Agar (Jim Martin), Jay Novello (Beebee), Morgan Woodward (Nathan Adams), Sarah Selby (Anna Prentiss), Dan Sheridan (Jake Summers), Harry Cheshire (Judge Traeger), Bruce MacFarland (Clerk), Don Dillaway (Judd).

Directed by Gunther V. Fritsch, Written by Jack Hawn, Producer: Coles Trapnell, Director of Photography: Willard Van der Veer, Art Director: Carl Macauley, Film Editor: Harry Reynolds, Sound: Samuel F. Goode, Music Editor: Donald K. Harris, Set Decorator: Gene Redd, Assistant Director: Richard L'Estrange, Supervising Hair Stylist: Jean Burt Reilly.

Synopsis: A woman is killed and her sister, with the help of a sketch artist, identifies the murderer as a friend of Troop's.

Commentary: Morgan Woodward makes an excellent final adversary for the marshal. As Troop and Johnny have done throughout the series, they must deduce the facts beyond lies and deceptions and also confront irrational anger even if they have to risk their lives to do so. This episode once again reveals Marshal Dan Troop's dichotomies: He is a hardnosed force of nature who is also compassionate and understanding about others' fragilities. In addition, he is very intelligent as he does some cross-examining of his own. One of Troop and Johnny's final dialogues sums up their work: Troop: "There's only one way to stop gunplay." Johnny: "I know, find the real killer."

Trivia: Morgan Woodward played Wyatt Earp's buddy, Shotgun Gibbs, in eighty-one episodes of *The Life and Legend of Wyatt Earp* between 1958 and 1961. His rugged, fuming face helped him get numerous parts as outlaws. Perhaps his most famous role was as the chain-gang overseer in *Cool Hand Luke* (1967). John Agar will always be remembered for his two young cavalry officers in the John Ford cavalry films, *Fort Apache* (1948) and *She Wore a Yellow Ribbon* (1949).

Recollections

Seven of the following recollections of *Lawman* are based on the author's phone interviews during the spring and summer of 2019. The reminiscences of Larry Blake's son, Michael F. Blake, were shared with the author via Facebook Messenger during the same period.

****

Larry Blake played Chuck Slade in the episode, "The Stranger," originally aired on January 17, 1960; Jennings in "The Go-Between" originally aired on September 25, 1960; Mr. Parker in "The Juror" originally aired on September 24, 1961; and Mr. Parker in "Change of Venue" originally aired on February 7, 1962. He also did an uncredited voice-over for Jack Lomas' Jess Brubaker character in "Riding Shotgun" originally aired on April 19, 1959.

Larry Blake
(Gifted to the Author by Michael F. Blake)

Michael F. Blake: "I was very young when Dad did the shows. I do remember watching some of them, and Dad brought home an autographed photo of John Russell – I wish I had it!

One episode that has stayed with me for almost 60 years was the one where Dan is in a well and can't get out. ['The Stalker' (1962)]."

"Most episodes were done in two to three days. Dad liked Russell, although he thought Peter Brown was a bit full of himself. Everything Dad did was filmed on the Warner Bros. lot, no locations at all. The studio had an area, 'The Jungle,' they'd use for exterior scenes away from the town. They brought in various fake rock formations and fake trees to dress up the area."

"Another episode I remember about *Lawman* was "Riding Shotgun" (1959). My dad is NOT in it, although he did get residuals for the episode. About two years ago, I watched it and realized what happened. Actor Jack Lomas, who was a good friend of my dad, played Jess Brubaker in that episode. Well, Lomas died on May 12, 1959. The episode aired on April 19. Well, my dad dubbed Lomas' voice for scenes in that episode. I do not know what Lomas died of, but wonder if he could not do his own dubbing for the episode and they had my dad step in. It was quite common in those days and through today that sometimes actors would have to re-dub their dialogue from outside scenes due to birds, cars, planes, etc."

"That's about all I can tell you about my dad working on the show. To him it was a job, usually working with people he liked, so coming home he'd say he had a fun day."

****

Robert Colbert played Breen in "The Locket" originally aired on January 7, 1962.

Robert Colbert
(Gifted to the Author by Robert Colbert)

"Peter [Brown] and I shared a house together for a year. He was very dedicated to his [acting] craft. He was constantly working at it. He was a good performer."

"Actor-director Marc Lawrence was a good friend; a talented and colorful guy."

"Although we [actors] bounced around from series to series, the crew, the wranglers, and the grips, usually remained with one show."

"Even though all of our [Warner Bros.] series were quickly produced on an assembly line basis and the same scripts were done over and over with no changes (they had this wax duplicator in which producers simply took an old script and substituted the name of another show), a lot of quality shows resulted thanks to the professionalism of the cast and crew."

****

Michael Dante played Jack McCall in "The Captives" originally aired on January 11, 1959:

Michael Dante
(Gifted to the Author by Michael Dante)

"Even though Warner Bros. was making all these series concurrently, there was no sense of rush. Everything appeared well-organized."

"The show had conscientious writers who wrote to satisfy the actors. The actors weren't wasted sitting around; you don't want unhappy actors."

"Both John Russell and Peter Brown knew what they were doing; they were well-prepared. Peter was a good actor, sincere and honest in his portrayals. You could always trust John to do a professional job in all of his scenes. Both were excellent in depicting two men staking their lives to serve and protect."

"Many of the Warner Bros. storylines were similar. Every time I saw a Warner Bros. script, it looked familiar."

"*Lawman* was special because it had no gimmicks, the plots were tight, and the dialogue didn't wander."

"Warner Bros. pushed us to work-work-work. One year I did fifteen TV shows plus three films!"

"The secret of a successful cowboy: The right hat, the right horse, and a good quality holster and pistol."

[With regard to his one *Lawman* episode, "The Captives"], "Stuart Heisler directed it. He was a good no-nonsense director, a real pro who was a caring individual. A few years later, I was in a show and Stuart wrote me a complimentary letter praising my work. That was rare in the industry."

"It was great to work with Edgar Buchanan with his distinctive voice."

"I really enjoyed playing Wild Bill's killer, Jack McCall. It gave me the chance to get my teeth into a role, show some versatility, and get away from typecasting. It was great to portray a dark character and explore what kind of soul he had, what element made him so one-sided, so evil, a killer in his soul."

******

Although he never appeared in a *Lawman* episode, Will Hutchins who starred in the Warner Bros. western series *Sugarfoot* from 1957 to 1961, was very familiar with the show. John Russell and Peter Brown were his good friends, and Hutchins worked with both actors in several productions.

Will Hutchins
(The Doug Abbott Collection)

"Peter Brown and Sammy Davis Jr. were famously fast with their draw – yep, and the dance girls were even faster. I was fast – but I cheated; before a gunfight, I'd pull the hammer back a notch to get one-up on the boys. One time I was too fast – I shot myself in the foot. That smarted. So did the tetanus shot."

"We Warner Bros. cowpokes never left the backlot. We shot everything either in indoor sets or on the backlot, which had been transformed into a jungle for the 1956 Alan Ladd movie *Santiago*. So, Warner Bros. television's Wild West exteriors were filmed on a football field-sized area landscaped with South American trees, bushes, and plants mixed with some huge fake plastic rocks and boulders thrown in."

"Actor-director Marc Lawrence was Hollywood's gangster par excellence. He played so many villains and outlaws named Lefty that they called him a Commie."

"It wasn't too cramped making those Warner Bros. series simultaneously and in close quarters. I'd be doing a quiet, romantic *Sugarfoot* scene with a pretty girl and suddenly, there's a loud *Lawman* shoot-out or a noisy posse chasing one of the Maverick brothers or a raucous *Cheyenne* saloon free-for-all ruining the moment."

"John Russell and Peter Brown were diligent professionals who made up a good team. They usually appeared serious in the show, but off camera they could be pretty funny. John especially could keep a straight face while he was ribbing you and pulling your leg."

****

Joyce Meadows played Elfreida Detweiler in "Detweiler's Kid" originally aired on February 26, 1961. She also played Barbara Harris in "The Cold One" originally aired on November 12, 1961.

Joyce Meadows
(Gifted to the Author by Joyce Meadows)

"There was good rapport between John Russell and Peter Brown. There was absolutely no rivalry; Peter knew he was second banana to John. Peter was a good spontaneous actor who had a beautiful way of listening."

"There was a scene in 'Detweiler's Kid' when I was supposed to do a fast draw. I didn't really know anything about guns and got very nervous about doing the scene. I was supposed to shoot bullets but I was sweating bullets. Finally, a friendly wrangler told me to draw slowly and they'd speed up my draw. That's exactly what they did."

"I loved working with Chad Everett in 'Detweiler's Kid.' Chad and I were old friends."

"At the conclusion of 'The Cold One,' I had a very dramatic scene that I carried off. I received a lot of compliments. Several people told me that it brought tears to their eyes."

"I may have looked like the 'leading lady type,' but inside I was always a character actor. I didn't plan it that way; it was a gift from God."

****

Jan Shepard played Madelyn Chase in "Change of Venue" originally aired on February 7, 1962.

(Gifted to the Author by Jan Shepard)

"I was double dating with my good friend, actress Valerie Allen, in late 1961. She looked a lot like Ava Garner and later married Troy Donahue. Anyway, the guy she was dating, Dick Sarafian, complimented me on my cheekbones. I knew he was a director for *Lawman* and so I immediately responded, 'So get me a job on the show.' He did."

"John Russell was very professional. He was a delicious-looking man; it looked like his clothes were glued onto him like an outer skin. And his hat – it looked more Spanish than western – added to his look."

"I loved movies and television photographed in black and white. It caught and held the drama,"

"Phil Carey was a very nice man. In the episode, there was a scene when we were in a cabin together. I remember that we worked late into Friday evening. On Saturday, I turned on the TV to hear that some huge crane broke and fell down exactly where we were in that building."

****

Roberta Shore played Millie Cotton/Johnson in "Owny O'Reilly, Esquire" originally aired on October 15, 1961.

Roberta Shore
(Gifted to the Author by Roberta Shore)

"What I remember most about that episode was singing the song 'Waiting for Me' in Lily's saloon with my vocal coach, Sy Miller, playing the piano. It was Sy who co-wrote the hymn, 'Let There Be Peace on Earth.'"

"Joel Grey was very nice and just slightly taller than me."

"Peter Brown was quite self-assured. He looked great in his tight-tight jeans."

"It cracked me up that in the episode, Joel described my character as 'six-foot eight with a voice like Niagara Falls.'"

"The episode was cute in the way Joel and I were pictured as naive adolescents making our way in an adult world."

****

Olive Sturgess played Wanda in "The Huntress" originally aired on May 3, 1959.

Olive Sturgess
(Gifted to the Author by Olive Sturgess)

"I'm only 5' 2 and because of this I've made lots of TV shows being romanced by shorter men. I did a *Wagon Train* episode once titled 'Wagons Ho!' with Mickey Rooney and I was taller than him! It was fun to be dwarfed by John and Peter."

"In those days they had great stories. Mary Tyler Moore said it exactly right in a *Hollywood Reporter* interview: 'Writing for television today is like writing shorthand. There's no depth to anything. We used to have stories that had a beginning, middle, and an end, that made you feel good about watching them. Not those terrible shallow shows of today. We had stories that were genuine, stories of the West done with humor or drama and romance. A good show you looked forward to seeing. You really felt good when you saw the TV shows of those days.' And when you see them today, they've aged wonderfully."

"Before Peter Brown began to star in *Lawman*, he and I co-starred in a *Cheyenne* episode called 'Renegades.' He played a soldier with issues and I played the colonel's daughter. It was such a pleasure to act with a tall romantic partner."

"I knew Peter better than John because of 'Renegades,' but both he and John Russell were excellent actors, very professional, and dedicated to making *Lawman* as good as they could make it."

Lawman Miscellanea

1. NIELSEN RATINGS: During its first season (1958-59), *Lawman* received a Nielsen rating of #27 of the top thirty shows on television in the United States. During its second season (1959-60), it received a rating of #15, ahead of *Cheyenne*, *Maverick*, and *The Life and Legend of Wyatt Earp*. During its third season (1960-61), it received a rating of #26. These ratings were impressive because *Lawman* was up against the second half of CBS's popular *The Ed Sullivan Show*. During its fourth and final season (1961-62), when *Maverick* was no longer slotted before it and NBC provided stiffer competition with *Walt Disney's Wonderful World of Color* and *Car 54 Where are You?*, *Lawman* was not listed in the top thirty shows.

2. AN EARLY ENCOUNTER: In 1949, two young actors did a screen-test for 20th Century-Fox, reading scenes from *Dinner at Eight*. The handsome twenty-eight year-old actor was John Russell. The pretty twenty-one year-old actress was Peggie Castle. They didn't work together again until *Lawman* ten years later in 1959.

3. COMICS: There were eleven *Lawman* comic books published by Dell and drawn by Don Spiegel between 1958 and 1962. Each consisted of two stories, a colored photograph of Marshal Dan Troop (John Russell) and Deputy Johnny McKay (Peter Brown) on the cover, and several pages of non-*Lawman* western filler stories. Each thirty-six-page issue cost fifteen cents.

4. *WHEN THE WEST WAS FUN*: In 1979, John Russell and Peter Brown appeared in the television show, *When the West Was Fun: A Western Reunion*, a fifty minute television special reuniting many of the TV cowboy stars of the 1950s and 1960s. Glenn Ford was the host, the setting was a western saloon, and there were numerous clips and humorous interchanges. Nine actors who guested on *Lawman* appeared: Iron Eyes Cody, James Drury, Harry Lauter, Doug McClure, Slim Pickens, Denver Pyle, Lee Van Cleef, Bill Williams, and Tony Young. The show concluded with everyone joining in with Roy Rogers and Dale Evans and singing "Happy Trails."

5. THE HOLLYWOOD WALK OF FAME: For her contributions to the television industry, Peggie Castle was awarded a star on the Hollywood Walk of Fame on Hollywood Boulevard. It was dedicated on February 8, 1960. Neither John Russell nor Peter Brown was so honored.

6. THE GOLDEN BOOT AWARD: John Russell in 1987 and Peter Brown in 2002 each received a Golden Boot Award. This award honored actors, actresses and production staff who made memorable contributions to movie and television westerns. Cowboy supporting-actor Pat Buttram originated the idea; the awards were presented annually from 1983 until 2007.

7. THE BACKLOT: All of the *Lawman* episodes were filmed at the Warner backlot, Stage 28, Warner Bros. Burbank Studios, 4000 Warner Boulevard, Burbank, California. "Laramie Street" was built in 1958 in an area alongside the studio's southeastern border known as "The Jungle." Encompassing numerous streets and buildings, the location was host not only to *Lawman* but to the other Warner Bros. western series when a

town scene was needed. Exteriors for the other series were occasionally shot at Warner's 2,800 acre Calabasas studio ranch, but the *Lawman* scenes were either shot on "Laramie Street" or stock footage was used.

8. *LAWMAN* THEME SONG: Jerry Livingston wrote the music and Mack David wrote the lyrics to the *Lawman's* theme song. The fourth stanza was never played on the show:

"The Lawman came with the sun
There was a job to be done
And so they sent for the badge and the gun
Of the Lawman"

"And as he silently rode
Where evil violently flowed
They knew he'd live or die by the code
Of the Lawman"

"A man who rides all alone
And all that he'll ever own
Is just a badge and a gun and he's known
As the Lawman"

"Till folks could walk thru streets unafraid
He would fight for what's right undismayed
When his job was complete he'd travel on
Lawman"

9. THE *LAWMAN'S* CREED: "The *Lawman's* Creed" was a sixty-second commercial for the series. It was first broadcast on ABC-TV's *Disneyland* episode, "The Nine Lives of Elfego Baca," on September 2, 1960. The creed was, "Draw quick or die." It currently can be seen on YouTube.

10. *TV GUIDE* COVER: John Russell was on the cover of *TV Guide* for its #330, July 25-31, 1959 issue. The story about him was titled, "*Lawman's* John Russell – All the Expression of a Rock."

11. NUMBER OF EPISODES: The first season of *Lawman* (1958-59) had thirty-nine episodes. The second season (1959-60) had thirty-seven episodes, the third season (1960-61) had thirty-nine episodes, and the fourth and final season (1961-62) had forty-one.

12. *LAWMAN* DVD SETS: Four DVD sets of *Lawman* are currently available from Warner Home Video. They became available to the public on July 7, 2015, August 25, 2015, December 1, 2016, and February 2, 2016 respectively. Each consists of five discs and thirty-nine episodes.

13. *LAWMAN* SITE ON FACEBOOK: In December 2013, Nancy Dale created Facebook's *Lawman* TV Series Fan Group and Facebook's John Russell Fan Group. As of October 1, 2019, there were over 950 active, passionate participants in the Lawman Group and over 580 members of the John Russell Group.

14. FAST DRAWS: Peter Brown and John Russell worked with Arvo Ojala ("The Gun Wizard") and Andy Anderson ("King of the Fast Draw") to improve and perfect their gunplay. During the run of *Lawman*, Brown wore an Ojala gun rig and later an Anderson "Walk and Draw" rig. There has always been speculation as to who was the fastest draw of all the Hollywood actors; among those considered were Brown, Sammy Davis Jr., James Arness, Glenn Ford, and Jerry Lewis.

15. *LAWMAN* MERCHANDISE: During the four-year run of *Lawman*, fans were offered the opportunity to purchase a variety of merchandise. In addition to the comics discussed above, other available products during the 1958-62 run of the show included lunch boxes, thermoses, Hartland figures, arcade cards, boots, puzzles, holsters, cap pistols, and toy rifles.

Epilogue

The last original *Lawman* episode, "The Witness," was aired on June 24, 1962. Reruns were broadcast throughout the summer and early fall until October 2, 1962.

There were several reasons why the show was cancelled. The dozens of westerns available on television during the late 1950s and early 1960s oversaturated the market. There was a movement against the violence inherent in the western genre. As writer Richard West suggested in his *Television Westerns*, "Heroes became passé – or at least heroes who rode horses and tamed the West." According to Peter Brown, "ABC was infatuated with movies on television, prime-time television. They wanted a two-hour run on Sunday nights." Beginning on April 8, 1962, *Lawman's* time slot was switched to the undesirable time of 10:30 to 11:00 on Sunday evenings. The writing was on the wall.

Lawman was the apex of the three stars' careers. After the series, each – in different degrees – experienced disappointments and misfortunes in their professional and personal lives.

After the show ended in 1962, Warner Bros. did not renew John Russell's contract and although Russell did work guesting in television westerns and dramas and playing supporting roles in occasional western movies (usually as a villain), he never again received star billing. Perhaps his most memorable post-*Lawman* role was Stockdale, the corrupt marshal in Clint Eastwood's *Pale Rider* (1985). Gary Yoggy, author of *Riding the Video Range: The Rise and Fall of the Western on Television*, describes Stockdale as "particularly chilling, a look at Dan Troop if he had changed sides in his later years." After a lingering illness, John Russell died of emphysema at the age of seventy on January 19, 1991.

Although he never became a major movie star, Peter Brown had a busy acting career after *Lawman* including co-starring in another television western series, NBC-TV's *Laredo* from 1965-67. He acted in over eighty movies and television shows and played Dr. Greg Peters in twenty-five episodes of *Days of our Lives* between 1972 and 1979 and Blake Hayes in 104 episodes of *The Bold and the Beautiful* in 1991 and 1992. He was married five times. Peter Brown died on March 21, 2016 at the age of eighty of Parkinson's disease.

After *Lawman* was cancelled in 1962, Peggie Castle had only one more acting credit, guesting on the western series, *The Virginian*, in the episode, "Morgan Starr," in 1966. During the 1960s and early 1970s she became an alcoholic and couldn't get work as an actress. She died on August 10, 1973 at the age of forty-five of cirrhosis of the liver and a heart condition.

Robert Malsbary, co-author of *Warner Bros. Television*, maintained that *Lawman* was "a good show to the end, " and added, "but Marshal Troop [and John Russell] learned that being good and dedicated to one's job does not make one immune to the blazing guns of Nielson."

Recommended Readings

Aaker, Everett. *Television Western Players of the Fifties.* Jefferson, NC: McFarland, 1997.

Abbott, Doug. *Television Westerns in Black and White.* Blurb Books, 2011.

Abbott, Doug and Jackson, Ronald. *50 Years of the Television Western.* Bloomington, IN: AuthorHouse, 2008; updated hardcover edition published by Blurb Books, 2012.

Anderson, Christopher. *Hollywood TV: The Studio System in the Fifties.* Austin, TX: University of Texas Press, 1994.

Barabas, SuzAnne and Barabas, Gabor. *Gunsmoke: A Complete History and Analysis of the Legendary Broadcast Series.* Jefferson, NC: McFarland, 1990.

Bianculli, David. *The Platinum Age of Television.* New York, NY: Doubleday, 2016.

Brown, Peter. *The Fastest Gun in Hollywood: The Life Story of Peter Brown.* Fort Worth, TX: Wild Horse Press, 2013.

Garner, James and Winokur, Jon. *The Garner Files.* New York: Simon & Schuster, 2011.

Grams, Martin and Rayburn, Leo. *The Have Gun – Will Travel Companion.* OTR Publishing, 2000.

Hardy, Phil. *The Western.* New York: William Morrow and Company, 1983.

Jackson, Ronald. *Classic TV Westerns: A Pictorial History.* Secaucus, NJ:

Carol Publishing, 1994.

Lentz, Harris M. III. *Television Westerns: Episode Guide*. Jefferson, NC: McFarland, 2012.

Levy, Bill. *Lest We Forget: The John Ford Stock Company*. Albany, GA: BearManor Media, 2013.

Magers, Boyd. *A Gathering of Guns: 50 Years of the TV Western*. Albuquerque, NM: Western Clippings, 2017.

_____. *So You Wanna See Cowboy Stuff? The Western Movie/TV Tour Guide*.

Madison, NC: Empire Publishing, 2003.

_____. "Western Clippings" bi-monthly western film newsletter.

Miller, Leo O. *The Great Cowboy Stars of Movies and Television*. New Rochelle, NY: Arlington House, 1979.

Parks, Rita. *The Western Hero in Film and Television: Mass Media Mythology*. Ann Arbor. MI: UMI Research Press, 1982.

Summers, Neil and Crowley, Roger M. *The Official TV Western Round-Up Book*. Vienna, WV: The Old West Shop Publishing, 2002.

Thomas, Bob. *Clown Prince of Hollywood: The Antic Life of Jack L. Warner*. New York: McGraw Hill, 1990.

West, Richard. *Television Westerns: Major and Minor Series, 1946-1978*. Jefferson, NC: McFarland, 1999.

Whittington, Harry. *Trouble Rides Tall, Cross the Red Creek, Desert Stake-Out* with an Introduction by David Laurence Wilson. Eureka, CA: Stark House Press, 2016.

Wooley, Lynn, Malsbary, Robert W., and Strange, Robert G. *Warner Bros. Television*. Jefferson, NC: McFarland, 1985.

Vahimagi, Tise. "Television Westerns." *The BFI Companion to the Western*, edited by Edward Buscombe. New York, NY: Plenum Publishing, 1988.

Yoggy, Gary A. *Riding the Video Range: The Rise and Fall of the Western on Television*. Jefferson, NC: McFarland, 1995.

Index

A **bold-faced** page number indicates a photograph of the subject.

1941, 93
"9:05 to North Platte" (*Lawman* episode), 76
100 Rifles, 45
77 Sunset Strip, 59, 64, 101, 146
3 Godfathers, 161

A
Abbott and Costello Show, The, 53
Abilene Town, 49
Ace in the Hole, 141
Aces of Action, 53
"Actor, The" (*Lawman* episode), **31**, 163
Adler, Robert, 150
Adventures in Paradise, 150
Adventures of Kit Carson, The, 163
Adventures of Mark Twain, The, 164
Adventures of Ozzie and Harriet, The, 121, 136, 145
Adventures of Red Ryder, 63
Adventures of Rin Tin Tin, The (TV series), 107
Adventures of Robin Hood, The, 80
Adventures of Robin Hood, The (TV series), 81
Adventures of Young Indiana Jones: Hollywood Follies, The (TV movie), 125

Affliction, 80
Agar, John, 20, 167
Ahearn, Jack, H., 124, 126, 147, 162
Ahn, Philip, 44
Alaskans, The, 39, 46, 59
Albertson, Frank, 38, 62, 153, 155
Albertson, Grace, 155,
Albertson, Jack, 152, 166
Alcaide, Chris, 77, 130
Alderson, John, 77, 78
Alfred Hitchcock Presents, 111
All About Eve, 113
All the King's Men (movie), 44
Allen, Corey, 142
Allison, Jean, 55
Allman, Sheldon, 112, 128, 129
Allyn, John, Jr., 84, 92, 103, 113, 124, 134, 144, 151, 160
Althouse, Charles, 72, 73, 78, 118
Altman, Robert, 111
Alzamora, Armand, 148
Anders, Luana, 96
Anderson, Anne, 64
Anderson, James, 104, 128
Anderson, John, 88, 116, 117
Anderson, Mary, 163
Anderson, Wesley, 41, 58, 60, 95
Andy Griffith Show, The, 40
Angel, Heather, 123, 124
Angel and the Badman (1947), 161
"Angry Sky, The" (*Cheyenne* episode), 94
Ankrum, Morris, 59
Annette, 136
Anthony Adverse, 80
Anton, Ron, 84
Antrim, Harry, 64, 100, 104
Apache Rifles, 49
Apache Woman, 141
"Appointment, The" (*Lawman* episode), 79, 141
Archer, Claude E., 67, 70, 97
Arizona Raiders, 49
Arlen, Richard, 52, 53, 78, 79, 120
Arliss, George, 9
Armen, Margaret, 88, 140, 146, 148
Armstrong, R.G., 21, 50, 51, 56, 57
Armstrong, Robert, 20, 81, 82, 107
Arness, James, 18, 26, 184
Arnsten, Stefan, 92, 128

Arrow in the Dust, 122
Arthur, Budd, 43
Arthur, Burt, 43
Arvan, Jan, 105, 136, 161
Ashby Hal, 110
Ashton, Tom R., 145, 147, 137
At War with the Army, 167
Ates, Roscoe, 22, **30**, 56, 57, 63, 67, 71-72, 80, 97
Atwater, Barry, 166
Austin, John P., 42, 159
Austin, Pamela, 165
Avery, Emile, 139, 142, 143, 145, 156
Avery, Tol, 55, 68

B
Babcock, Fay, 36, 108
Babe Ruth Story, The, 11
Babes in Toyland/March of the Wooden Soldiers, 72
"Baby It's You," 115
Backman, Lonie, 46
"Badge, The" (*Lawman* episode), 42
Bailey, Rex, 113
Baird, Jimmy, 64, 76
Baker, Benny, 140
Baker. Carroll, 107
Baker, Roy, 63
Baldwin, Walter, 62, 76
Ball, Lucille, 161
Ballad of Cable Hogue, The, 104, 157
"Ballad of Cat Ballou, The," 115
Bambi, 153
"Bandit, The" (*Lawman* episode), 64
"Barber, The" (*Lawman* episode), 152
Barclay, Jerry, 130
Barcroft, Roy, 59, 60, 89, 150
Bare, Richard L., 38, 41
Barnes, Rayford, 66, 72
Barnett, Jim, 62
Barrett, Claudia, 108
Barrett, Hoyle, 135, 137, 142, 144, 150, 164, 165
Barron, Baynes, 53, 122, 155
Barry, Don (Donald), 62, 63, 89, 116, 137
Batanides, Arthur, 74
Bateman, Charles, 542
Bat Masterson (TV series), 50
Battle Cry, 157
"Battle Scar" (*Lawman* episode), 22, 56, 122

Bau, Gordon, 35
Baxter, Alan, 157
Baxter, Anne, 113
Baxter, Lex, 128
Baylor, Hal, 53, 72, 162
Baywatch, 120
Beachcomber, The, 105
Beau Geste (1966), 150
Beaumont, Jud, 123
Becker, Ken, 65, 96
Beddoe, Don, 41, 64, 117
"Belding's Girl" (*Lawman* episode), 89
Bell, Charles Alvin, 101, 138
Bell, Cliff, 108, 114, 132, 133, 150
Bell, James, 48, 64
Bell, Rodney, 97
Bellinger, Ted, 74
Bellows, George, 59
Bend of the River, 129
Benedict, Dick, 141, 144, 163
Benedict, Greg, 158
"Benefit of Doubt" (*Maverick* episode), 146
Bennett, Norman, 45, 117, 129, 135, 162
Benson, Hugh, 11
Beradino, John, 104
Berger, Carl, 55, 67, 74
Berkeley, Mowbray F., 64, 146
Berle, Milton, 46
Bernardi, Hershel, 112
Bestar, Barbara, 73
Betz, Carl, 95
Beverly Hillbillies, The, 49
Bewitched, 71
"Bibbidi-Bobbidi-Boo," 115
Bid Time Return (novel), 103
"Big Hat, The" (*Lawman* episode), 53
Big Jake, 55
Big Valley, The, 43, 64, 136
Billy the Kid, 54, 149
Binyon, Claude Jr., 67
Biscuit Eater, The, 50
Bishop, Rummy, 93
Bissell, Whit, 39, 40, 116, 125, 136, 137, 161
Bite the Bullet, 41
Black, John D.F., 131, 134, 135, 141, 148, 152, 161, 163, 165
Black Saddle, 43, 50, 97
Blair, Don, 80

Blake, Amanda, 77
Blake, Ann, 157
Blake, Larry, 21, 24, 80, 100, 133, 150, **170**
Blazing Saddles, 78, 93
"Blind Hate" (*Lawman* episode), 127
"Bloodline, The" (*Lawman* episode), 43
"Blue Boss and Willie Shay" (*Lawman* episode), **33**, 119
Blyth, Ann, 162
Bob Cummings Show, The, 145
Boetticher, Budd, 154
Bogart, Humphrey, 9, 55, 85
Bohanan, Fred M., 54, 63, 71, 89, 155
Bold Venture, 93
Bonanza, 56
Bone, Ben, 44, 46, 87-89, 92-96, 98, 101-107, 110-111, 115
Bonney, Gail, 116, 152
Bonnie and Clyde, 39
Boone, Richard, 65
Booth, Billy, 143, 144
Booth, John Wilkes, 166
Booth, Nesdon, 60
Boots and Saddles, 78
Bouchey, Willis, 38, 60, 61
Bounty Hunter, The, 158
Bourbon Street Beat, 59, 64
Bow, Clara, 37
Bowie, Jim, 96
Bradford, Lane, 44, 62, 100
Bradley, Bart, 84
Bradley, Stewart, 50
Brady Bunch, The, 88, 113
Brady, Scott, 128
Brain from Planet Arous, The, 118
Branded, 140
Brandon, Henry, 72, 82, 83
"Brand Release, The" (*Lawman* episode), 50
Braus, Mortimer, 54
"Break-In, The" (*Lawman* episode), 128
"Breakup, The" (*Lawman* episode), **30**, 72
Breck, Peter, 43, 132, 165
"Bride, The" (*Lawman* episode), 156
Bridges, Lloyd, 141, 158
Briggs, Charlie, 76, 145, 159

Brigham Young – Frontiersman, 164
Brinegar, Paul, 53
Brocius, Curly Bill, 62
Bromley, Sheila, 120
Bronco, 11, 59, 61
Brooke, Hillary, 63
Brown, Howard, 117
Brown, Mina 143, 144
Brown, Peter, **2-6**, 9, 12-15, 17, 19, 23-25, **30-33**, 36-167, 170, 172-176, 178, 179, 182, 184-186
Browne, Howard, 117
Browne, Kathie, **33**, 155
Browning, Robert, 140
Bryar, Claudia, 126
Bryon, Keith, 61
Buchanan, Edgar, 48, 49, 173
Buckskin, 48
Buetel, Jack, 20, 124, 125
Buka, Donald, 49, 72
Bullitt, 133
Buntline, Ned, 143
Burke, Walter, 67, 73, 106, 144, 145
Busey, Gary, 88
Bush, George W., 49
Bush, Owen, 142, 152
Butch Cassidy and the Sundance Kid, 74
Butler, Ralph, 130
"By the Book" (*Lawman* episode), 141, 144
Byrnes, Edd (Edward), 20, **32**, 36, 37, 100, 101, 147

C
Cabaret, 92
Caddyshack, 83
Cagney, James, 9, 73
Caine, Howard, 52
Calamity Jane, 154
Calamity Jane (movie), 129, 151
Calder, King, 98, 114, 143
Cameron, Rod, 62
Campbell, Howard, 36, 38-46, 49, 51, 52, 54-67, 70, 77, 96
Campbell, William, 134
"Captives, The" (*Lawman* episode), 48, 172, 173
Carey, Harry, 160
Carey, Harry Jr., 38, 160, 161
Carey, MacDonald, 151
Carey, Olive, 38, 159, 160
Carey, Philip, 20, 150, 151, 177

Carlisle, Spencer, 81
Carlson, Doug, 117, 120
Carlyle, Richard, 138
Carr, Paul, 97
Carr, Vicki, 115
Carradine, David, 164
Carradine, John, 20, **31**, 38, 163, 164
Carradine, Keith, 164
Carradine, Robert, 164
Carroll, Dee, 48, 97, 136
Carson, Johnny, 139
Carter, Ellis W., 78, 86
Casablanca (TV show), 11
Case, Allen, 59, 60
Cason, John, 43, 144
Cassavetes, John, 135
Castle, Peggie, **2-7**, 9, 13, 15-17, 19, 20, **33**, 47, 63, 68-167, 181, 182, 185, 186
"Catalog Woman, The" (*Lawman* episode), **7**, 22, 138
"Catcher, The" (*Lawman* episode), 107
Catching, Bill, 92
Catlow, 166
Catron, Jack, 155
Cattle Queen of Montana, 140
Centennial, 118
Challee, Bill (William), 74, 81
Chambers, Phil, 99
Chandler, Lane, 36, 37, 46, 58, 59
Chaney, Lon, 149
Chaney, Lon Jr., 20, **32**, 148, 149
"Change of Venue" (*Lawman* episode), 21, 150, 169, 276
"Chantay" (*Lawman* episode), 105
Charney, Kim (Kimm), 69, 107
"Chef, The" (*Lawman* episode), 54
Cheshire, Harry, 37, 41, 46, 54, 58, 107, 112, 116, 118, 132, 148, 151, 155, 162, 167
Cheyenne, 11, 13, 59, 93, 112, 152, 157, 175, 179, 181
Chisum, 120
Christy, Ken, 46, 58
Chudnow, Byron, 120
Cimarron (1931), 71
Cinderella, 115
Citizen Kane, 74, 76
Clark, Dane, 93
Clark, Robert, 72
Clarke, John, 61, 72, 87
Cliff, John, 39, 120, 121
"Clootey Hutter" (*Lawman* episode), 154
Coburn, James, 21, 42, 79, 80, 107

Cody, Iron Eyes, 52, 182
Cohen, Carl, 142
Colbert, Robert, 146, **171**, 172
"Cold Fear" (*Lawman* episode), 130
"Cold One, The" (*Lawman* episode), 139, **175**, 176
Colman, Ronald, 79, 80
Colmar, Andrew, 72
Colt .45, 11, 59, 66
Comancheros, The, 45
Comanche Station, 65, 154
Comi, Paul, 71, 100
Conagher, 39
"Conclave" (*Lawman* episode), 66
"Conditional Surrender" (*Lawman* episode), 129
Connecticut Yankee in King Arthur's Court, A (1949), 52
Connors, Mike (Michael), 46
Conrad, Robert, 56. 57
Conway, Gary, 100
Conway, Russ, 125
Cool Hand Luke, 70, 167
Cooper, Charles, 56
Cooper, Clancy, 68, 69, 71, 72, 74, 78, 80, 82, 83, 87, 88, 91, 93, 95, 98
Cooper, Gary, 11, 19, 150
Corman, Roger, 141
"Cornered" (*Lawman* episode), 108, 115
Cornthwaite, Robert, 123
"Cort" (*Lawman* episode), 154, 160
Costello, Lou, 53
"Counterfeit Mask" (*The Lone Ranger* episode), 121
Courtleigh, Stephen, 39, 64
Courtney, Chuck, 43
Coy, Walter, 56, 57
Crane, Fred (Frederick), 100, 107, 123
Crawford, Oliver, 50, 64
Crawford, Robert (actor) 68
Crawford, Robert, (film editor) 77, 93, 119, 135, 162
Crazy Horse, 49, 140
Cronin, Dermot, 89
Crosby, Bing, 52, 98
Crosland, Alan Jr., 46, 60
Curwood, James Oliver, 42
Custer (TV series), 49
Cyrano de Bergerac, 128

D
Dakotas, The, 88, 118, 152
Dancer The (play), 74

Dante, Michael, 23, 25, 48, 49, **172**, 173
Danton, Ray, 21, **31**, 68, 69, 103
Darby's Rangers, 14
Dark at the Head of the Stairs, The, 127
Darrell, Steve, 72
Darrin, Diana, 145
David, Mack, 21, 35, 115, 183
Davis, Bette, 9
Davis, Karl, 57, 133
Davis, Michael, 122
Davis, Sammy Jr., **33**, 119, 120, 174, 184
Davy Crockett and the River Pirates, 39
Davy Crockett at the Alamo, 96
Day of the Badman, 65
Days of Our Lives, 125, 134, 186
de Corsia, Ted, 45, 62, 127
de Havilland, Olivia, 9
de Kova, Frank, 21, 108, 109
Dean, Eddie, 71
Dean, James, 167
Deane, LeRoy, 68, 69, 72, 73, 97
DeBenning, Jedd, 113
DeCarlo, Yvonne, 66
Decision at Sundown, 95
Defenders, The, 88
Dehner, John, 153
Del Ruth, Roy, 11
Dennis, Nick, 100
Dennis the Menace, 144
Denver and Rio Grande, 71
"Deputy, The (*Lawman* episode), 9, 36
Deputy, The (TV series), 60
"Detweiler's Kid" (*Lawman* episode), 118, 128, 135, 175, 176
Devereaux, Rex, 148
Devil and Daniel Webster, The (1941), 127
Devil's Doorway, 77
"Devil's Godson, The" (*Colt .45* episode), 66
Devine, Andy, 53
Dick Van Dyke Show, The, 113
Dick Tracy (TV series), 166, 167
"Dilemma" (*Lawman* episode), 104
Dillaway, Don, 167
Dinehart, Mason Alan, 19
Disney, Walt, 10, 96, 97, 153, 181
Distant Trumpet, A, 51, 95
Dobkin, Lawrence, 66
Dobson, James, 48

"Doctor, The" (*Lawman* episode), 161
Dolan, Bill, 98
Donahue, Troy, 20, **32**, 51, 56, 93, 94, 95, 177
Doucette, John, 36, 54, 55, 1123
Douglas, Burt, 62, 89
Douglas, Kirk, 141
Downing, John, 122
Dragon Teeth (novel), 78, 79
Drake, Tom, 20, **33**, 64, 69, 70, 84, 104
Dr. Strangelove: or How I Learned to Stop Worrying and Love the Bomb, 92
Drums Along the Mohawk, 21, 101
Drury, James, 18, 21, 26, 47, 48, 57, 58, 182
Dr. Who, 78
Drysdale, Don, **33**, 81, 82
Dubberly, Ginger, 84
Duggan, Andrew, 94, 113, 114, 158, 159
Duncan, Archie, 81
Duncan, Craig, 86
Dunn, George, 153
DuPar, Edwin, 42, 46, 55, 57, 99
Duryea, Dan, 157

E
Earp, Virgil, 117, 119
Earp, Wyatt, 45, 78, 125, 153, 167
Eastwood, Clint, 18, 109, 123, 186
Edwards, Saundra, 104
Eimen, John, 103
Elam, Jack, 21, 36, 37, 49, 62, 63, 87, 88, 134, 154
Ellery Queen (TV series), 135
Elliot(t), Laura, 70, 71
Elliott, Cecil, 62
Elliott, Sam, 39
Ellsworth, Stephen, 64, 114
Elson, Donald, 66, 96
Emanuel, Jack, 40
"Empty Gun, The" (*Cheyenne* episode), 13, 93
"Encounter, The" (*Lawman* episode), **32**, 49, 50
Eric, Martin, 103
Erway, Ben, 103
"Escape of Joe Kilmer, The" (*Lawman* episode), 109
Essay, Chris, 97
Evans, Richard, 99, 158, 159
Evans, Robert, 106
Everett (York), Chad, 20, 118, 134, 135, 176
Evers, Jason, 127
"Exchange, The" (*Lawman* episode), 71

"Explosion" (*Lawman* episode), 22, 164

F
F Troop, 74, 109
Facebook's John Russell Fan Group, 184
Facebook's *Lawman* TV Series Fan Group, 23-26, 184
Fadden, Tom, 48, 62
Fail Safe, 130
Fancher, Hampton, 129
Fantasia, 153
Far Country, The, 129
Farfan, Robert, 41, 60
Faris, Jim, 86, 102, 105, 114, 116, 120-122, 140
Farr, Lee, 50
Farrar, Stanley, 36
Fastest Gun Alive, The, 129
"Fast Trip to Cheyenne" (*Lawman* episode), 98
Father Knows Best, 26, 136
Faulkner, Ed, 130
Fawcett, William, 52, 98, 102, 103, 138, 152, 156
Fein, Bernie, 104, 105
Ferguson, Frank, 100, 123, 124, 147, 165
Ferguson, Perry, 73-76
Fernstrom, Ray, 72, 75, 80, 109
Fields, W.C., 162
Fifteen Flags (novel), 76
Fighting Kentuckian, The, 80, 158
Fighting Man of the Plains, 121
Fighting Sullivans, The, 12, 99
Fink, Mike, 39
Finnerman, Gerald Perry, 70
Finnerman, Perry, 68-70, 72, 97
Firecreek, 51
"Firehouse Lil" (*Lawman* episode), 19, 112
Fix, Paul, 59, 60
Flaming Star, 45, 120, 135
Fletcher, Louise, **32**, 49, 50
Flory, Med, 107, 108, 124, 156
Flynn, Errol, 9, 93, 129
Flynn, Gertrude, 147
Fogetti, Howard, 67, 70
Fonda, Henry, 60, 70, 108
Fong, Frances, 44
Foran, Dick, 20, 40, 41, 157
"Forbidden City, The" (*Maverick* episode), 146
Ford, Glenn, 182, 184
Ford, John, 13, 21, 38, 61, 66, 70, 98, 101, 124, 160-162, 167, 168

Forest, Michael, 52
Forever Amber, 13
Forster, Bill, 102
Fort Apache (1948), 124, 167, 168
Foster, Zach, 141
Foulger, Bryon, 54
"Four, The" (*Lawman* episode), 134
Four Faces West, 65
Four Queens and a King, 41
Fox, Frederick Louis, 58
Foy, Fred, 85
"Frame-Up, The" (*Lawman* episode), 112
Franklin, Harry, 93
Fredericks, Charles, 45, 100
Fredericks, Dean, 105
Freeman, Kathleen, 136, 137
Fremont, John, 88
French, Victor, 149
"Friend of the Family, A" (*Lawman* episode), 147
"Friend, The" (*Lawman* episode), 67
Fritsch, Gunther V., 161, 167
Frontier Circus, 120
"Fugitive" (*Lawman* episode), 122
Fuller, Lance, 140, 141
Fuller, Robert, 21, 58, 67, 68
Fury at Furnace Creek, 122

G
Galante, Jim, 110, 124
Gale Storm Show, The, 111
Gallant Men, The, 70, 71
Gallison, Joseph, 134
Gallo, Lew, 52
"Gang, The" (*Lawman* episode), 18, 26, 57
Garcia, Stella, 105
Garland, Judy, 69
Garland, Richard, 97
Garner, Ava, 177
Garner, James, 137, 147,
General Mills, 36
George, Anthony, 41
Geronimo, 140
Gerstle, Frank, 117
"Get Out of Town" (*Lawman* episode), 125, 141, 163
Gibson, C. Carter, 36, 137
Giler, Berne, 93, 149, 157
Gilligan's Island, 50, 150

INDEX

Gilmore, Johnathan, 78
Gilson, Tom, 59, 100, 114, 139, 159
"Girl from Grantsville" (*Lawman* episode), 18, 89
Glass Key, The, 50
Glennon, Bert, 21, 100-108, 110-133, 135-137, 138, 139, 141-144, 146, 148, 150-152, 154-156, 159, 161-166
"Go-Between, The" (*Lawman* episode), 100, 169
Go-Between, The (1971 movie), 100
Gomer Pyle, 40
Gone With the Wind, 71, 124
Goode, Samuel F., 44, 47, 56, 57, 60, 73, 96, 98, 99, 102, 108, 113, 114, 119, 127, 128, 167
Goodrich, J. A., 49
Gordon, Don, 133
Gordon, Leo, 124, 125, 163
Gordon, Louis W., 86, 111, 114, 125, 139, 153, 166
Graham, Fred, 38, 44
Graham, James W., 97, 99
Graham, Tim, 126, 163
Granger, Bertram C., 148
Granger, Farley, 71
Grant, Cary, 75
Granville, Joan, 62
Grapes of Wrath, The, 162, 164
Gray, Coleen, 121, 122
Great Bank Robbery, The, 143
Great Santini, The, 22
Greatest American Hero, The, 163
Greatest Show on Earth, The, 122
Greco, George, 152
Green Acres, 49
Greene, Angela, 166, 167
Greene, Richard, 81
Greer, Dabbs, 112, 113, 166
Gregg, Virginia, 154
Grey, Duane, 46, 124
Grey, Joel, 21, **30**, 91, 92, 102, 103, 135, 136, 178
Griffith, James, 21, 165, 166
Griswold, Claire, 129
Gruber, Frank, 38
"Grubstake, The" (*Lawman* episode), 123
Guadalcanal Diary, 120
Guilfoyle, Paul, 72, 73, 77, 97
Gun Fury, 151
Gunderson, Bob, 137
Gunfight at the O.K. Corral, 45, 96, 160
Gunfighter, The, 56, 65, 120

Gunga Din, 120
"Gunman, The" (*Lawman* episode), 52
Gunman's Walk, 75, 76
"Gun-Shy" (*Maverick* episode), 102
Gunslinger, The, 75
Gunsmoke, 11, 20, 26, 60, 77, 102, 113, 119, 139, 144, 149
Gun That Won the West, The 77
Guys and Dolls, 88

H
Haffen, John M., 100
Hagen, Kevin, 148, 160
Haggerty, Dan, 131
Haggerty, Don, 130, 131
Haglund, Oren W., 36-100
Hale, Barbara, 163
Hale, Richard, 90, 91
Hall, John, 129, 163
Hall, Lee C., 45
Hallelujah Trail, The, 40, 117, 153
Hamill, Mark, 88
"Hanging Tree, The" (song), 115
Hanks, Harold, 87, 88, 92
Hansen, Franklin, 126
"Hardcase, The" (*Lawman* episode), **33**, 81, 128
Hardin, Ty, 61
Hardman, Ric, 75, 81, 84, 85, 90-92, 101, 102, 104, 105, 107, 110, 112, 116, 118, 119, 133, 136, 138
Harmon, John, 65
Harris, Donald K., 83, 91, 104, 119, 126, 132, 142, 154, 167
Harris, Gary, 163
Harrison, Jan, 58
Hart, Dolores, 151
Harte, Kathryn, 87
Harvey, Don C., 76
Harvey, Harry Jr., 40
Harvey, Harry Sr., 163
Harvey, Jean, 54
"Hassayampa" (*Lawman* episode), 116
Hawaiian Eye, 57, 59, 93
Hawks, Howard, 37
Hawn, Jack, 167
Hayden, Sterling, 71, 122
Haynes, Roberta, 79
Hayward, Jim, 79, 101, 133
Hayworth, Rita, 112
Hayworth, Vinton, 75, 92, 101, 120, 132, 138, 147, 152, 163, 166

He Rides Tall, 157
Heath, Dody, 81
Heisler, Stuart, 39, 40, 44, 45, 47-58, 60-63, 100, 102, 103, 106, 119, 173
Hellzapoppin', 38
Helton, Percy, 73, 74, 104, 139
Hendry, Marsh, 67, 77
Hengen, Debby, 65
Henry, Buzz, 153, 158
Henry, William, 37, 38
Hepburn, Katherine, 80
Herbert, Pitt, 98, 152
"Heritage of Hate" (*Lawman* episode), 22, **33**, 155
Herman, Woody, 108
Heston, Charlton, 89
Hickok, Wild Bill, 48, 173
Hicks, Chuck, 116
High Noon, 42, 80, 87, 133, 159
Hill Street Blues, 142
"Hoax, The" (*Lawman* episode), 76
Hodgins, Earle, 47
Hoffman, Morris, 116, 121
Hoffman, Robert, 90, 98
Hoffman, Theodore B., 40, 45, 52, 55, 62, 97, 109
Hogan, Jack, 76, 100, 132, 133, 154
Hogan's Heroes, 105
"Hold-Out, The" (*Lawman* episode), 102, 151
Holland, Tom, 46
Holliday, Doc, 43, 65, 66
Holliday, Doc (TV series), 66
Holliman, Earl, 58
Hollingsworth, Elbert K., 36, 39, 51, 57, 59, 70, 81, 85, 87, 94, 95, 101, 109, 160
Holman, Rex, 118, 119
Holmes, Wendell, 75, 152
"Homecoming" (*Lawman* episode), **7**, 115
Homeier, Skip, 64, 65
Hondo (movie), 125, 140
Hondo (TV series), 140, 155
Hope, Bob, 98
Hope, James, 43
Hopkins, George James, 57, 58, 61, 64-67, 119
Horan, James, 124
Horse Whisperer, The, 58
Horvath, Charles, 106, 116
Hoskins, Bob, 152
Hotel de Paree, 58
Hound of the Baskervilles, The (1931), 124
How the West Was Won (movie), 107

Howard, John, 79, 80
Howitzer, Bronson (Ric Hardman), 75, 114, 122, 124, 137
Hoyt, John, 44, 94
Hubbard, John, 45, 66, 76, 163
Hudson, Larry, 98
Hudson, Rock, 94
Huffaker, Clair, 45, 49, 53, 57, 59, 61, 63, 65, 67, 68, 72, 76, 78, 80, 82, 83, 90, 97
Hughes, Everett A., 134, 136, 145, 146, 149, 157, 159, 160
Hughes, Howard, 125
Hugueny, Sharon, 105, 106
"Hunch, The" (*Lawman* episode), **33,** 69, 107
Hunter, Jeffrey, 51, 88
Hunter, Tab, 75, 94
"Huntress, The" (*Lawman* episode), 61, 178
Hurst, Ralph S., 55, 91, 109
Hutchins, Will, *xi, xi, xii,* 147, **174,** 175

I
I Am Legend (movie), 103
I Am Legend (novel), 103
I, the Jury, 15
"I'll Always Love You," 94
Iceman Cometh, The, 22
Iglesias, Eugene, 52
Inditement: The McMartin Trial, 127
Informer, The, 124
Inge, Joe, 79, 81, 88, 98, 99, 105, 119, 133, 137, 148, 164
"Inheritance, The" (*Lawman* episode), 44, 118
"Intruders, The" (*Lawman* episode), 22, 44
Ireland, John, 37
Irvine, Eugene, 76, 79, 82, 116, 121, 133
Irving, Charles, 134
"It Must Be Him," 115
It's a Mad Mad Mad Mad World, 46

J
Jackson, Andrew, 117
Jackson, Tom, 41
Jacques, Ted, 52
Jaeckel, Richard, 119, 120
Jahns, Robert, 101, 117, 124, 126, 137, 139, 142, 152, 156, 159
"Jailbreak" (*Lawman* episode), 154
James. Jesse, 40
Janiss, Vivi, 56
Jara, Maurice, 90
Jay, Steven, 46

INDEX

Jennings Louis, 153, 157, 159
Jensen, John, 84
Jeremiah Johnson, 129
Jesse James Rides Again, 143
Jesse James' Women, 15, 63
Johnny Guitar, 124
Johnson, Arch, 21, 101, 102, 141, 142, 151
Johnson, Chubby, 128, 129
Johnson, Erskine, 15
Johnson, Russell, 49, 50
"Joker, The" (*Lawman* episode), 39, 73
Jolley, I. Stanford, 39, 42, 86, 112, 139, 161
Jolson, Al, 9
Jones, Gordon, 53, 72
Jones, L.Q., 156, 157
Jones, Miranda, 47, 48, 113, 164
Jones, Spike, 166
Jones, Stanley, 36, 57, 69, 74, 114, 119, 161
"Journey. The" (*Lawman* episode), 60
Joyce, John, 127, 137, 138, 144
Joyce, William, **33**, 155
Judge Roy Bean, 49
"Judge, The" (*Lawman* episode), 94
"Juror, The" (*Lawman* episode), 19, 132, 169
"Jury, The" (*Lawman* episode), 41

K
Katt, William, 163
Kean, John K., 51, 95, 100
Keast, Paul, 62
Keel, Howard, 156
Kegerris, Alfred E., 132, 134, 141, 159
Kelley, Barry, 47, 48, 135
Kelley, DeForest, 85, 114, 115
Kellogg, John, 121, 122, 141
Kelly, Don (O'Kelly), 39, 58, 85, 86, 125, 147
Kelly's Heroes, 109, 123
Kemmerling, Warren, 111, 163
Kennedy, Burt, 53, 154, 157, 158, 160
Kennedy, George, 82, 83
Kennedy's Children, 127
Kevin, Sandy, 123, 139
"Kids, The" (*Lawman* episode), 84
King Creole, 151
King Kong (1933 movie), 82
King of the Royal Mounted, 94
King, Brett, 58

King's Row (TV show), 11
Kirbach, Arthur, 75
Kirkwood, James Jr., 51
Kit Carson and the Mountain Men, 88
Kitty Foyle, 124
Kleinberg, Milt, 82, 83, 98, 143, 145, 148, 165
Knight, Fuzzy, 118, 119
Knight, Shirley, 21, 126, 127
Knight, Ted, 83
Kolster, Clarence, 58, 85, 97
Komant, Carolyn, 87, 130
Konrad, Dorothy, 122, 134
Korngold, Eric Wolfgang, 80
Korngold, George W., 80
Krieg, Frank, 108
Kubrick, Stanley, 47
Kuehl, William L., 45, 48-54, 56, 90, 112, 160, 163, 166
Kung Fu, 121
Kuter, Leo K., 43, 45, 47, 48, 50, 53

L
L'Estrange, Dick (Richard), 102, 159, 166, 167
Ladd, Alan, 52, 174
"Lady Belle, The" (*Lawman* episode), 92
"Lady in Question" (*Lawman* episode), 46
Lairden, George, 99, 100
Lambert, Jack, 21, 45
Lancaster, Burt, 45, 56, 160
Lancer, 114
Landau, Martin, 21, 40
Landers, Harry, 62
Landis, Kenesaw Mountain, 117
Landon, Michael, 157
Landry, Richard (Dick), 107, 121
Lane, Allan, 20, 93, 94
Lane, Charles, 161
Lane, Rusty, 46
Lang, Barbara, 15, **30**, 47, 53, 54, 57, 58, 59
Lang, David, 44, 46, 96
Langton, Paul, 43, 44
Langtry, Lily, 20
Lansing, Joi, 141
Laramie (TV series), 68
Lasky, William, 68, 69, 72, 73, 77, 97
Lassie (TV series), 100, 132
"Last Bugle, The" (*The Zane Grey Theater* episode), 140
Last Command, The, 13

Last Man on Earth, The, 103
"Last Man, The" (*Lawman* episode), 53, 72, 79
"Last Stop" (*Lawman* episode), 78
Latell, Lyle, 161
Lau, Wesley, 42
Laurel and Hardy, 72
Lauter, Harry, 137, 138, 182
Lawrence, Marc, 21, 104, 108, 113-116, 118, 119, 121-123, 126, 127, 129, 133, 172, 175
Leader, Anton M., 46
Leary, Nolan, 76
Lee, Bo, 112
Lee, Robert B., 58, 112, 126, 137, 147, 148, 151, 153
"Left Hand of the Law" (*Lawman* episode), 88
Left Handed Gun, The, 51
Legend of Tom Dooley, The, 157
Leicester, William, 39-41, 47, 51, 55, 60, 65, 67, 69, 70, 73, 74, 79, 81, 86, 89, 104, 108, 114, 155
Leslie, Edith, 105
Levin, Erma E., 73, 76, 77, 87, 96, 100, 103, 106, 118, 131, 140-142, 157, 165
Levin, Sam E., 75, 77, 89, 102, 103, 108, 116, 126, 137, 148, 161, 163
Lewis, Harrison, 108, 118
Lewis, Jerry, 137, 167, 184
Lewis, Victor C. Jr., 115
Life and Legend of Wyatt Earp, The, 11, 19, 113, 117, 131, 167, 181
Lifeboat, 124
Life with Father, 41
"Lily" (*Lawman* episode), **31**, 68
Lincoln, Abraham, 117
Little Big Man, 104
Little House on the Prairie, 63, 113, 148
Livingston, Jerry, 21, 35, 115, 183
Llewellyn, Russell, 152
Lloyd, Suzanne, 89
"Locket, The" (*Lawman* episode), 146, 171
Lomas, Jack, 59, 169-171
London, Julie, 93
London, Tom, 141, 163
Lone Ranger, The (TV series), 26, 85, 121
Lone Ranger, The (movie), 50
"Long Gun, The" (*Lawman* episode), **5**, 153
Long, Richard, 63, 64
Long Riders, The, 164
Longmire, 12
Loos, Ann, 117
"Lords of Darkness, The" (*Lawman* episode), 102, 141
Lormer, Jon, 37, 39, 41, 43, 47, 53

Lost Horizon (1937), 80
Lubin, Arthur, 98
Luciano, Michael, 84
Luckenbacher, George E., 75, 76, 96
Luddy, Barbara, 105
Lukas, Karl, 51
Lukather, Paul, 51, 67
Lullaby of Broadway, 38
Lusk, Freeman, 115
Lyden, Pierce, 85
Lydon, James, 40, 41
Lynch, Ken, 74, 109, 130
Lynch, Warren, 44, 76, 79, 81-85
Lynn, Betty, 39, 40
Lynn, Cherrill, 127
Lynn, Rita, 53, 78

M
Macauley, Carl, 72, 74-96, 98-133, 135-157, 159-167
Macbeth, 58
MacDonald, Kenneth R., 43
MacDuff, Tyler, 129
MacFarland, Bruce, 121, 133, 142, 162, 167
Macready, Michael, 47, 55
"Mad Bunch, The" (*Lawman* episode), **32**, 100
Magnificent Seven, The (1960), 40, 42, 80, 111
Mahoney, Maggie, 130
"Mairzy Doates," 115
Major Dundee, 51, 107, 157
Maltese Falcon, The, 55
Man Behind the Gun, The, 151
"Man Behind the News, The" (*Lawman* episode), 162
"Man Called Ragan, A" (*Cheyenne* episode), 152
Man from Colorado, The, 12
Man from Galveston, The, 51
Man from God's Country, 113
"Man from New York, The" (*Lawman* episode), 120
"Man on a Mountain" (*Lawman* episode), **31**, 73, 97
"Man on a Wire" (*Lawman* episode), 95
Man Who Shot Liberty Valance, The, 61
Man Without a Gun, 98, 136
Manley, Joann, 76
Mannix, 46
"Mano Nera" (*Maverick* episode), 95
Mansfield, Rankin, 36
Manson, Maurice, 128
March of the Wooden Soldiers/Babes in Toyland, 72

INDEX

Marden, Adrienne, 115
Margulies, William, 48, 52-54
Marjorie Morningstar, 14
"Marked Man, The" (*Lawman* episode), 113
"Mark of Cain" (*Lawman* episode), 121
Marks, Dave, 74
Marley, J. Peverell, 65, 73
Married with Children, 137
Marsh, George E., 82, 90, 102, 108, 121, 128, 145, 150, 156, 159
Marshall, Craig, 127
Marshall, Joan, 92, 93
Martin, Andra, 61
Martin, Strother, 69, 70, 87
Martinson, Leslie H., 39, 42, 43, 59, 63, 67, 68, 70, 112, 117, 136, 138
Marx Brothers, 55
Marx, Groucho, 84
Mary Tyler Moore Show, The, 83
MASH (movie), 111
"Master, The" (*Lawman* episode), 46
Masterson, Bat, 19, 96
Mather, Jack, 81
Matheson, Richard, 87, 103, 106, 108, 115, 163
Mature, Victor, 122
Maverick (TV series), 11, 43, 59, 64, 95, 102, 146, 153, 175, 181
Maxwell, Charles, 68, 142, 166
Mayberry, Richard, 109, 131, 132
Maynard, Ken, 41
Maynard, Kermit, 20, 41
Maynor, Asa, 100, 101
Mayo, Ray, 163
McBain, Diane, 94, 95
McCabe and Mrs. Miller, 111
McCall, Jack, 48, 49, 172, 173
McCallion, James, 43
McCann, John, 104
McCarty, Marc, 124
McCay, Peggy, 124, 125
McClay, Booker, 63
McCloud (TV series), 110
McClure, Doug, 56, 182
McCord, Evan, 123, 134, 159, 160
McCrea, Joel, 65
McDermid, Finlay, 39, 42, 43, 46, 62, 96
McDonald, Francis J., 80
McEveety, B.F., 158-160, 161, 165
McGavin, Darren, 155
McHale's Navy, 165

McKay, Don, 77, 82, 90, 93
McKennon, Dal, 74
McKinley, J. Edward, 71, 117
McLaglen, Victor, 44
McLeod, Catherine, 56, 93, 94, 122, 143
McLintock!, 66, 125
McMahon, David, 44, 103
McMahon, Ed, 139
McNally, Stephen, 62
McQueen, Steve, 133
McQueeney, Robert, 70, 85, 93, 142, 143
McVeagh, Eve, 83
McVey, Pat, 42
McWhorter, Frank, 152
Meadows, Joyce, 118, 139, 140, **175,** 176
Medical Center, 118
Meek, Rusty, 71
Meet Me in St. Louis, 69, 70
Megowan, Don, 104, 105
Meigs, William, 46
Men into Space, 52
Menkin, Larry, 57
Meredith, Charles, 54
Merlin, Jan, 91
Merrick, M.A., 40, 42, 60, 63, 64, 80, 86, 142, 156, 164
Meyer, Emile, 39, 89
Milford, John, 70
Millard, Harry, 60
Miller, Frank M., 62, 63, 68, 77
Miller, Lester, 138
Miller, Peter, 111
Miller, Sy 178
Milletaire, Carl, 66
Mills, Mort, 135, 136
Mims, William (Bill), 86, 87, 112, 156. 157
Minter, Harold, 68
Miracle in the Rain, 15
Miss Grant Takes Richmond, 161
Mission:Impossible, (TV series), 40
Mitchell, Cameron, 105
Mitchell, Frank, 110
Mitchell, Steve, 108
Mitchum, Robert, 100
Mohr, Gerald, 84, 85
Mondo, Peggy, 162
Montez, Maria, 20
Montgomery, George, 62, 113

Moody, Ralph, 64, 157, 160
Moore, Clayton, 143
Moore, Irving J., 131, 144, 149
Moore, James, 36, 38-104, 109-111
Moore, Mary Tyler, 179
Moore, William W., 107, 147, 166
"Morgan Starr" (*The Virginian* episode), 186
Morgan, Bob, 92
Morgan, Boyd "Red", 146
Morris, Edmund, 38, 41, 44, 46, 48, 50, 54, 56-58, 60, 63, 65, 66, 71, 77, 88, 96
Morris, Eric, 59
Morris, Jeffrey (Jeff), 106
Morris, Wayne, 20, 46, 47
Morrow, Jo, 156, 157
Morrow, Russ, 139
Morrow, Susan, 89
Most Outstanding Newcomer Award, The, 15
"Mountain Man" (*Lawman* episode), 18, 156
Mr. Ed, 94
Mr. Lucky, 75
Mr. Peabody and the Mermaid, 162
Muni, Paul, 9, 118
Munroe, Tom, 151
Murphy, Donald, 91
Murphy, John F., 112, 134
Murray, Zon, 50
Music Man, The (movie), 162
My Fair Lady (movie), 78
My Friend Flicka (TV series), 124

N

Nanny and the Professor, 64
Nashville, 111
Navarro, Anna, 77
Nebraskan, The, 151
Neff, Thomas, 48, 60, 67
Negley, Howard, 44, 53
Nelson, Bek, 15, **30**, 36, 37, 39, 42-47
Nelson, Ozzie, 145
Nelson, Robert J., 76
Nevada Smith, 40, 41
Newhart, 145
Newman, Paul, 51
Newton, Theodore, 121
"No Contest" (*Lawman* episode), **31**, 54, 149
Nolan, Jeanette, 58
Nolte, Nick, 80

North by Northwest, 123
Nosler, Lloyd, 78, 113, 118, 161, 163
Novello, Jay, 53, 54, 167
NYPD Blue, 127

O
O'Brien, Edmond, 71
O'Connor, Arthur, 152
O'Flynn, Damian, 142
O'Hara, Maureen, 76, 98
O'Kelly, Don, 39, 58, 85, 86, 125, 147
O'Malley, J. Pat, 60, 96. 97
O'Neill, Frank, 42
O'Toole, Ollie, 96
Oates, Warren, 107
"Oath, The" (*Lawman* episode), 39
Odney, Douglas, 113
"Old Stefano" (*Lawman* episode), 110, 120
"Old War Horse, The" (*Lawman* episode), 101
Oliphant, Tom, 119, 120
Omega Man, The, 103
On Moonlight Bay, 11
One Flew Over the Cuckoo's Nest, 50
One Life to Live, 151
Onionhead, 14
Orr, William T., 9-13, 22, 35, 147
Otis, Joyce, 83
"Outcast, The" (*Lawman* episode), 40
Out of Africa, 129
Outlaw, The, 125
Outlaw Women, 158
Outrage, 128
"Outsider, The" (*Lawman* episode), 22, 47
Overell, Hal, 100, 143, 148, 151-155, 157, 164
Overton, Frank, 130
Owen, Ross, 68, 71, 83, 86, 90, 94, 106-108, 131, 137, 140, 141, 148, 150, 159, 162
"Owny O'Reilly, Esquire" (*Lawman* episode), 92, 135, 177

P
Page, Don, 62
Page, Joy, 147
Paiva, Nestor, 67
Pale Rider, 18, 186
Paley, Charles, 82, 90, 101, 112, 122, 130, 138, 152, 158, 164
Palmer, Byron, 63
Palmer, Gregg, 110
Palmer, Robert, 130, 137

INDEX

Palmer, Tom, 50, 57, 58, 63, 64, 76, 81
Paradise, Hawaiian Style, 151
Parker, Charlie, 108
Parker, Edward M., 86
Parnell, Emory, 40, 43, 57, 58, 62, 65-67, 96, 97
Parnell, James, 53, 71, 115
Parrish, 99, 106
Parsons, Milton, 104, 164
"Parting, The" (*Lawman* episode), 96
Partington, Dorothy, 53
Pat Garrett and Billy the Kid, 51, 80, 120, 157
Pate, Michael, 139, 140
Paths of Glory, 47
Patrick, Lee, 54, 55, 101
Patrick, Millicent, 90
Patterson, Hank, 99
Patty Duke Show, The, 87
Pawl, Nick, 142
"Payment, The" (*Lawman* episode), **32**, 93, 122
Payne, John, 122
Pearce, Wynn, 109
Peck, Gregory, 56, 133
Peckinpah, Sam, 51, 70, 80, 107, 157
Peil, Paul Leslie, 163
Pendleton, Steve, 38, 97, 98
Perkins, Anthony, 89
Perkins, Barbara, 71
Perkins, Kenneth, 60
Perry Mason, 136, 163
"Persecuted, The" (*Lawman* episode), 123, 134
Peter Gunn (TV series), 112
Peters, House, 132
Peters, House Jr., 132
Peterson, Nan, 62, 68, 69, 72
Petrie, Howard, 69
Petticoat Junction, 49
Peyton Place (TV series), 44, 71, 159
Phil Silvers Show, The, 52, 105
Philadelphia Story, The, 80
Phillips, Robert, 85, 94, 107, 114, 127, 136, 147
Pickard, John, 61
Pickens, Slim, 92, 93, 126, 182
Pickup on South Street, 12
Pierce, Shanghai, 45
Pingitore, Carl, 69
Pistols 'n' Petticoats, 165
Pittman, Montgomery, 36, 94, 128

Pitts, James, 109
Plainclothesman, The (TV series), 110
Plainsman, The (1966), 150
Player, The, 111
Plenty, Gilbert, 110
Pleshette, Suzanne, 93, 95
Pollack, Sydney, 129
"Porphyria's Lover" (*Lawman* episode), 140
"Posse, The" (*Lawman* episode), 55
"Post, The" (*Lawman* episode), 61, 104
Potter, Stephen A. (Steve, Steven), 69, 72-74, 97
Powell, William, 104, 162
Powers, Mala, 127, 128
Prentiss, Ed, 85
Presley, Elvis, 135, 151
"Press, The" (*Lawman* episode), 75
Price, Sherwood, 188
Prickett, Maudie, 76, 77
Pride and Prejudice (1940), 124
Prinz, Eddie, 38-40, 42-61, 63-66, 82-96, 98, 99, 101-103, 105, 106, 108, 110, 111, 114-116, 118-120, 122-130, 133, 135, 136, 138, 140-148, 150, 153-157, 162-164
"Prisoner, The" (*Lawman* episode), 37, 55, 123
"Prodigal, The" (*Lawman* episode), 74
"Prodigal Mother, The" (*Lawman* episode), 122, 143
"Promise, The" (*Lawman* episode), 130
"Promoter, The" (*Lawman* episode), 117
Provine, Dorothy, 21, 46
Psycho, 136, 154
Pyle, Denver, 38, 66, 164, 165, 182

Q
Qualen, John, 38, 64, 110, 127, 164
Quillin, Ted, 147

R
Rage at Dawn, 128
Rancho Notorious, 124
Randall, Stuart, 40, 130
Rangno, Terry, 59, 99
Rankin, Gil (Gilman) 81, 164
Ransom of Red Chief, The (TV movie), 87
Rare Breed, The, 76
Rawhide, 53
Raymond, Paula, 76, 77
Raynor, Grace, 66
Reach, John, 41

Reagan, Ronald, 140
Reason, Rex, 98
Rebel Without a Cause, 142
Red Hair, 37
"Red Ransom" (*Lawman* episode), 66
Red River, 37, 60, 122, 161
Red Ryder films, 94
Redd, Gene S., 47, 76, 77, 79, 81-86, 113-115, 117, 118, 122, 123, 125-131, 133, 136, 138-140, 143, 145, 149, 156, 158, 167
Reed, Donna, 95
Reed, Lewis, 93
Reed, Marshal, 148
Reed, Ralph, 42
Reed, Robert, 88
Reed, Walter, 125
Reese, Ray, 112
Reese, Tom, 134, 135
Reeves, Richard, 53, 85, 148
Reilly, Jean Burt, 98-167
Remington, Frederic, 83
Requiem for a Gunfighter, 62
Rettig, Tommy, 99, 100
"Return, The" (*Lawman* episode), 62, 128
"Return of Owny O'Reilly, The" (*Lawman* episode), 18, **30**, 92, 102, 136
Return of the Gunfighter, 118
"Reunion in Laramie" (*Lawman* episode), 86
Rey, Rosa, 47
Reynolds, Debbie, 107
Reynolds, Harry, 111, 121, 131, 142, 148, 151, 157, 167
Rhodes, Grandon, 62
Rich, Dick, 55, 97, 99
Richards, Addison, 151
Richards, Frank, 88
Richards, Keith, 122
Richards, Paul, 109
Ride Lonesome, 154
Ride the High Country, 51, 107, 157
Ridgely, Robert, 111
"Riding Shotgun" (*Lawman* episode), 59, 169, 170
Riesner, Dean, 36, 52, 68, 77, 111
Rifleman, The, 60, 120
Rin Tin Tin, 9
"Ring, The" (*Lawman* episode), 63, 119
Rio Bravo, 18, 135
Rio Conchos, 45
Rio Grande, 21, 98, 101, 161
Riordan, Robert, 75

Ritch, Ocee (Oc; Rich, OCee), 151, 161
River of No Return, 100
Riverboat, 45
RJ Reynolds Tobacco Company, 36
Road to Singapore, 98
Road, Mike, 47, 48, 71, 96, 120, 121
Roaring Twenties, The, 46, 48, 59, 111, 112, 165
"Robbery, The" (*Lawman* episode), 79, 111
Roberts, Lenore, 109
Roberts, Pernell, 45, 46
Roberts, Roy, 155
Roberson, Chuck, 38, 66
Robinson, Edward G., 9
Rock, Blossom, 164
Rocky Mountain, 93, 129
Rodgers, Mark, 139, 142, 150
Rogers, Kasey (Laura Elliot), 70, 71
Rogers, Richard, 149
Rojo, Gustavo, 95
Roman, Ric, 84, 112
Romano, Tony, 40, 48
Roosevelt, Franklin, 117
Root, Wells, 165
Roth, Gene, 87, 159
Rough Riders, The, 91
Rowland, Henry, 166
Rubine, Irving, 39
Rudie, Evelyn, 84
Rudin, Herman, 72
Rudley, Herbert, 73
Ruman, Sig, 54, 55, 59
"Runaway, The" (*Lawman* episode), 51
Ruskin, Joseph, 109, 151
Russell, John, **2-7**, 9, 12-14, 17-19, 23-26, **30-33**, 36-130, 132, 134-167, 170, 173-177, 179, 181, 182, 184, 186
Rust, Richard, 76
Ryan, B.F., 38, 41, 43, 46, 54, 97, 101, 104, 105, 111, 115, 117, 122, 135, 154, 155, 163, 165, 166

S
Sakal, Richard, 126, 127
"Salvation of Owny O'Reilly, The" (*Lawman* episode), 91
"Samson the Great" (*Lawman* episode), 44, 106
Sanders, Hugh, 51
Sands, Lee, 117
Sandwich, Jr., Mark, 66, 67, 96
Sarafian, Richard C. (Dick), 123, 126, 128, 130, 132, 134, 135, 137, 139, 142, 145,

147, 148, 150-153, 157, 165, 164, 177
Saturday Roundup, 42
Savage, Paul, 114, 121, 143
Savage, The, 89
Sawtell, Paul, 73-127, 133
Scannell, Frank, 156
Schallert, William, 86, 87
Scheid, Francis J., 39, 50
Schermer, Jules, 9, 12-15, 21, 22, 36, 38-164
Schermer, Peter, 114
Schermer, Victoria, 114
Schneider, Sam, 117, 149
Schoenfeld, Bernard C., 43
Scott, Noel L., 79, 106, 108, 134, 136, 141, 154, 157
Scott, Randolph, 49, 65, 95, 121, 128, 154, 158
Searchers, The, 57, 72, 160, 161
Searl, Jack, 148
Sebern, Theo W., 74, 78, 97, 109, 115, 120, 134, 143, 149, 155, 159
"Second Son, The" (*Lawman* episode), **3**, 107
Selby, Sarah, 167
Selk, George, 103
Senator was Indiscrete, The, 104
"Senator, The" (*Lawman* episode), 62
Sergeant Rutledge, 101
Sergeants 3, 120
Sessions, Almira, 137
Seven Brides for Seven Brothers, 156
Seven Hills of Rome, The, 15
Seymour, Harry, 163
"Shackled" (*Lawman* episode), 70
"Shadow Witness" (*Lawman* episode), 73
Shadows, 135
"Shady Deal at Sunny Acres" (*Maverick* episode), 153
Shalako, 166
Shampoo, 93
Shane, 89
Shannon, Harry, 76, 107
She Wore a Yellow Ribbon, 44, 94, 161, 168
Shea, Jack, 62, 81, 156
Shearman, Roger, 77
Shefter, Bert, 73-127, 133
Shelby, Alfred, 70
"Shelter, The" (*Lawman* episode), 73, 77
Shenandoah, 56
Shepard, Jan, 21, 150, 151, **176**, 177
Sheridan, Dan, 62, 63, 68, 69, 101-103, 105, 106, 108, 112, 113, 116-118, 121, 122, 124, 125, 130, 132-134, 136, 137, 141, 142, 144, 148, 152, 153, 156, 158, 159,

163, 166, 167
Sherlock Holmes (TV series), 81
Sherman, Fred, 85, 121, 142
Sherman, Orville, 92
Shirelles, The, 115
Sholem, Lee, 43, 64, 65
Shore, Roberta, 135, 136, **177**, 178
"Short Straw" (*Lawman* episode), 45
"Showdown, The" (*Lawman* episode), 79
Shrader, George C., 72, 88
Shreve, Leo, 39, 43, 44, 52, 55, 56, 60
Silva, Henry, 65
Simmons, Jean, 48
Simon, Robert F., 67, 129
Simpson, Mickey, 38, 44, 61, 82, 93, 106, 165
Simpsons, The, 56
Sinatra, Frank, 117, 142
Sinclair, Robert B., 104, 105, 107, 110, 115, 124, 137, 142, 143, 146, 155, 156, 159, 162, 166
Singin' in the Rain, 137
Sitting Bull, 140
Sloane, Everett, 73, 74
Smith, Andrea, 76
Smith, Cecil, 89
Smith, Charles B., 166
Smith, John, 68
Smith, Justin, 154
Smith, K.L., 37, 142
Smith, Kent, 141
Smith, Leonard Paul, 123
Snyder, J. Earl, 85
Soble, Ron, 59
Sokoloff, Vladimir, 111
Soldiers of Fortune, 13
Somewhere in Time, 104
Son of Paleface, 41
"Son, The" (*Lawman* episode), 134
Sorenson, Rickey, 99
"Souvenir, The" (*Lawman* episode), 58, 73
Sparr, Robert T., 40, 49, 50, 57, 69-72, 75-96, 98-101, 109
Spielberg, Steven, 93
Spin and Marty, 97
Spinner, Anthony, 151, 160
Springfield Rifle, 151
"Squatters, The" (*Lawman* episode), 114, 143
Stagecoach (1939), 21, 101, 161, 164
Stahl, Francis E., 48, 53, 66, 77, 120, 123, 138, 139, 142, 143, 144

"Stalker, The" (*Lawman* episode), 91, 137, 170
Stanton, Anjo, 137
Stanton, Hank, 137
Stanwyck, Barbara, 140
Stapleton, James, 100
Star Trek (TV series), 70, 119
Stark, Sheldon, 125, 156
"State of Mind" (*Trials of Rosie O'Neil* episode), 125
Staunton, Ann, 46
Steele, Bob, 20, 61
Steele, Karen, 95
Stern, Walter S., 53, 63
Stevens, Inge, 155
Stevens, Warren, 82, 83
Stevens, William L., 161
Stevenson, Venetia, 42
Stewart, James, 51, 56, 61, 76
Stewart, Paul, 74, 75
Stewart. Art, 163
Stine, Harold, 43, 47, 62- 64, 66, 67, 71, 96, 126
Stine, Jan, 112, 157
Stockwell, Dean, 150
Stockwell, Guy, 149, 150
Stone, Eric, 159
Stoney Burke (TV series), 107
Storm Rider, The, 128
Storm Warning, 50
Storrs, Suzanne, 98
Strang, Harry, 38, 156, 161, 162
"Stranger, The" (*Lawman* episode), 80, 169
Strangers on a Train, 71
Stricklyn, Ray, 115
Stuart, Barbara, 39, 40
Stuart, Randy, 94, 112, 113
Sturgess, Olive, 61, **178,** 179
"Substitute, The" (*Lawman* episode), 19, 136
Sugarfoot, xi, 8, 11, 59, 66, 174, 175
Sullivan, Barry, 70
Sully, Frank, 53
Summer Place, A, 93
Sun Shines Bright, The, 13
"Sunday" (*Lawman* episode), 154, 158
Sundberg, Clinton, 162
Sunshine Rider (novel), 76
"SuperSax" (musical ensemble), 108
Support Your Local Gunfighter, 88
Support Your Local Sheriff, 67, 88, 137, 154

"Surface of Truth, The" (*Lawman* episode), 90
SurfSide 59, 93, 95
Sutton, Grady, 22, 101, 112, 117, 126, 128, 132, 134, 135, 141, 153, 156
"Swamper, The" (Lawman episode), 96
Sweet Bird of Youth, 127
Swoger, Harry, 61

T
Taeger, Ralph, 155
Tait, Don, 57, 165
Talbot, Lyle, 144, 145
Talbot, Stephen, 56
Tales of the Texas Rangers, 138
Tall in the Saddle, 58, 131
Tall T, The, 65, 154
Tall Texan, The, 158
Tannen, Charles, 38, 130
"Tarnished Badge, The" (*Gunsmoke* episode), 149
"Tarnished Badge, The" (*Lawman* episode), **32** 148
"Tarot" (*Lawman* episode), 142
Taylor, Buck, 39
Taylor, Dub, 39, 61
Taylor, Forrest, 97, 98
Taylor, Joyce, 51, 52
Taylor, Kent, 91
Tea for Two, 38
Tead, Phil, 42, 48, 50
Teal, Ray, 126, 127
Teleplay (book), 146
Temple Houston, 88
Terhune, Bob, 156
Terry, Philip, 123
"Thimblerigger, The" (*Lawman* episode), 22, 84, 143
"Thirty Minutes" (*Lawman* episode), 22, 49, 87
Thirtysomething, 127
Thomas. Bob, 10
Thomas, Dean, 91
Thomas, Dolph, 46, 54
Thompson, Glenn P., 71, 75, 78, 80
Thordsen, Kelly, 42
Thorson, Russ, 42, 50
"Threat, The" (*Lawman* episode), 22, 125
Three Texas Steers, 71
Time Tunnel, 146
"To Capture the West" (*Lawman* episode), 82, 86
To Catch a Thief (TV series), 96
To Kill a Mockingbird, 60, 91, 104, 130

INDEX

Tobey, Kenneth, 96, 145
Todd, Holbrook N., 90, 104
Tom Brown's School Days, 41
Tombstone, 161
Tomerlin, John, 113, 119, 126, 137, 144, 145, 147, 157, 159, 162
Tonka, 151
Tooney, Regis, 88
Tootsie, 129
Torey, Hal, 111
Torn Curtain, 136
Toughest Gun in Tombstone, 62
"Town Boys, The" (*Lawman* episode), 22, 99, 159
Trader Horn, 160
Trader Tom of the China Seas, 138
Trapnell, Coles, 128, 130, 132, 134-150, 154-156, 162, 164-167
"Trapped" (*Lawman* episode), 132
Treacy, Emerson, 55
Trevor, Claire, 15
"Trial, The" (*Lawman* episode), 126
"Trial of the Canary Kid, The" (*Sugarfoot* episode), 66
Trials of Rosie O'Neil, The, 125, 147
Tribute to a Bad Man, 125
"Trojan Horse" (*Lawman* episode), 22, 145
Trouble Rides Tall, 11, 37, 45, 64
Troupe, Tom, 108, 109
"Truce, The" (*Lawman* episode), 85
Tryon, Tom, 90
Tully, Phil, 37
Turnbull, Lee, 111
Tuttle, Lurene, 64, 118
"Twelfth of Never, The," 115
Twelve O' Clock High (TV series), 114, 130
Twilight Zone (TV series), 104, 146
Two Faces West, 118
Tyler, Harry, 38, 50, 61

U
U.S. Marshal, 126
"Ugly Man, The" (*Lawman* episode), **5**, 83
Ulzana's Raid, 120
Unforgiven, The (1960), 56
"Unmasked, The" (*Lawman* episode), 166

V
Valentine, Nancy, 96
Vallejo, Victor, 104
Van Cleef, Lee, 21, **31**, 36, 7, 42, 66, 97, 102, 136, 182

Van der Veer, Willard, 160, 167
Van Dreelen, John, 117
Van Zandt, Julie, 146
Vanquished, The, 122
Vaughn, James T., 75-79, 81, 100
Vaughn, Jeanne, 140
Vaughn, Mina, 68, 83, 83, 103, 106
Vestuto, Louis, 112
Vigran, Herb, 138, 139
Vincent, Sailor, 103
Vinson, Gary, 42, 164, 165
"Vintage, The" (*Lawman* episode), 147
Virginian, The (TV series), 48, 56, 136, 186
"Visitor, The" (*Lawman* episode), 56
Vittorio, 140
Vollaerts, Rik, 120, 127, 130, 164
Von Beltz, Brad, 67
Voyage to the Bottom of the Sea, 107
Vye, Murvyn, 52, 86

W
W. Hermanos, 94, 95, 98,
Wadsworth, Jack B., 86, 95, 110
Wages, David, 41, 46, 47, 64, 66, 90
Wagner, Maxine, 132
Wagner, Walter, 129, 132
Wagon Master, 101, 161
Wagon Train, 20, 68, 179
Waldis, Otto, 118
Walker, Clint, 143, 146, 155
Walker, Ray, 46
Wallace, George, 67, 116
Wallace, William, 59, 60, 70, 97
"Wanted" (*Lawman* episode), 42
Wanted Dead or Alive, 126
"Wanted Man, The" (*Lawman* episode), 41, 154, 157
War Wagon, The, 45, 154
Ward, Larry, 151, 152
Warlock, 70
Warner Bros., 9-11, 13-15, 21-23, 36-39, 41, 43, 46, 48, 51, 57, 59, 61, 66, 70, 95, 96, 99, 105, 106, 116-118, 121, 127, 146, 147, 150, 156, 165, 170, 172-175, 182, 183, 186
Warner, Jack L., 9, 10, 106, 147
"Warpath" (*Lawman* episode), 22, 52
Warren, Ruth, 63

INDEX

Warwick, Robert B. Jr., 61, 73, 82, 91, 103, 110, 119, 125, 149, 153, 159
Waterman, Willard, 76
Waters, James, 119-121, 144
Watkins, Frank, 84, 149, 152
Watts, Robert, 38, 65, 112
Way We Were, The, 129
"Wayfarer, The" (*Lawman* episode), 65
Wayne, John, 11, 18, 55, 57, 71, 80, 94, 122, 125, 131, 158, 161
We Wish You a Merry Christmas (Warner Bros. album), 156
Weaver, Doodles, 85, 89, 92, 96
Weaver, Ned, 56
Weaver, Sigourney, 89
Webster, Frank, 81
Welch, Jerry, 38-41 43, 46, 60, 67, 99, 138
Welcome to Hard Times, 154
Welles, Orson, 58, 74, 76
Wells, Dawn, 21, **31**, 149, 150
Wescoatt, Rusty, 1156
Wessell, Dick, 55, 57
West, Adam, 65, 66
Westbound, 49
Westerfield, James, 134
Weston, Brad, 80
"Whiphand" (*Lawman* episode), 22, 124
Whirlybirds, 96
Whispering Smith (movie), 52
White Heat, 73
White, Ted, 87, 166
Whitney, Peter, 90, 91, 137, 138
Whittington, Harry, 9, 11, 37, 45, 63, 64
Wiard, Bill, 146
Wilbanks, Don, 62, 96, 108, 126
Wild Bunch, The, 39, 107, 157
Wild Wild West, The (TV series), 57, 120
Wilke, Robert (J.), 21, 42, 60, 75
Wilkerson, Guy, 57, 108
Willard, Elen, 141
Willes, Jean, 41, 123
Williams, Adam, 123
Williams, Bill, 20, 163, 282
Williams, Jack, 150
Williams, Robert (B.), 37, 53
Williams, Rush, 89
Williams, Van, 59
Willson, Henry, 94
Windsor, Marie, 20, 157, 158
Wings, 53

223

Winterhawk, 49
Winters, Johnathan, 77
Wissmann, Joseph T., 59, 64, 65, 67, 103
"Witness, The" (*Lawman* episode), 54, 167, 185
Wolfe, Ian, 80
Wolfe, Robert L., 123
"Wolfer, The" (*Lawman* episode), 81, 120
Woods, Harry, 130, 131
Woodward, Morgan, 167
Woolem, Dee, 165
Woolley, Shep, 42
Woolsey, Ralph, 21, 22, 36, 38, 39, 40, 43, 46, 49, 50, 51, 54, 56, 57, 60, 63, 87-90, 96, 100, 134, 137, 140, 145, 147, 149
Wrangell, Basil, 43, 126
Wright, Robert Vincent, 154
Wright, Will, 43, 44, 118
Wright. Theresa, 94
Wyatt, Al, 153
Wyoming Outlaw, 63

Y
Yancy Derringer, 50, 146
"Yawkey" (*Lawman* episode), 103
Yellow Mountain, The, 128
Yellow Sky, 13
York, Jeff, 39, 65
You Bet Your Life, 84
Young and the Reckless, The, 146
Young Mr. Lincoln, 21, 101
"Young Toughs, The" (*Lawman* episode), 19, 22, 55, 59
Young, Carleton G., 75
Young, Tony, 74, 75, 157, 182
"Youngest, The" (*Lawman* episode), 134, 159

Z
Zane Grey Theater, The, 140
Zane, Edgar, 80
Zeigler, William, 62
Zimbalist Efrem Jr., 48
Zint, Karl E., 89
Zorro (TV series), 112
Zuckert, Bill, 142

About the Author

Born in California and raised on Long Island, Bill Levy is a retired New York City and Hopatcong, New Jersey special education teacher who now devotes his time to writing. He is the author of *John Ford: A Bio-Bibliography* (Greenwood Press, 1998), *Beyond the Beach: The Wit and Wisdom of Nevil Shute* (BLS Publishers, 2012), and *Lest We Forget: The John Ford Stock Company* (BearManor Media, 2013). He has been writing a monthly movie column for the New Jersey publication, *Fifty Plus*, since 2001, and has also co-written with Frank Fredo a western screenplay, *The Battle of Adobe Walls*. Bill is currently completing two speculative fiction books, *Meets* and *Meets II*, each consisting of 100 fictitious celebrity encounters during the past 150 years, as well as an autobiographical novel about his thirty-five years of teaching.

www.ingramcontent.com/pod-product-compliance
Lightning Source LLC
Chambersburg PA
CBHW071432150426
43191CB00008B/1104